OUT OF THE GHETTO

OUT OF THE GHETTO

THE SOCIAL BACKGROUND OF
JEWISH EMANCIPATION, 1770–1870

JACOB KATZ

HARVARD UNIVERSITY PRESS
CAMBRIDGE, MASSACHUSETTS   1973

PREFACE

The title of this book indicates its intent: it is the description and analysis of the process through which the Jews, isolated in ghettos on the fringe of society until well near the end of the eighteenth century, made their first steps toward integrating into the mainstream of European life. That the escape from the ghetto represents a turn in Jewish history has been recognized ever since. At the same time, the entrance of Jews into European society must also be considered a momentous event in European and subsequently American history, in light of the active role of Jews in contributing to all fields of endeavor as well as their passive role as targets of social antagonism.

One cannot complain that the theme has not attracted the attention of historians, but the treatment of the subject only rarely escaped the partisanship which clung to the topic by its very nature. It would be presumptuous to claim that where others failed, the present author succeeded. What he is permitted to say is that the subject held his attention for some thirty-odd years — having written his doctoral dissertation on the assimilation of German Jews in the year 1934 — and that he saw the danger of subjectivity and tried to beware of it.

The composition of this text itself extended over eight years. The first version had been written in 1962–63 at Harvard University, where I served as a visiting professor. Writing in English, I needed the help of someone and found it in the stylistic ability and friendly assistance of Neal Kozodoy. I wrote the final version in Jerusalem in the late sixties and once again relied upon others' help. Mrs. Etty Aman's linguistic vigilance oversaw the English style, taking care at the same time to preserve the exact thoughts of the author. Miss Shoshana Friedman gave the last touch to the English text.

I have discussed the composition of this book with my friend

Professor Shmuel N. Eisenstadt, who was good enough to read an early draft. Yakov Guggenheim helped me in the preparations of the manuscript and the verification of my sources. It is a pleasant duty to thank all those who aided me in the publishing of this book, and they have my gratitude.

Jerusalem, March 1972
The Hebrew University of Jerusalem

CONTENTS

OUT OF THE GHETTO

I SOCIAL REVOLUTION —
WITH A DIFFERENCE

One hundred years of history — starting in the last third of the eighteenth century — wrought profound changes in the countries of Europe. In economics, politics, in social structure, as well as in the ideological realms that govern these fields, acute transformations took place. These changes affected all nations in Europe, but particularly the Western countries. Nowhere was life affected more deeply than in the Jewish community, which existed among these nations and was regarded until then as apart from the rest. But whereas the European nations were transformed economically, politically, and socially, the change seems to have gone deeper in the case of the Jews, transmuting the very nature of their entire social existence. For at the beginning of this period, in the decade of 1760–1770, Jews were regarded as no more than a part of one dispersed Jewish nation. But by 1860, though it was still doubtful as to how the Jews should be defined, this description would certainly have failed to do them justice. In the first period a Jew might have been designated as English, French, or German depending on his land of residence. At that time, however, this was only a geographical description and gave, perhaps, a hint of some collective characteristics that the members of each respective community may have manifested. A hundred years later, if a person was called a French, English, or German Jew, he was taken to belong in some way to both the social units implied in the compound expression: he belonged to one of these nations and was, in addition, a Jew.

During the century under question, Jewish communities underwent a transformation that changed their legal status, their occupational distribution, their cultural habits, as well as their religious outlook and behavior. The process had been referred to by contemporaries of that time, and by historians in retrospect as

1

well, by different terms: naturalization, reform, civic betterment, amalgamation, assimilation, emancipation — the last being the most widely accepted, used sometimes in its limited, political or legal, sense, and at other times in a more comprehensive way. These terms indicate the different aspects of the process.

In all these respects, Jews moved from their former distinct Jewish pattern toward the standard common in their non-Jewish surroundings. Some sectors of the community in fact were entirely absorbed by the environing society: those who left the Jewish fold intermarried and converted to Christianity. It seemed at times to contemporaries that this ominous defection would result in the decomposition of the Jewish community. This prognosis did not materialize; the result of the political, social, and cultural changes was not the disintegration of the Jewish community but its thorough transformation. At the end of the period under consideration, the community is still very much extant, albeit differing greatly from its structure of a century earlier. The task of this book is to describe and analyze the process of change which so affected Jewry in Central and Western Europe in this interim period.

What happened to Jewry in the Western countries in the hundred years between 1770 and 1870 (approximately) became a pattern later followed by Jewry in other parts of the world. The proximity of the Jews of Eastern Europe to Western Jewry made it inevitable that Jews of Poland and Russia would be aware of what was happening in the West. Actually there is no strict division of boundaries between the East and West. The Jews of Galicia, for instance, historically and culturally belong to "Eastern Jewry." Owing to political incidents, namely the partitions of Poland in 1772–1795, Galician Jewry came under the sovereignty of a Western-oriented country, namely Austria. In this manner, Galician Jewry came under political pressure to adapt itself to the demands of an enlightened and enlightening regime. The response of Galician Jewry to these stimuli was, on the whole, a negative one. A real process of social and cultural transformation started much later in Galicia — about the middle of the nineteenth century — and much the same happened in Russia. In the beginning only the echoes of what was happening in the West penetrated to Russia; only in the 1840's and 1860's, when initial response to Western stimuli had been strengthened by the expectation of political improvement and social acceptance, did the movement of enlightenment gather momentum.

In other communities, such as the Moslem, the change started even later. In Algiers it came in the wake of the French conquest (1830) and colonization in the late nineteenth century; and in Iraq only after the First World War. Although influenced by Western Jewry and even partially initiated by their agencies (as, for instance, the Alliance Israélite Universelle), the process of change was different here owing to different circumstances. The same applies, although for different reasons, to countries such as the United States, South Africa, and Australia to which Jews emigrated. Here a great many Jews underwent a process of change where the characteristic features of Jewish metamorphosis mingled with the process of adaptation forced upon any group of new immigrants.

It was only in Western Europe — Germany, Austria, Hungary, France, Holland, and England — that Jewish emancipation, in its wider sense, occurred more or less simultaneously. It can also be said to have followed a similar, if not identical, course. For even Western countries differ from one another in many respects that condition the process of Jewish absorption; the number of Jews accepted varied from place to place; the historical background was different; the kind of memories pertaining to the Jewish-Gentile past that had to be overcome were certainly not identical; the political institutions and social conditions on which formal and actual integration depended varied from country to country. Add to this the accidental factor of the type of personality involved in directing the political struggle and giving direction to the social and cultural adaptation and there emerges a special set of agents contributing to the history of Jewish emancipation in any of these countries.

Indeed, the story of Jewish emancipation in any of the Western European countries could be told separately but not for each country in isolation. For there is a reciprocal influence here that

cannot be ignored. The example and teaching of German re-
formers like Moses Mendelssohn had their effect on French Jews;
and the political advances gained by French Jews through the
French Revolution had their impact on German Jewry. Dutch
Jewry was granted citizenship after the French conquest of Hol-
land in 1795, with the Dutch National Assembly emulating the
French example. Later, in the 1830's, the very term "Jewish
Emancipation" had become a political slogan and spread from
England to the Continent, where the struggle for equality was at
its height.[1]

There is no doubt that events in the various countries were in-
terrelated. Still, the actual course of events and their results were
different in the respective countries. Their presentation as one
fabric entails the neglect of details and the omission of special
features of development in each separate country. This, however,
is the price to be paid for a compound picture based upon observations on what was occurring simultaneously in different
countries.

The presentation of Jewish emancipation in the West as a
meaningful whole is legitimate. For even if the results of the process differed from place to place, the underlying forces effecting
these changes were identical. The trend of change encompassed
all estates and classes of Western nations, and although it
reached Jewish society at a later stage, once it did so it had a
deeper impact than in most cases. The transformation of Jewish
society from its prerevolutionary state represents perhaps the
greatest upheaval of any sector of European society at that time.

The very deep effect of the revolutionary era in European society on the Jews could not have been accidental. The reason for it
must be sought in the unusual nature of Jewish society in its earlier state. In general, Jewish society at that time could be designated as a traditional society, using this term in a very special
sense. Jewish society derived its religion and cultural values, its
very mainstay, from the past; it adhered to them as a source of
orientation in the present; and relied upon them as a means of
ensuring its continuity in the future.[2] The past to which Jewish
society related lay in the remote antiquity of Talmudic and Bib-

lical times. This in itself was nothing unique, for Christian society also cherished its traditions, which were to some extent identical with those of the Jews and, at least partly, derived from the same historical period. In each case, however, the connection with antiquity was of a different nature. Christian society accepted a certain literary tradition from ancient times as a source of religious guidance in the present. Some institutions, for instance the Catholic church, trace their origins to the remote past, while others such as the state and its law, schools, and so on, rely more on the immediate past. The special feature of Jewish society was its total reliance on the distant past; for Jewish tradition regarded everything of value in Jewish religion — law, learning, and culture — as stemming from ancient times, the period of the Bible and the Talmud.

There is yet another difference between the two societies. Christian society regarded its tradition as inherited from peoples who had once lived and disappeared. If and when an identification with peoples of antiquity — especially the Biblical Israelites — was suggested, it pertained to the level of symbolism. In the realm of reality, Christian society found identity in its concrete time and environment. Jewish society, however, regarded itself as directly descended from the ancient people of Israel. It was not only the heir of a religion and a cultural inheritance, but the sanguinal perpetuation of those who bequeathed its values. According to their own historical tradition, echoed by the prevalent tradition of their Christian (and for that matter, Muslim) environment, Jews did not belong to the place in which they lived but, expelled from their own country, had found a *temporary* abode among the nations. Tradition also envisaged a termination of exile with the advent of the Messiah. In the meantime, there were no other means of self-identification but the adherence to tradition. Admittedly, not all parts of the tradition could function successfully in exile, and some parts of the Biblical and Talmudic law, including the prescribed religious obligations, had to be waived. Nevertheless, the theory was maintained that life, public and private, could be regulated by the law and endowed with meaning by adherence to tradition. In spite of basic changes in their environment and in spite of the constant exchange of environments in the wake of voluntary and compulsory emigration, Jewish society contrived to keep a balance between the irresistible demands of the conditions of life and the essential demands of tradition. To be sure, this was achieved at a double price. First, there was the curtailment of possible spheres of life and the distortive adjustments of tradition. The one-sidedness of Jewish life in the Middle Ages and the ghetto period is well known, as is the forcible adjustment of tradition to the exigencies of life. On the other hand, no matter how much tradition was changed, adjustment was always achieved within its terms. All the changes that evolved or came about by adaptation were somehow justified in terms of tradition. Therefore it is possible to say that this society was a traditional one in a very special sense. Tradition played a much greater part in its life than in that of the people among whom it dwelt. When the framework of traditional society all over Europe disintegrated, the more traditional a society had been, the deeper was its transmutation.

Here is an intermediate answer to the question of why Jewish society was more deeply affected than others. A more detailed answer will be forthcoming later. First it is necessary to give a concrete description of traditional society in the countries where the subsequent upheavals occurred.

Although this book throughout will especially focus on Jewish society in its various metamorphoses, attention will be given to the history of these societies which at first surrounded, and then gradually, although not entirely, absorbed Jewish society. This partial absorption of Jews by the surrounding societies introduced a new element into the life of these societies and contributed to their complexity. In terms of challenge and response, the process of absorption elicited a reaction out of proportion to the size of the group absorbed. The transition from the ghettolike existence of Jewish society to a partial inclusion in society-at-large was nowhere a smooth or unobserved social process, as was the case with the French Huguenots, who had lived in the countries of their exile in separate colonies, often alongside the Jewish ghettos. In the course of time, these Huguenots simply disappeared as a group, retaining at most a slight institutional or cultural distinctiveness.[3]

Jewish integration, on the other hand, even where its end result may have resembled the case of the Huguenots, remained very different during its process of realization. The change of the Jews' civil status — the transformation of strangers into citizens — was in no European country the result of general legislation, and their acceptance as equal members of society nowhere the natural result of mutual adaptation. Both the political and the social aspects of the problem were envisaged as special issues and discussed with great passion in the legislative bodies of each country and in the arena of public opinion. The most protracted and vehement controversy took place in Germany, but its parallel, on a less extensive scale, is to be seen all over Western Europe.[4]

When an explanation is sought for the intensive reaction on the part of non-Jewish society to the process of Jewish integration, it is necessary once again to resort to the burden of the past. Jewish-Gentile relations had a longstanding tradition; time-honored notions cleaved to the very name of Jew and strongly stereotyped features attached to his image. A historically and theologically well-defined evaluation attached itself to Jews in Christian tradition.[5] Their lot as eternal exiles was considered the direct result of their rejection of Christianity or, in its cruder version, as divine retribution for the crucifixion of Christ. This tenet served as an explanation as well as a justification of their status as aliens. If Christian society wished to embrace Jews as an integrated group, it had to overcome its stereotyped associations and prejudices against things Jewish. This could, at best, only be a slow process — as indeed it turned out to be. The lingering force of the stereotype was evident first of all from the opposing attitudes, which drew most of their arguments against Jewish emancipation from the ancient anti-Jewish armory, with slight adaptations to the new situation. But the stereotype was no less present in the mind of the advocates of emancipation, who made their recommendations dependent on a radical transformation of what they imagined to be traditionally Jewish.

The history of the Jews at this time may be said to be an interplay between changes in condition, alteration of types, and shifts in institutions on the one hand, and a reshaping of ideas, images, and stereotypes on the other. It is sad to observe that the latter process was generally slower than the former. This is well demonstrated by the fact that the latter process is still continuing in the twentieth century. Such an observation is apt to cause the historian to become unduly involved with the history of the events themselves and to become a partisan in the struggle he is called upon to describe. Historical detachment, however, demands a limitation on the historian's task; he must record and analyze events as well as ideas and their underlying passions with equal objectivity and allow the reader to draw his own conclusion.

II GHETTO TIMES

The dissolution of traditional society began in Western Europe. From there waves of change and disintegration spread to other countries. As the concern here is with the first appearance of disintegration, it would be best to describe traditional society in its historical reality, where it served both as background and battleground for incipient change.[1] More accurately, a factual and an analytical account of Jewish society as it existed between 1650 and 1750 in Germany, Austro-Hungary, France, Holland, and England must be given.

Statistical data about the Jewish population before the end of the eighteenth century is lacking. But some idea may be formed of the numerical state of affairs before statistics were available by working backward from the figures given for the end of the eighteenth century.

The most conspicuous Jewish communities at this time were in Germany and in the Austrian Empire. In Germany the number of Jews at the end of the eighteenth, century was assessed at 175,000. Jews in the Austrian Empire, where in effect they were to be found only in Moravia, Bohemia, and Vienna, numbered 70,000. In Hungary, at this time, there were 100,000. In the West, France had not more than 40,000, the greater number being the Ashkenazi community of Alsace-Lorraine and a small group of Sephardim in southern France. In Holland and in England there were again two communities, Sephardim and Ashkenazim, numbering 50,000 in Holland and in England some 25,000.[2]

English Jews were, for the most part, a recent influx, the result of a vigorous immigration. Around the middle of the eighteenth century they did not number more than about 8,000.[3] The Dutch Jewish population grew from a slow but steady absorption of immigrants of Sephardic origin, among them Marranos who had escaped the Spanish and Portuguese inquisitions, and Ashkenazim from Germany and Poland. This process started at the beginning of the seventeenth century and continued unabatedly.[4] Most of the 100,000 Jews in Hungary were also immigrants, some from Bohemia and Moravia and some who came from Galicia in the wake of the reconquest of Hungary by the Austrian Empire from the Turks at the end of the seventeenth century. At this time there were fewer than 20,000.[5] In other countries, too, a certain amount of mobility and fluctuation in the Jewish population must be reckoned with. But in Germany and in Austria not only was immigration opposed, but even the natural growth of the Jewish population was rigorously controlled by the authorities with the restriction of marriages. Nevertheless, since the eighteenth century is marked by a rapid population growth in general, it must be assumed that the number of Jews, too, was growing at this time at an increased rate not only in countries of immigration but everywhere. The figures of the late eighteenth century require a thorough correction when used as a starting point for estimating the figures of a hundred or a hundred and fifty years earlier.

Similar uncertainties prevailed in estimating the ratio between the Jewish and the general population. At the end of the eighteenth century the 50,000 Dutch Jews lived among a population of two million, representing 2.5 percent — the highest percentage in all Western Europe. The 100,000 Jews in Hungary were part of a population of seven million, that is, 1.4 percent. In other countries the percentage was much lower — in Germany less than one for every hundred and in France only two in a thousand. It may safely be assumed that during the seventeenth century not even this ratio was reached in any of these countries.

However, to assess the economic, social, and religious role of the Jews in European society at this time according to their comparative numbers only would be a gross fallacy. First, the Jews, even in countries where they were admitted, did not live divided and dispersed over the land, for they were still not allowed to settle where they pleased. In France the Edict of Expulsion, inherited from the Middle Ages, had never been repealed. On the contrary, it was reissued as late as 1615 by Louis XIII. The Sephardic Jews of the South came into the country disguised as Christians. When their identity was discovered, the prohibition against their presence was overlooked by the authorities but not legally revoked. Later, in the reign of Louis XV, letters patent were granted to individuals and even entire communities expressly mentioning Jews.[6] Such official documents simply disregarded the Edict of Expulsion without invalidating it. The Jews of Metz, Alsace, and Lorraine were an involuntary acquisition of France through the annexation of these districts during the war with Germany in the sixteenth and seventeenth century, especially between 1648 and 1681.[7] Had they wished, the French could have executed the Edict of Expulsion. The rigor of the law was waived, however, and the Jews of Alsace remained within the boundaries of France. But the actual permission to reside in any locality depended on the good will of the local authorities, and many towns, such as Strasbourg Colmar and Münster, continued to remain closed to Jews.[8] Those towns and villages that permitted Jews to reside there granted this privilege in exchange for the payment of special levies and by strictly limiting the field of occupation in which Jews were permitted to engage.

Holland has been pointed to as the place where Jews found friendly abode and a tolerant attitude earlier than in any other European country. This is not unwarranted praise, for as early as the beginning of the seventeenth century, Jews in Holland felt themselves to be more free religiously and economically less hampered than in any other country in Europe. Still the advantages enjoyed by Dutch Jews over Jews in other countries are only comparative, for their better situation resulted only from circumstances — the expanding Dutch economy and the atmosphere of religious tolerance following a period of religious strife — and not from a change of status. Basically the legal status of Dutch Jews, like that of their brethren elsewhere, remained unchanged. Jews admitted into the country still had to secure the right of residence from some district or municipality, and this was not always and unreservedly granted. The towns of Utrecht, Gouda, and Deventer denied access to Jews.[9] Moreover, even if born in Holland, the

Jew remained an alien who could, in theory, have been expelled without violation of the law.[10]

Essential deviation from the current pattern was to be found in England. Although the legal status of Jews admitted since Cromwell's time remained unclarified, permission to stay meant freedom to live in any part of the country. True, a Jew who emigrated from abroad remained an alien, but one born in the country was a British subject.[11] Political and occupational disabilities he had to put up with were the results of the constitutionally enacted laws of the country, which limited certain offices to members of the Anglican church. These restrictions were not aimed against Jews but against non-Anglican Christians, so that the Jews had no reason for feeling discriminated against.

Returning to the Continent, the same timeworn pattern is found in Germany, Austria, and Hungary. There were many places in these countries, even whole districts, from which Jews were excluded, and townlets and villages cherished their privilege — inherited from the Middle Ages — *non tolerandis Judaeorum.* There is no rational explanation in economic or other terms for the presence or absence of Jews in particular localities. In Fürth there was a thriving Jewish community but in neighboring Nuremberg a Jew could appear only in daytime and only in the company of a local inhabitant.[12] Halberstadt and Magdeburg, both important centers of commerce and administration and Prussian dominated since the middle of the seventeenth century, differ greatly in their attitude to Jews. Halberstadt harbored one of the earliest Jewish communities uninterruptedly since the Middle Ages. In Magdeburg, Jews struggled for mere admission even during the comparatively tolerant rule of the Prussian kings.[13] In Leipzig, Jews played an important role in the great fairs and, while these were being held, they were allowed to hold their religious services and maintain their kosher kitchen. But only in 1713 was one Jewish family permitted to settle in Leipzig and, forty years later, a second one. Jews were allowed to establish a recognized community and maintain some public institutions as a synagogue and the like only as late as 1837.[14] Jews were expelled from Vienna in 1670 but some families, headed by the rich court Jew Samuel Oppenheimer, were readmitted after a lapse of five years. The next generation of Jews filled an important function in the economic life of the Austrian Empire. They also played a conspicuous role in the life of Western Jewry. Still, they were not allowed to form a community until 1849.[15] In the twin towns of Buda and Pesth on the banks of the Danube different conditions prevailed. Buda had had a mixed Sephardic and Ashkenazi community since the time of the Turks. In Pesth no Jews could remain overnight and escape a fine.[16] In the province of Hungary admittance or exclusion depended on the decision of the municipalities or the wish of the landed aristocracy. The former were usually against the Jews, sometimes prohibiting their free passage. Among the latter there were those who favored Jews and protected them. Thus, in order to attend fairs in Ödenburg, Jews had to plead with the municipality, while in the localities of the neighboring district belonging to Count Esterhazy the so-called seven communities, Eisenstadt being foremost among them, thrived.[17]

Why were such contradictory rulings accepted for seemingly similar circumstances? A specific answer for any community can only be given on the basis of its history. Still, two general rules governing the situation may be suggested. First, the disjunction of the political authority in a double sense, both horizontally and vertically. The horizontal dispersion (no central authority) is particularly distinct and far-reaching in Germany where, following the Peace of Westphalia in 1648, actual sovereignty is divided by some three hundred commonwealths of varying sizes. The supremacy of the emperor exists only in name and, at best, affects only external policy. The admittance or exclusion of Jews, being an internal matter, is decided by local authorities. But even where the central authority of a state has a large jurisdiction, it does not necessarily mean that Jewish admittance or exclusion is decided by this authority. The Empress Maria Theresa was competent to expel the Jews of Prague in 1744 and equally able to readmit them after three years. Of course, Bohemia was a patrimonial dominion of the Hapsburgs and there the empress ruled supreme. In Hungary she felt herself entitled to impose a tax on every Jewish soul as the price of imperial protection.[18] This, however, remained a formality. The actual protection of Jews, that is, permission to live in certain towns, depended upon the Comitate, the municipality, or on the owner of the estate. In France, too, royal permission for Jews to remain in that country did not entail the right to reside in any town or village; this had to be acquired, or rather bought, from the authorities existing in the various villages or towns.[19]

Sometimes rival claims were made by the local and the central authorities for the right to decide on Jewish admittance or exclusion and the issue decided by the relative strengths of the political forces involved. The favorable situation of the Jews in Halberstadt as against that of Magdeburg under the Prussian government is a case in point. The central government of Prussia supported Jewish settlement in both cities despite reluctance on the part of the local estates. In Halberstadt the local agencies yielded to superior stress of the central government. In Magdeburg, on the other hand, the resistance of the estates turned out to be so formidable that the central government withdrew.[20]

The admission or rejection of Jews being a controversial matter, ideological consideration could influence the decision taken. The wavering nature of public opinion with regard to Jews was the second factor to influence the decision on their acceptance or rejection. Since the Middle Ages, Christian authorities, though they strove for complete religious unity in their respective countries, made an exception in the case of the Jews.[21] This exception was based on theological reasoning. The Jewish nation was to be preserved in a suppressed state in order to testify to the truth of Christianity. This argument, however, only allowed for the possibility of accepting the Jews, though it in no way commended their toleration. Whether they were in fact accepted, depended upon how the Jew was evaluated by the authority that would eventually make the decision. Different reasons, economic and religious, were advanced pro and con. With the advent of the Reformation and the ascendancy of the centralized state based on a money economy, new arguments emerged that could be used in both directions. The Reformation did not abandon the basic ideology of tolerance toward the Jew as history's witness to Christianity. In some instances, as in Cromwellian England, new religious principles were evolved to be used in justification of admitting the Jew. Some of the Purtian groups, having identified themselves with the Israelites of the Old Testament, evolved a kind of philo-Semitism whereby they created a favorable atmosphere for contemporary Jews. Menasseh Ben Israel, the promotor of Jewish resettlement in England (he was a Sephardic sage from Amsterdam), could plausibly argue that the return of Jews to England was in accordance with Biblical prediction that total dispersion would preccdc the Redemption.[22] With the fervent Puritan, who regarded Puritanism as the precursor of the millennium, such an argument was bound to carry weight. But in other countries the Reformation and Counter-Reformation sometimes induced a religious fervor that operated against the acceptance of Jews.[23] The practice of tolerance that was imposed on the parties within Christianity did not necessarily apply in the case of Jews. And even after the practice of tolerance had assumed the nature of a principle in the seventeenth century, the basic situation of Jews remained unchanged for a long time.

The same is true for the development in the field of economics. As money became more important for conducting the affairs of the centralized state, Jewish capitalists had a better chance of admittance. The court Jew became a ubiquitous figure in German principalities after the middle of the seventcenth century. He served as an agent, purveyor, contractor, mediator, and banker.[24] However, these functions could have been filled by other agents — as was illustrated in France, where Jews played a comparatively minor role. But even if the centralized economy demanded the presence of the Jew, it was not the only factor to be considered; for the city burghers, living on their crafts and trades, were apprehensive of Jewish activity along lines that would represent competition. From these quarters an objection to Jewish acceptance was almost traditional. In any case, the question of admitting Jews was not a settled issue anywhere; rather, it was precariously dependent on the balance of economic and religious forces.

The description of the facts of Jewish residence in European countries reveals, at the same time, the underlying legal conception according to which they were admitted. The Jew had no legal claim to acceptance or toleration, and if he was admitted, it happened on the basis of a contract between the Jewish community and the relevant political authority. The Jewish contractor might even in some cases have been only an individual who received the right of residence for himself and his family. Sometimes a whole community slipped in under the shadow of an influential individual who had received the necessary permission. There was also a great difference as to the times the contracts were concluded, some having been drawn up within the memory of contemporaries and some going back to remote times. When the latter was the case, the terms of the agreement had often become vague and the identity of the non-Jewish partner was no longer clear. In fact, the legal title to the contract was often contested by rival claimants and these were the very situations that often produced conflict between the central and the local authorities. But the unclarified origin of the contract notwithstanding, the *fact* of the contractual origin for Jewish residence was never doubted. Jews at no time used the obscure origins of their domicile in a given place as an argument to prove precedence over their non-Jewish neighbors there. Had this been the case, their right of residence would have existed independent of any concession.

Such contention, it seems, was unthinkable because of Christian and Jewish tradition alike, which accepted Jews as strangers and exiles. The political and legal inference from this fact amounted to the assumption that Jews had no residential rights beyond what was granted them by the respective political authorities. As a famous eighteenth century jurist put it: "Although they are tolerated in some provinces and towns of Germany, they are nevertheless still *in civitate* but not *de civitate*." [25] A concomitant was the inevitable conclusion that the contract could be terminated at any time. In fact, Jews were forced sometimes to leave their places of residence because their non-Jewish contractors decided to expel them. The best-known examples are the expulsion of Jews from Vienna in 1670 and from Prague in 1744. Jews tried

OUT OF THE GHETTO

to counter such terminations of their contract by means of persuasion and pressure but did not question the legitimacy of the action.[26]

As late as 1777 Mendelssohn intervened in favor of the Dresden Jews. Hundreds of them faced expulsion for failing to remit the annual head tax — an oversight for which the penalty was expulsion, as determined by a regulation passed five years previously. Mendelssohn appealed to the benevolence of the ruler of Saxonia and his high officials and asked them as friends of the human race to reconsider their decision but did not question the legitimacy of the expulsion. Expulsion was for a Jew, Mendelssohn declared, the hardest of all punishments "since it banished him, as it were, from the surface of the earth of the Lord, on which prejudice with armed hands repulses him from every frontier." [27] Here Mendelssohn voices the painful fact that the Jew was utterly dependent on authority for the right to reside anywhere.

The status and position of the individual Jew depended therefore upon possession of the right of residence that would enable him to establish his family and set about earning his living in an orderly fashion. The retention of the right of residence and its procurement for those who had none was the vital concern of every Jewish individual and his family. For not every Jew was privileged in this way. A great number of Jews, sometimes amounting to a whole layer of society, were denied this fundamental right of belonging to a place where they could spend their lives. Lacking a place of residence in their own right, these individuals conducted an insecure existence in the shadow of the privileged — serving in a Jewish household, or holding the post of teacher or acting as beadle on behalf of a community — who gave them residence for as long as their services were required. Others, either because they did not find an occupation or did not aspire to any, turned into wanderers, going aimlessly from community to community. They relied on the charity of Jewish individuals and institutions, often becoming a burden on their Jewish brethren and a liability to Jewish and non-Jewish society alike.[28]

Those who were privileged to have the coveted right of residence were still bound by certain occupational limitations. The Jewish contract with the authorities always contained some provisions stating either what occupations were open to them or setting out those from which they were debarred. The type of enterprise allotted to Jews varied from place to place. Occupations that were allowed or even encouraged in one place would not be permitted in another. By and large, however, Jewish business activities were always variations on a single theme: enterprise connected with the investment of money. The practical and, in a certain sense, even conceptual association of Jews with money had a long history. Jews had been conspicuous in trade ever since they began to live dispersed among other nations. Yet this became a distinguishing characteristic only during the Middle Ages when, through a combination of causes, Jews were dislodged from almost all occupations besides trade and the lending of money. In an age of a preponderantly natural and self-contained economy, the Jews were one of the few agencies that maintained the channels of exchange between countries and continents. They also provided the money for the marginal activities that had to be based on investment even at that time of natural economy. With the expansion of the field of money-based economy in Europe during the sixteenth and seventeenth centuries, Jews had more opportunities to invest their money and use their financial acumen. In some places, notably in Moravia, Bohemia (Prague), and especially in Poland where their settlements were crowded together, some of them formed an outlet for handicraft of various sorts. Still, the most conspicuous Jewish source of livelihood remained the investment of capital in profit-making ventures. These ventures differed in extent, from the large amount of capital invested by a court agent in a great kingdom to the modest sums of the peddler, very often borrowed from a capitalist. In both cases the profit expectation was based on the potential of capital joined to a perception of the customer's need and its possible satisfaction from a source of which he was unaware. In any case, it was the possession of capital or the ability to acquire it that recommended the Jew to those interested in the results of such activity. Because of the benefit expected from the Jews' activities, their presence was tolerated or even pleaded for by those who perceived their usefulness.[29]

Jews who found an abode and livelihood in one of the states became a part of the social structure at least insofar as economics was concerned. They also became subject to the prevailing political authority and legal institutions. Political and juridical authorities, however, did not take cognizance of Jews as individuals. Jews were expected to form a community and the community was expected to deal with a good many aspects of the life of the individual. Personal matters like marriage, divorce, inheritance, and so forth came under the jurisdiction of the Jewish institutions, though in most places marriage contracts — which were a key to the population policy of the state — demanded special permission. Jewish institutions dealt with these matters on the basis of Jewish, that is, Talmudic law. Talmudic law also served as a source and authority for Jewish courts dealing with litigations between Jew and Jew. In most places, non-Jewish courts were also available to Jews, either in the first or second instance, and Jews sometimes availed themselves of this. Appeal to non-Jewish courts, however, was regarded by the proponents of Jewish tradition as a deviation from the prescribed religious obligation and, at most, suffered as a compromise under the pressure of circumstances. In principle all litigation between Jews should have been brought before a Jewish court and dealt with in accordance with Jewish law. This attitude toward the non-Jewish legal agencies is a clear indication that the demand of the non-Jewish authorities for the creation of Jewish communities was in no way complied with only as a necessity. On the contrary, it corresponded fully with the Jewish aspiration to retain as great a measure as possible of self-government.[30]

In many of the German states Jews lived dispersed in small groups in the villages and townlets. Unable to create a proper community in one locality, the Jews of a particular district would join in establishing a common organization. This organization, the so-called *Landgemeinde*, mediated between Jews and the existing powers, obtained the taxes that were to be paid collectively, and exercised some control over the life of members. The authorities were interested in seeing these organizations functioning and, in any case, they could only be maintained with their consent and active assistance. But the organization served also to satisfy Jewish needs. The rabbi it employed supervised the religious life of his scattered constituents and mediated between conflicting parties. These organizations were typical for western Germany, and those existing in Cleves, Paderborn, Mainz, and elsewhere have been described by historians in detail.[31] Other types of association between Jews living in different localities existed in Bohemia and Moravia. In Bohemia the great Prague community represented all Jews until the middle of the seventeenth century. About this time the provincial communities succeeded in establishing an independent organization to represent the Jews outside Prague.[32] In Moravia all the communities affiliated with one dominating organization, while the great community of Nikolsburg, the seat of the Chief Rabbi, enjoyed some few prerogatives.[33]

Jews lived out their lives in the Jewish community. Non-Jewish society, in fact, served them only for the acquisition of means. Family life, educational endeavor, the adult pursuit of study, and religious services and ceremonies were, of course, conducted in exclusively Jewish institutions and environment. In most cities where Jews lived together in any considerable numbers, they also lived in special quarters, compelled by non-Jewish authorities or as a natural result of concentrating around their own institutions. In this second case, Jews might have lived some distance from the Jewish quarter proper or, where they lived in the country, altogether scattered among the non-Jewish population. Nevertheless, barred from social contact with Christians by their own religious prescriptions and convictions as well as by those of their Christian neighbors, they must still sociologically be called a group apart.[34]

When the Jews of a given locality gained sufficient numbers to constitute a community, all the functions of group life manifested themselves, even if only in a rudimentary fashion. The community leadership was elected by the members or by a privileged number of them. The leaders exercised the measure of political power conceded to the community by the non-Jewish authority. This meant the coercive power of taxation for the collective payment due the Gentile authorities and the maintenance of Jewish institutions. It also meant the authority to control the behavior of members of the community, their business conduct (especially in dealings with non-Jews), their social behavior, and their religious observance. As a means of control, there were at the disposal of the leaders all the usual means of coercion short of capital punishment: fines, imprisonment, pillory, and different grades of religiously sanctioned bans.[35]

In addition to the community organization, there were other institutions to which people resorted for the satisfaction of certain needs and to whose maintenance they contributed more or less voluntarily. These included the synagogues, houses of study, the schools for indigent children, and in many places *yeshivot,* schools for higher Talmudic learning. Then there were societies for charity or other ethically laudable activities such as catering for the sick and providing opportunity for communal study. A special place was occupied by the burial society, which was ubiquitous. Where, as for instance in Prague, a group of artisans existed, they were organized in a type of guild association.[36]

Behind this formalized framework of the community, as expressed in organizations and associations, there loomed an informal stratification, a recognizable range of higher and lower status based mainly on two criteria: wealth and Talmudic learning. Attainment in these fields was considered necessary for those aspiring to positions in the formal organization; to reach office a candidate had either to belong to the hierarchy of higher-grade taxpayers, or, as a full or partial substitute, to hold one of the honorary titles, *morenu* or *haver,* accredited to the learned. Within the range of two or three generations at least, wealth and learning supported each other; the sons of the rich and the learned had a better chance to become both learned *and* rich through better educational facilities and through marriage. As, however, both wealth and learning are by their very nature attainable qualities, even the highest rungs of these societies were in theory accessible to everybody. In practice, although social mobility was not excessive by modern standards, the channels of advancement were open for the economically ingenious and the academically gifted.[37]

Another characteristic of this society was its horizontal mobility. No community, even the largest, could be said to have been self-contained and self-sufficient. Business transactions brought members of different communities into touch through correspondence or personal contact. It was a typical feature of Jewish economic activity that it could rely on business connections with Jewish communities in even far-flung cities and countries. This pertains especially to the activity of the upper class, the bankers, court agents, and purveyors. The more humble businessmen, retailers, and peddlers, even if they did not travel great distances or even go abroad, still visited in the neighborhood. Jews who made a living by sitting in their shops waiting for clients were the minority rather than the prevalent type. Outside contact being an ever-present reality for the Jewish businessman, it was not unusual for him to move from one place to another. It was not uncommon for marriages to be arranged between individuals whose communities were far apart — especially for the sons of the wealthy. Youths were, in fact, already a mobile element during the years of their education, for to attend a *yeshiva*, that is a Talmudic academy in one of the famous communities, was a commendable educational course. Those who made study and communal service a career remained, throughout their lives, ready to attend the call of another community. The greater a rabbi's fame, the larger the possible geographical circumference of his service.[38]

These channels of contact and mobility broadened the scope of Jewish society beyond the local boundaries. In fact, they extended beyond the boundaries of the Western countries. At least for the students and the learned, an exchange among Poland, Austria, Germany, England, Holland, and the French Alsace was not at all uncommon. The Sephardic communities of England, France, Holland, and northern Germany (Hamburg and vicinity), on the other hand, maintained similar cultural and religious connections with their sister communities in Italy and the

Levant. Parallel to the cultural connections were the business activities of the capitalists. Thus, besides loyalty to the local community, its tradition, and customs, there evolved a consciousness of a broader society and, beyond this, a commitment to the idea of a Jewish nation that included every Jew in the world.[39]

The common ideological commitment went far beyond the established organizational units. It was based on the strong identification with the idea of a Jewish nation, to which one belonged by birth and religious obligations and which created a demand for mutual responsibility. Therefore, it was the commitment of the individual to the Jewish tradition with its symbols and tenets that tied him to the community in both its broad and narrow sense. This attachment was achieved in the case of each individual through the process of his initiation into Jewish life, its rites, and teachings. It is true that Jewish teachings were left very much undefined and that the period from the sixteenth to the eighteenth century lacked a systematic exposition of Jewish tenets and beliefs. But such tenets were nonetheless held, exposed, and interpreted within the context of study of the holy texts, of ethical admonition, and by way of homiletic exposition. Teachers and preachers of this period drew the substance of their teachings from the Talmud and medieval sources, which were imbued with the notion of Jewish nationhood, its metaphysical origin, its religious implications, and its historical destiny. Thus, the conception of nationhood and the individual's allegiance to it, as it was expounded by philosophers and kabbalists in the Middle Ages, was easily disseminated and absorbed.[40]

The fact that the exponents of Jewish teaching could afford to indulge in homiletic exercises, displaying the well-known and playing upon it, is an indication that the fundamentals were taken for granted, that their systematic exposition was not deemed necessary. However, if the fundamentals seemed in danger of being contradicted, a theoretic deviation met with no less opposition than a practical transgression of law or custom. This is well borne out in the history of the heretical movement that emerged in the wake of the false Messiah, Sabbatai Zevi. Upon his appearance in Turkey in 1665, Sabbatai Zevi was hailed by virtually the entire nation, with a few notable exceptions, as the true Messiah. But his claim was rejected by the majority after his defection to Islam to save his own life. A minority of his believers, however, would not repudiate their own great religious experience during the excitement of the Messianic year; they preferred to accept the idea that the Messiah's apostasy belonged to the preordained course of the Redemption rather than reject his Messianic claim altogether. This led to the metaphysical conclusion that wrong might be an instrument in the divine course of events and, ultimately, to the assumption of a duality in the essence of the deity Himself, a clear heresy in the view of orthodox Judaism. The following hundred and fifty years of Jewish history is full of the constant harassment of the sect, or those suspected of belonging to it, by the exponents and guardians of Jewish orthodoxy.[41]

The most conspicuous case was that of Jonathan Eibeschütz, the rabbi of the important community of Hamburg, a great Talmudist and preacher who fell under suspicion of upholding the Sabbatian doctrine.[42] The line of defense in this controversy, as in all similar ones, was either a flat denial of the accusation or an interpretation of the suspect writings that blunted any heretical connotation. No one ever came forward with the latitudinarian argument that there is no limit to the freedom of dogmatic exposition in Judaism. True, the Sabbatians were suspected not only of holding heretical views but also of indulging in immoral practices. But there is no doubt that the dogmatic deviations were of no less concern to the guardians of official Judaism than moral infringements.

The essentially traditionalistic character of Jewish society is demonstrated perhaps even more in its attitude toward innovations on the basis of mystical experience than by its proscription against dogmatic deviations. A full-fledged religious movement of a mystical character — Hasidism — did not appear until the second half of the eighteenth century in Poland. This, therefore, lies outside the area of principal interest. On a more limited scale, however, there were also mystical eruptions in the West at an earlier date and the reactions to them provide sufficient evidence for ascertaining the position taken on such issues by the traditional society. Here the best-known case was that of Moses Hayim Luzzatto (RaMHaL), who in 1727 experienced a kind of mystical revelation and became a spiritual leader of a small group of initiates in Padua. The group seems to have regarded him as the incarnation of the Messiah and perhaps even the chosen agent of Redemption. The scene of this phenomenon was Italy, but rumors of the Paduan goings-on reached the German and Polish communities. Luzzatto himself passed through Frankfurt am Main in 1735 on his way to Amsterdam, the place of an involuntary exile. In Frankfurt he was apprehended and cited before a rabbinical court, where he was sentenced to keep a strict silence on mystical matters.[43] The main argument of Luzzatto's accusers was that by promulgating writings revealed to him through automatic speech or writing, he invited possible deviations. Essentially, they maintained that today he has pretended to write new versions of Psalms or the Zohar; "tomorrow he may appear on the scene with a new version of the Pentateuch"; [44] the apprehension, in other words, was that Luzzatto might be on the verge of trying to displace the traditional law with a new one.

Thoroughly embedded in his own tradition, the Jew felt himself bound to his own community and therefore clearly separated from Christian society. Slight though his ideological training may have been, the Jew at least knew that Judaism and Christianity were mutually exclusive and therefore that defection to Christianity meant a complete abandonment of the true faith for a false one. Non-Jewish society kept its doors open to Jews, theoretically for the whole community, but practically for individuals who accepted Christianity and joined one of the Christian churches. Such cases occurred wherever Jews lived surrounded by Christian communities. But in this period actual instances of this were not too important for the communal existence of Jews. Halakic literature, it is true, mentions cases of apostasy, as it had to determine the law for the exception as well as the mean, but Musar literature neglects the problems almost entirely.[45] Certainly, such cases could not have been too frequent at this time, in spite of some attempts on the Christian side to revitalize the evangelist spirit through the pietistic movement. A special institute for a mission to the Jews, the *institutum judaicum,* was established in Halle in 1724;[46] its records, incidentally, provide an important source for an evaluation of the attempt and its results. A thorough analysis reveals that despite the great effort of the missionaries, actual cases of conversion were few and far between. What is more important, the type of Jew who *was* attracted to the missionary movement turns out to be, in most cases, the individual who would probably have left Judaism even without such outside influence: the unfortunate, marginal Jew who had difficulty not only in making a living but even in finding a place of residence.[47] This marginal nature of the prospective convert explains the indifference of Jewish society toward the whole problem. From the seventeenth until the second half of the eighteenth century, there is no record of any lay leader or rabbi of any standing converting to Christianity, a phenomenon which did occur quite often in earlier periods of Jewish history.

The outside world did not overly occupy the Jewish mind; it was neither a field of social aspiration nor a source of acute spiritual danger. It was, however, a field for possible encounter in business dealings and contact with government authorities. The Jewish community was vitally concerned that the conduct of the individuals involved in such contact would be as unimpeachable as possible. To this end, the community exercised a far-reaching control over the dealings of the individual with the outer world. Transgressors of community regulations in this field were threatened by severe disciplinary measures and were rebuked like all who failed to uphold a fair standard of conduct in any other sphere of activity. That such control and admonition could not have taken care of the total situation is obvious. Much of the contact between Jew and non-Jew took place outside the geographic area of the community. Many Jews were not even affiliated with any community but wandered about from place to place, conducting a disjointed, unsettled life. With no fixed place of residence, they failed to develop a responsibility to institutions and their ethical demands. These Jews represented a constant danger of felony and even criminality and were a permanent source of embarrassment to the well-settled communities.[48]

Contact with the non-Jewish world also presented a problem for the well-settled. The great social hiatus that lay between the two societies could not fail to engender a double standard of obligations toward each other. In both Christian and Jewish society, it was not taken for granted that moral precepts evolved for the inner group were valid for the outer group as well. The very fact of two different systems of law governing the internal life of each society must have led to the conclusion that the yardsticks to be applied to cases of social interaction depended upon the group membership of the individuals involved. Add to this the religious biases of the two groups, and some idea of the extent of the problem emerges.

On the Jewish side, attempts were made in the period from the sixteenth to the eighteenth century to overcome these deficiencies. Theories were advanced to prove that some common basis existed for the two religions, which lead to the idea of a de facto ethical equality. The precarious situation of Jews among non-Jews was also used as a moral appeal to the individual to refrain from deeds that might endanger the physical well-being of his fellow Jews.[49]

These ideological and educational endeavors may have had some effect. They certainly did not change the basic situation, which was one of a social cleavage and moral double standard. Those who, with the emergence of a new social aspiration, attempted to remove the cleavage itself, found enough to criticize in the old situation because of its moral deficiencies and dangers.

III THE PORTENTS OF CHANGE

The picture of traditional society presented in the previous chapter was a static one giving the permanent ingredients of Jewish life during the hundred years preceding the great changeover that took place in the following century. The static picture is, however, deceptive and should not mislead us into believing that no changes occurred in Jewish society during the period between 1650 and 1750. This period, especially the second part of it, is regarded in European history as a time of slow preparation for the great upheaval that shook European society to its very foundations. The inclination is to examine events preceding this period in an effort to detect the dominating causes for later developments.

This is a delicate piece of historical accounting. The historian moves here on slippery ground, for much that seemed insignificant at the time is likely to be viewed in retrospect by him as heralding or even directly influencing later events. Common sense, however, as well as social theory assume that turning points in history, like the French Revolution or the dissolution of traditional society, cannot be sufficiently explained in terms of immediately visible causes. This assumption prompts the historian to turn to the more remote past to trace the beginnings of tears in the fabric of the old society or the emergence of a new design, new ideas, and aspirations indicating the beginning of something new.

Jewish traditional society, too, has been under scrutiny by historians who are attempting to discover the cracks in an overall structure that seemed to be unimpaired. These were interpreted as the first signs of the coming transformation of the whole traditional Jewish society. Indications, which were interpreted as the signs of change, were detected in four aspects.

The social ascent of the court Jews in the seventeenth and

eighteenth centuries has been pointed to as an undoubtedly new feature of Jewish society at that time.[1] As a result of their important economic role, these rich Jews acquired positions of influence with those in power — the emperor, king, princes, and bishops whom they served. In return for their services, they often secured privileges for themselves. Some of them were exempted from paying the *Schutzgeld* (protection money) that was a basic condition of the Jew's right to toleration in a certain place. The court Jew might also secure the right of residence for his family, his widow, or his sons-in-law. More than that, communities were founded or enlarged owing to the influence of a court Jew. In addition, court Jews were exempted from the jurisdiction of both Jewish and Gentile courts and were accountable for their actions only to the Royal Court (*Hofgericht*) like other officials of the ruler. Indeed, the court Jew's status resembled that of high officials in other respects as well. He was appointed to his post by his lord; he bore the title *Hoffaktor* or *Hofagent* and other similar titles, and received a salary. Finally, the court Jew also demonstrates his high standing by outward appearance. He is clad, if not entirely in the fashion followed by one of the other estates then, in any case, differently from his Jewish brethren. In his household his attire and equipage exhibit his wealth and influence.[2]

This type of Jew who acquires forbearance and standing by serving the politically powerful is no novelty in Jewish history. He is found wherever Jews lived amongst Gentiles and relied on the protection of the mighty. To serve the masters of the country with money and business acumen gave Jews their best chance to ascend beyond the level of the underprivileged. The Jewish financier and tax farmer of Muslim and Christian Spain are perhaps the most conspicuous examples of this.[3] Still, the court Jews of the seventeenth and eighteenth centuries seem to have surpassed all their precursors. They were more numerous, their business activities were more extensive, and their influence increased; so did their proximity to those in power. No wonder that historians came to regard them as prime movers in what was happening in Jewish society at that time.

The era of the court Jew was followed by that of Jewish emancipation. Court Jews were active in the struggle for Jewish rights — at least in the first phase of the era of emancipation — and the whole process could therefore easily be attributed to their weight and influence. This was done in a most consistent fashion by the German historian Heinrich Schnee, who more than anyone else contributed to our knowledge about the activities of the court Jews. According to Schnee, the *"emancipation of the Jews was the work of the Hoffactoren."* Not the Enlightenment, nor the message of 1789 were decisive for the emancipation of the Jews, but the numerous court Jewry (*Hoffactorentum*).[4]

Whether the ideas of 1789 can be dismissed as irrelevant to Jewish emancipation can only be determined if the process that led the Jew to make his debut into society is examined.[5] But accepting the Enlightenment and what it stands for as one of the factors does not exclude giving the court Jew his due as another of the factors that advanced emancipation. That court Jews, or better, their descendants or those that inherited their wealth and influence, pulled their weight in the negotiations that resulted in acts of legislation favorable to Jews cannot be denied. But not all legislation in favor of Jews was supported by court Jews nor owed its origin to their influence. The two perhaps most important acts, the Edict of Tolerance of the Emperor Joseph II in Austria in 1781–82 and the granting of citizenship in France by the National Assembly in 1790–91, were accomplished without a contribution by Jewish notables.[6]

The rich Jews of Amsterdam looked askance at the Dutch revolution which, in the wake of the French conquest of 1795, swept away the House of Orange under whose protection these notables ruled the Jewish community — and flourished. They thwarted rather than supported the measures intended to grant full citizenship that were taken by the Dutch National Assembly.[7] David Friedländer in Berlin had done his best since the death of Frederick the Great to improve the status of the Prussian Jews but with only small success. The Edict of 1812, which granted almost complete emancipation, was part of the general reform of the Prussian state that followed the Prussian defeat at the hands of Napoleon in 1806. In the shaping of this edict, Friedländer played the role of adviser, the expert on things Jewish. He certainly cannot be regarded as a prime mover of events.[8] The Arnsteins in Vienna worked — with doubtful results — behind the scenes during the Congress of Vienna in 1814–15 when the future status of Jews in the German countries was discussed.[9] More success met the endeavors of the Rothschilds in the ensuing decades in Frankfurt and elsewhere.[10] By then conditions had changed and the Jewish banker was no longer a court Jew proper.

For the political, economic, social, and intellectual changes of these times affected also the position and the character of court Jews. How this came about and what it meant will become clear during the course of this analysis. At any rate, the exertions of their wealthy leaders to secure a new basis of existence for the Jewish community are not unrelated to these changes. Had there been no connection, there is no reason why the wealth and influence of the court Jew should not have achieved similar results fifty or a hundred years earlier when the court Jew was at his zenith. At that time the assistance the court Jew was able to render his brethren was spasmodic and restricted to some alleviation — the repeal of the Prague Edict of Expulsion in 1745,[11] ensuring right of residence in some places, and similar activities.[12] No one at that time even remotely envisaged the possibility of the naturalization of all Jewish communities or had even considered the desirability of such an event.

It is true that the attitude of the state to the Jewish community underwent change during the Old Regime and these fluctuations may, in historical retrospect, be interpreted as heralding the impending change in the status of the Jews. At the beginning of this period, about 1650, the comparative independence and self-government of the communities or the *Landgemeinde* was taken for granted; the non-Jewish authorities demanded only that the Jewish communities control the behavior of their members and collect the taxes due them. As the idea of the centralized state progressed and its instrument, the all-pervasive bureaucracy developed, the state began also to intervene in the inner life of the Jewish communities. From this time the state laid down procedures for the election of elders, controlled the administration of communal finances, and supervised the growth of Jewish population by limiting the establishment of new families. Some of the regulations touched on practices closely bound up with the cultural habits of the Jews. In order to enable the state to control the administration of community affairs, transactions and accounts had to be recorded in German.[13] This transition from the comparatively free self-government of the community to a state-controlled organization has been exhaustively described by Selma Stern in her books on Prussian Jewry.[14]

Similar findings have been presented about many other communities — about Württemberg by A. Weber;[15] for the *Landgemeinden* of the South, recently by Daniel J. Cohen.[16] These processes of transition may be said to be a characteristic feature of the whole of German Jewry in the eighteenth century. Selma Stern saw in this growing intervention of the state into the affairs of the community an indication of the coming emancipation. She conceded that, from the standpoint of contemporary Jewry, the steps taken by the state were of a restrictive and even irksome character. But she saw in them the seeds for future liberation. "If we look at the effect of the Police State on the Jewish community from the standpoint of emancipation, then the beginnings of decomposition of Jewish self-government (*Eigenverwaltung*) cannot mean anything but the beginning of political integration of the Jews into the state. If the state superseded the self-government of communities, then it simultaneously destroyed the barriers that separated it (the state) from this corporation . . . If it compelled Jews to use the German language in bookkeeping, it at the same time laid the foundations for the cultural assimilation of the Jews." [17]

When reference is made to a relation between bureaucracy's intervention in the life of the Jewish community in the early eighteenth century and the granting of citizenship some generations later, the concern is not with observable facts: rather, it is assumed that a causal connection between events separated in time existed — but it can scarcely be corroborated by direct evidence. If it is to be substantiated at all, it must be done by critical analysis of the facts in their relation to one another.

It is true that the intervention of bureaucracy in the life of the community was steadily growing, keeping pace with the demand of the centralized state to take over such functions as taxation and jurisdiction from the estates and corporations. Estates and corporations yielded their autonomy; so did the Jewish community.

Obviously the autonomous Jewish community of the seventeenth century could not continue to function in the nineteenth. The dissolution of the autonomous community would therefore, in any event, have posed a problem to the state: what to do with the Jews who were formerly members of such communities. The granting of full emancipation was one possible solution and was, in fact, finally used. But it was not the only possible answer to the problem, and it was not given as a matter of course but only after much heart-searching, struggle, and public discussion. Other solutions were considered: the expulsion of the Jews was aired, at least theoretically; some suggested that Jews be settled in separate colonies where they be given a chance to prove their ability and willingness to provide for themselves through hard work as peasants and craftsmen before being accepted as citizens; still others wished to place the Jews in a special category of aliens who would be entitled to legal protection but, because of their different religion and culture, would not be recognized as forming part of the country's citizenry.[18] That such suggestions were in the long run discarded in favor of full emancipation has to be attributed to the trends of that time that were instrumental in shaping modern society. These were, on the one hand, the prevalence of rationalistic ideas, the secularization of the state or, at least, a loosening of the bonds that bound church and state and, on the other hand, the increasing number of Jews who were shedding tradition in favor of the cultural habits of their environment. In short, the emancipation of Jews, even in its political aspect alone, cannot be attributed only to political forces but must be ascribed also to these nonpolitical factors.

It has however been argued — and this is the third avenue to the problem — that a process of slow but significant acculturation took place among Western Jewry at least some fifty years before the breach in the structure of traditional Jewish society became visible. Sephardim are known to have acquired education and knowledge in their respective countries — France, Holland, England — since the end of the seventeenth century. In some cases, as for instance in the case of the economist Isaac de Pinto, they actively contributed to the culture of their country.[19] The early cultural adaptation of Sephardim is a well-known fact. German Jews, on the other hand, used to be regarded as living in isolation socially and culturally almost until the threshold of modernity, that is, the second half or perhaps even the last third of the eighteenth century. This assumption has lately been contested by Azriel Shohet, who maintains that the incipient dissolution of traditional Jewish society has to be antedated by a good half a century.[20] Shohet has assembled an imposing amount of data to prove that German Jews began departing from the traditional patterns of their lives as early as 1700. Shohet's data pertain to the standard of living, the laxity of religious observances, the waning of traditional evaluation of religious education and learning and the like. At the same time Shohet gives a reassessment of non-Jewish society and its values as they were seen by Jewish contemporaries. Philosophy, science, and other branches of knowledge of non-Jewish origin — banned by earlier generations — began to be cultivated, and the acknowledgment by non-Jewish society became a coveted good. In many cases this led to conversion to Christianity. As all these features are the obvious characteristics of the ensuing era of assimilation, the predating of them seems to anticipate the turning point by some two generations.

The facts as presented by Shohet cannot be discussed here in detail. Some of them can certainly be contested but others will stand examination. What calls for elucidation is their significance as an indication of change.[21] The issue to be decided is whether the new phenomena appearing in the late seventeenth and early eighteenth century in Jewish society were in the nature of variations or deviations from the traditional pattern, or if they were the elements of a new process that would lead ultimately to a new structure of society. The test for this distinction is to be found in the consciousness or mental attitudes of those who performed the acts that count as mere deviations or innovations. It depends on the ideas of the performers themselves and how they regarded the actions they took. What activated those who displayed greater than the customary luxury, who condoned greater religious laxity, who tolerated values deriving from the non-Jewish world? Did they do so because of a new outlook on life? Or did they find justification for their attitude in terms of tradition — not discarding the possibility that they might be called upon to atone. There is no doubt that the second alternative is the correct one.

The variations of the traditional pattern, even if they were conspicuous, could still be woven into the old fabric. A life of luxury was not unknown in traditional society either. If self-indulgence became excessive, compensation could easily be attained by offering more to charity or supporting the needy and the learned — as was indeed the case. The rich German Jews of the seventeenth and eighteenth century are known to have contributed liberally for all such commendable causes.[22] If laxity in observance and perhaps even gross offenses against the religious law became more recurrent, it did not mean that the transgressor had a quiet conscience. Most of the evidence for this kind of occurrence derives from the works of the moralists, the authors of Musar literature. By the very fact that they recorded these acts and condemned the practices, they testify to the sentiments the public associated with these acts. There is no reason for assuming that another attitude existed below the surface of public opinion. Appeals to rabbis by people who had committed what was regarded as a grave sin — mostly of a sexual nature — to prescribe a course of self-mortification in atonement are not less common at this time than in earlier times. If some rabbi was inclined to grant a less severe punishment — though even then it would be exorbitant by twentieth century standards — this was only a variation of an old pattern.[23] The system remained uncontested. The real turning point would arrive only when deviation was justified on the basis of new concepts that contradicted the value system of tradition.

This difference between a deviation that could be neutralized by the traditional system and one that undermined the system itself can best be demonstrated in connection with the study of science and philosophy deriving from non-Jewish sources. Shohet has adduced proofs that the two great eighteenth century rabbis, Jacob Emden (1698–1776) and Jonathan Eibeschütz (1690–1764) were familiar with current thought that could have reached them only through contact with non-Jewish sources. Both knew about the new theories and discoveries of science; they had some notion of rationalism in philosophy and of the theories about the nature of the state and human society and made use of this knowledge in their sermons and Talmudic dissertations. On the basis of his findings, Shohet concluded that Moses Mendelssohn — usually regarded as the first Jewish European thinker — had no historical claim to the title. Indeed, he had nothing new to add to what his predecessors had known.[24]

Had mere contact with ideas and concepts represented absorption, the conclusion would be valid. However, the great rabbis knew about the new ideas but did not accept them as elements of a new system of thought. They integrated them into the context of traditional thinking, which was that of homiletic exposition of the Bible and the Talmud. The new elements forfeited their original revolutionary character and were neutralized. In spite of using the new concepts, the rabbis continued to follow their medieval patterns of thought. The method of homiletics has been recognized as an adequate means of expression of traditional society. Emden and Eibeschütz were committed to this method and may rightly be regarded as exponents of traditional society. Moses Mendelssohn, on the other hand, although he succeeded in retaining his orthodox Jewish faith — that is, the acceptance of revelation and compliance with the requirements of religious law — was a modern thinker, for the justification of his faith was advanced by means of rationalistic philosophy. Not the elements nor the conclusions of thought are relevant in fixing a place in history, but the system of thought resorted to.[25]

Some of the newly evolved concepts of the postmedieval world were absorbed by Jews, but did not usurp the system of thought on which the traditional interpretation of Jewish existence was based. It was still taken for granted that the Jews were a nation whose members were scattered among the peoples of the world. The Messianic belief in an ultimate redemption and ingathering was, despite the great disappointment caused by the Sabbatian fiasco, fully retained as were other basic tenets of the Jewish tradition. Speculation was rife, even outside Sabbatian circles, as to the exact date of the Messianic appearance.[26]

Only insfoar as it can be proved that some of the basic tenets of Judaism were called in question can there be talk of an indication of change. There was, in fact, a report on a group of Sephardim living in Holland at the beginning of the eighteenth century that allegedly rejected the belief in the sacred nature of the land of Israel and refused to acknowledge the special merit claimed by the inhabitants at all times — even when the Temple lay in ruins.[27] There is scanty evidence of what was actually said, and since Rabbi Moses Hagiz was a Palestinian preacher and a propagandist for the support of Palestinian Jewry by the Diaspora, he may have been oversensitive to remarks made by people disclaiming their responsibility toward Palestine. But it is no accident that such remarks were made. Some Sephardic Jews probably felt themselves to be secure in Holland, ridiculed the idea of a return to Palestine, and rejected the financial obligation to support those who were living there. These were sporadic rather than consistent and serious convictions as is borne out by the fact that they did not find written expression and were not disseminated at that time. Though without visible effect, these feelings were indicative of a trend that might have developed under different conditions.

The position of Jews was dependent not only on their attitudes but on those of their neighbors. When did the first signs of change appear among the Gentiles? European literature in this early period of the seventeenth and eighteenth centuries has often been scrutinized by Jewish scholars for traces of a change in attitude on the part of those Gentiles whose writings and ideas represent the trend of change in other fields.[28] Following such a course of inquiry, it is necessary to guard against accepting variations within the old system for ideological innovations. As observed, the Christian conception of the Jews' place in society allowed for contradictory attitudes. It vacillated between the wish to avoid contact with Jews and the concessions that allowed Jews to live among them. The latter attitude was encouraged by economic interest combined with leniency in religious matters; or, it was prompted by the hope of gaining converts. Thus, if in seventeenth century England the admittance of Jews was recommended — motivated by economic interest but justified in theological terms — this did not mean a departure from the old conception but merely a variation on a familiar theme.

For a significant change in attitude the writings of those who anticipated the conception of a civil society and a state separated, or at least partly detached from religion and its institution, the church must be examined. It was only when a sphere of life divorced from religion evolved that a situation was created for the Jews to be included on a comparatively equal footing with Gentiles in a single social and political unit. Religious tolerance, in the sense of accepting various religious systems and institutions in one society, and the concomitant idea of the moral self-sufficiency of the state paved the way for the inclusion of the Jew in Gentile society. The early promoters of the secular basis for the state were also the forerunners of the idea of accepting the Jew into society without the expectation of his ultimate conversion. It is not surprising, therefore, to find in the works of John Locke the classic statement of the idea of a secular state and, at the same time, the recommendation for the inclusion of the Jews in it.

Although Locke's direct concern in his *Letter Concerning Toleration* (1689) was the relation between Christian denominations, his consistency led him to the conclusion that "neither Pagan, nor Mahometan nor Jew ought to be excluded from the civil rights of the commonwealth because of his religion." [29] Twenty-five years later John Toland spelled out the consequences of religious tolerance for Jews in a Christian society, though he did not adhere to the principle with full consistence.[30] Toland's starting point was not a theoretical but rather a practical one of a possible law of general naturalization that had been a political issue in England ever since the Restoration.[31] Such a law would have permitted any professing Protestant to become an English citizen. Though countenancing the exclusion of Catholics, Toland recommended the inclusion of Jews in the law. The reason for admitting aliens into the country rested on the widely held opinion that the increase of population would contribute to the wealth of the country. Unless the religion of the newcomers was politically subversive — as Toland and most of his countrymen considered Catholicism to be — there was no reason for exclusion. Jews could therefore be accepted without hesitation. In view of the fact that the admittance of Jews had been an issue in England since the time of Cromwell, Toland may be said only to have taken a stand on an old question. The novelty of his attitude lies not in the unqualified acceptance of Jews but rather in the underlying reasons for this argument. Here admittance is not to be granted as a concession on the part of Christianity to those who deny its truth, but because of the elimination of Christianity as a factor in the policy making of the commonwealth.

Yet religion continued to influence the rights of the naturalized as well as those of citizens born in the country. For Toland, perhaps inconsistently, did not surrender the idea of an established church. State offices could therefore be reserved for the adherents of the church but others, most importantly in the field of economics and public administration, would be open to Jews as well. In this Toland certainly deviated from the prevailing theory and practice throughout European society, for Jews were traditionally limited to trades and it was assumed that they would be neither capable of nor willing to take up other occupations. Toland announced his conviction that human nature was essentially the same, a basic principle of the spreading idea of rationalism — and predicted that Jews, once granted the opportunity, would take to all occupations like any other human beings.

Here, perhaps even more than in his pronouncements in favor of religious toleration, Toland anticipated a social trend that was to emerge at a later date.

In their time the conceptions of Locke and Toland were isolated phenomena. Historically they indicate a possibility rather than an expression of social reality. That they had no social impact in their own time is proved not only by the fact that these ideas raised no interest but, even more so, by actual events, which demonstrated that with the public at large the case of the Jews still turned on the traditional issues. A generation after the appearance of Toland's pamphlet, *Reasons for Naturalizing the Jews* (1714), a Naturalization Bill was introduced (1753) by the government and passed both by the House of Lords and the Commons. This bill had a most limited application. It granted individual Jews the right to be naturalized by Act of Parliament if they could meet the costs of such an expensive procedure and procure a majority vote in both Houses for their special case. This bill was duly enacted but it had to be repealed under pressure of a public outcry. The controversy engulfed the entire country. It was, as modern historical research has amply established,[32] fostered on purpose by the opposition Tory party in view of the pending elections. But this does not diminish its significance as an indication that the image of the Jew as depicted by Christian tradition and popular prejudice was predominant in the public mind.[33] But it is even more important to know that the promoters and advocates of the Jew Bill had never advanced an argument of toleration that disregarded religious considerations in civil matters. Rather, they kept to the line of a lenient Christian attitude, pointing to the economic advantages that would accrue from accepting rich Jews into the country and hinting at the prospect of eventual conversion.

The Jew Bill in England had some impact on the thought of those who dealt with the problem of the Jews on the Continent. Voltaire mentioned it in his *Essai sur les moeurs* as an example of the populace's negative attitude toward Jewish aspirations.[34] In Germany, it was a Jew, Levi Israel, who — in a pamphlet[35] written before the bill had been repealed — used the occasion to air the idea of permitting Jews to settle in the country on equal terms. The interest of the state and its material progress could be furthered by encouraging new settlers, who, together with local Jews, would contribute to the economy. The author himself had doubts, however, whether the well-understood economic interests could overcome the ingrained prejudices against Jews. The pamphlet had few reverberations, and no practical consequences. By the eighties, when the idea of Jewish integration had become a public issue, there was no mention made of Israel's pamphlet.

The hundred years from 1650 to 1750, preceding the period of change, reveal some shifts in the social position and the economic role of Jews. Some alterations in both Gentile and Jewish ideologists in defining their attitudes to one another became evident. But, on the whole, the structure of society as well as the systems of thought by which it was justified and supported, remained intact. Only sporadically are there some indications of change that, at the time, were scarcely discernible as carrying the seeds of future disruption but which, in retrospect, appear to have held out prospects for a new configuration on the plane of reality as well as in the realm of thought.

IV THE SEMINEUTRAL SOCIETY

Tangible results of a changing mentality would have manifested itself in the state or in society. The political status of Jews could have been altered — as indeed happened later, beginning with the Edict of Tolerance granted by the Emperor Joseph II in Austria in 1781–82 and followed by the various acts of emancipation. This edict did not explicitly acknowledge Jews as subjects of the emperor but, by accepting responsibility for their welfare no less than for that of other estates and denominations, implied such acknowledgment.[1] Other acts of legislation, particularly the decisions of the National Assembly of France made on January 28, 1790, and on September 28, 1791, turned the Sephardim of the South and the Ashkenazim of Alsace into full citizens. These events, however, took place at a comparatively late date when the trends of change, first appearing in ideas and concepts, had already penetrated into the apparatus of state and society, affecting the impulse to reform from above or the revolution from below. It is no wonder that the legally acknowledged acceptance of Jews as members of the body politic, being the culmination of integration, was slow in arriving. It was different where social connections were concerned. Change in the nature of social relations between Jews and Gentiles came about spontaneously and could easily reach fruition under the influence of concepts of toleration and broad-mindedness.

A new approach in the field of social relations can be said to have been achieved when Jews and Gentiles began to meet each other in situations not governed by the immediate purpose of business. At the time of traditional society, every meeting between Jews and Gentiles had its well-defined aim. The transaction of business, the teaching of Jew by Gentile or vice versa, treatment by doctors of a patient of the other community, are the recurrent patterns of social encounter between Jews and Gentiles.

These situations, although differing from one another in the grade of intimacy involved, are still defined and limited by the practical purpose behind them. Between the court Jew and the master he served in a variety of capacities, a mutual attachment may have sprung up. Nonetheless, the relation between the two remained hierarchic, with each side aware of the social distance;[2] such a relationship could continue only for as long as the manifest purpose justified it. It never would have been perpetuated for its own sake or undertaken for the purpose of cultivating spiritual interests. Sociability for its own sake or association to arrive at moral, religious, or aesthetic values are the signs of social acceptance. To locate the place and time of the new kind of social relationship between Jews and Gentiles, it is necessary to look for the first signs that heralded this new kind of meeting.

Moral (Musar) literature of the late seventeenth and early eighteenth centuries contains many complaints about Jews attending comedies and theaters.[3] The extent of such occurrences is difficult to judge; the source available is, by its nature, liable to exaggeration. But since an understanding and appreciation of theater depends on some measure of acculturation, it may be assumed that attendance was more common among Sephardim in Holland, England, and France than among the Ashkenazim, especially in Germany. The frequenting of such places of entertainment presupposes, firstly, the aspiration of Jews to join a Gentile audience; secondly, the willingness of the latter to tolerate them in their midst. For although sitting in an audience does not require active relationships among those present, it does create a measure of belonging together. That this could be achieved between Jews and Gentiles at that time indicates a diminished desire for disassociation by both groups.

A greater measure of involvement is presupposed in meetings of individuals for the pursuit of common scholarly or educational endeavor. The growing interest in Jewish culture, customs as well as literature, in non-Jewish circles brought many a non-Jewish scholar into contact with learned Jews.[4] On the other hand, Jewish students sought the instruction of non-Jewish teachers — especially in medicine — and since the last third of the seventeenth century, students were admitted to some universities, not only in Italy (where this had been quite usual for many generations) but also in Germany.[5] Still, such encounters did not necessarily make for a common ground. The Jewish student could enter the non-Jewish university with reservations against its cultural background, limiting himself to the study of his subject in the purely technical sense. The Christian scholar, on the other hand, could regard his Jewish informant as the source for those hidden facts that, Christians surmised, lay dormant in the Jewish mind and literature. In the last third of the seventeenth century, Johann Andreas Eisenmenger collected much of his data through personal contact with Jews in Frankfurt and Amsterdam and used this data afterward in his notorious "Entdecktes Judenthu." [6] On the other hand, there can be no doubt that, in many cases, association between students and teachers of the different communities created some spiritual communion between them.

Still, such random associations can scarcely be regarded as signs of the new times. Indeed, occasionally such connections had occurred even when the gap between Jewish and Gentile societies was at its widest. An indication of change can be conjectured only when the neutral or value-oriented meetings between Jews and Gentiles assumed some institutionalization or at least some permanence.

There does exist a case of institutionalized neutrality where, at least according to the declared intention, there was a basis for sociability and even the cultivation of values could be undertaken in spite of the gulf between existing religious churches and denominations. I refer to the case of the Freemasons.

I have dealt extensively with the Freemasons elsewhere[7] and shall here limit myself to summarizing the main text as it concerns the problem under discussion. Freemasonry proper — if any supposed or real forerunners of it are ignored — started in Britain in the second decade of the eighteenth century and spread in the following decades to France, Holland, Germany, and many other countries. It developed out of the craftsmen's associations which, from the seventeenth century, began to accept nonoperative, or speculative, members — that is, people who were not of the craft but found an interest in the social and spiritual life of the members of these craftsmen's associations which were known as "lodges." For these associations were not concerned only with the professional interests of their members. They provided opportunities for social contact and cultivated a special tradition of doctrine, passwords, and symbols. By 1717 many lodges consisted almost exclusively of nonoperative members. In that year four London lodges united to establish a Grand Lodge and some years later accepted a new constitution, formulated by the Reverend James Anderson, and based on some of the old traditions.

Who would and who could join the lodges? The constitution states that in ancient times masons were "charged in every country to be of the religion of that country or nation" but at the time the constitution was promulgated, it "was thought more expedient only to oblige them to that religion in which all men agree, leaving their particular opinions to themselves." [8]

This sounds like a declaration of absolute religious tolerance. Indeed, it approaches this ideal. The current trend of religious thought was deism, the postulation of a Supreme Being who can be conceived of by any rational being. In addition, it was assumed that this religion of reason was at the root of every historical religion. The assumption is clearly indicated by the wording of Anderson's constitution. It expressed in unmistakable words the intention to ignore the differences of conflicting religious doctrines. Anderson was a Presbyterian, and other members of the lodge, adherents of other Christian denominations, apparently thought it proper that there should be, apart from the chapels and churches, a neutral place where they could meet on the basis of the religious minimum they had in common.

Did they embrace Jews by their concept of the religious minimum? There is no indication whatsoever on which to base either a positive or a negative answer. Taking into consideration the social and cultural status of English Jews of that time, it is improbable that their possible aspiration to be accepted in the lodges did influence the wording of the constitution. Yet the constitution is worded in a way that includes Jews as possible members. Thus, when a Jew appeared on the scene asking for admission in 1732, one of the lodges in London did indeed accept him. For some time after his acceptance it was nonetheless debated in London lodges whether a Jew is eligible for membership. Still, English Freemasonry accepted the consequences of its avowed toleration and there was never any attempt, as far as can be learned, to change or reinterpret the first paragraph of the constitution. Thus, the doors of the lodges remained — in principle — open to Jews.

In principle. It does not follow that there was in practice no discrimination against Jews. It was the uncontested right of the old members of the lodges to reject by blackballing any candidate who did not appeal to them. There are traces of discrimination in some of the records of the English lodges but the general picture is one of comparative toleration of Jews, not only in theory but also in practice.

Good will and tolerance on the part of the Christian members did not solve all the problems of a Jewish candidate. For the deistic declaration of the constitution did not remove the traces of Christian practice in the life of the lodges. Besides some neutral symbols of Freemasonry such as the circle and triangle, he also found the Bible, including of course the New Testament, to which a Jew could not be expected to pay allegiance. Two New Testament figures played a special part in the life of the lodges: St. John the Baptist and St. John the Evangelist, whose festivals (June 24 and December 27) were accepted as Masonic celebrations. Some Jews may have been careless, others may have found some excuse to salve their consciences, but there were conscientious Jews in the lodges who cared to keep the tenets of their creed within the Masonic fraternity. For the benefit of these, special Jewish prayers were printed in 1756, avoiding any Christian references.[9] Perhaps Jews had separate lodges. Admittedly, this was an ad hoc solution. But it was not limited to England. In Holland, in France, and even in Germany, a similar approach was to be found. A Berlin lodge accepted a Jew in 1767 and permitted him to take the oath on the Five Books of Moses. It was the general climate of the eighteenth century, when religious zeal

OUT OF THE GHETTO

was receding and forbearance became a virtue with rationalists and the enlightened, that made such solutions possible.

In spite of the seemingly absolutely tolerant declaration of the Freemasons, they can hardly be considered as more than a semineutral society. This holds true even for the original English pattern. Some of its variations in prerevolutionary France, Germany, and the Scandinavian countries assumed an outspoken Christian character. The so-called Scottish rite, originating in France about the middle of the eighteenth century, tried to trace the origins of Freemasonry back to medieval Christian orders and introduced Christian elements into Masonry. Jews, unless they were ready to make far-reaching concessions, were automatically excluded.

Therefore the Jews who joined the Freemasons were few in number. Besides, since the Freemasons tried to avoid being too much in the public eye, Jewish acceptance in the lodges could scarcely represent a breakthrough for the idea of toleration. It remained a marginal affair and had no direct historical consequences.

It was just the open and unfettered behavior of Moses Mendelssohn's circle in Berlin — emerging in the 1760's and 1770's — that made it so conspicuous. Here Jews and Gentiles mingled as though the barriers separating the two societies had already been torn down. As Mendelssohn's example as well as his philosophy and teaching will be discussed on more than one occasion in this book, it is well to record here his well-known life story.[10]

Born in Dessau in 1729, the son of a Torah scribe, Moses Mendelssohn excelled in his studies with the local rabbi, David Frankel. When Frankel moved to Berlin in 1743, Mendelssohn followed him there and used the opportunity to add secular knowledge to his profound rabbinical scholarship. He was lucky to find a teacher in the person of Israel Levi, a Polish Jew from Szamos who excelled in mathematics and Jewish philosophy and must be considered one of the first promoters of Enlightenment in Jewish society, with all that this implies. On leaving the yeshiva, he made his living in Berlin, first as a bookkeeper in one of the Jewish firms and later as a textile merchant. Through these occupations he might have met non-Jews, in the traditional pattern of contact in business. But he was drawn into a more intimate relationship with non-Jews through a common interest in the study of what was called in Jewish parlance at that time "secular knowledge" — languages (German, French, English, Latin, and later even Greek), mathematics, and all branches of philosophy. The story goes that Mendelssohn met Ephraim Gotthold Lessing at the chess table. What bound them, however, in a lifelong friendship was the common pursuit of philosophical inquiry and literary creativity. For Mendelssohn stood out from other Jewish youth who might have taken up the study of similar subjects. He not only absorbed the elements of European culture — to be sure, mainly in its German version — but also became creative himself.

Mendelssohn's first publication had as its title *Philosophical Conversations* (1755); this was followed by other essays of similar nature. His European reputation was based on his *Phädon* (1767), which set out to prove the immortality of the soul, a tenet that was being damaged by the skepticism of the rationalistic philosophers. European society could ill afford to give up this tenet, universally regarded as the pillar supporting the whole edifice of the morality of man. Thus, by a timely reaction to an acute problem, Mendelssohn proved his involvement with society. What is more, the literary composition of *Phädon* is an expression of Mendelssohn's intellectual journey from the exclusively Jewish environment to European society. According to his own testimony in a Hebrew letter to his friend Naphtali Herz Wessely, he had originally intended to deal with the problem of the immortality of the soul in a Hebrew treatise based on a collection of Jewish sources. Had this plan been realized, the Hebrew book would have represented a continuation of an earlier attempt by Mendelssohn to address himself to a Hebrew-reading Jewish public through a periodical he had started in about 1755.[11] His intention with this publication was, no doubt, to introduce enlightenment to his Jewish contemporaries. This earlier attempt was discontinued, probably for lack of response. Mendelssohn's remark that he had originally intended to write a Hebrew version of *Phädon* reveals

OUT OF THE GHETTO

that he had not yet relinquished the idea of addressing himself to a Jewish audience. His reasons for finally abandoning this idea are not known but the result is clearly stated in Mendelssohn's own words in the letter mentioned. "A change in the language has brought a change in the subject matter." [12] In fact, instead of inquiring into the problem in its Jewish context, Mendelssohn followed the example of a Greek dialogue and, as for the content, if he was inspired at all by his Jewish sources pertaining to the problem, he succeeded in suppressing them. For the arguments in favor of the immortality of the soul were finally put forward along the lines of Leibnizian-Wolfenian philosophy. Had other sources not clearly revealed that the author was in full command of another cultural tradition, it would not have been possible to surmise it from perusing the *Phädon*. Perhaps it is superfluous to state that the changeover to another cultural tradition goes hand in hand with visualizing other social goals. Instead of writing for the Jewish reader, Mendelssohn addressed himself to the German and European public. Not only intellectually but also socially Mendelssohn now transcended the confines of the Jewish community and became part also of the non-Jewish environment.

The philosopher's home had always been a magnet for the intellectuals of the day. When he became a celebrity, his home became a target for travelers and often the meeting with Mendelssohn was one of the main attractions of their stay in Berlin. Mendelssohn also participated in the activities of some of the learned societies, where lectures were held and appropriate subjects discussed.[13] As Berlin had no university, the societies served as social centers for the learned and the educated. To be admitted to one of these meant acknowledgment of membership to the intellectual elite of the town and perhaps even of the country.

To be sure, Mendelssohn was neither the only nor the first Jew to achieve this status in Berlin. His friend Aron Gumperz, son of a wealthy Berliner, had already preceded him.[14] Gumperz had had the usual Jewish education, to which he added a knowledge of philosophy, mathematics, and literature. It was he who helped Mendelssohn to pursue the same course of self-education. Gumperz frequented the houses of enlightened Christian scholars and also became a member of the coffeehouses where Mendelssohn followed him and surpassed him by far in actively contributing to the intellectual endeavors of these societies. Mendelssohn in his turn set a precedent to be followed by others. The best-known among his followers is Dr. Marcus Herz, a physician who was one of the first to understand the new Kantian philosophy. Herz lectured on problems of philosophy and science to a largely Gentile audience.[15] Another philosopher of standing, originally a Lithuanian Talmudist — a mixture of an original thinker and a bohemian — was Salomon Maimon.[16] Maimon attracted attention in Berlin, Bresslau, and other towns where he came into contact with those interested in philosophy. Other Jews, less conspicuous perhaps in their scholarly achievements, were nonetheless given access to the circles of the intellectual elite.

This social leniency was the work of the generation of the 1770's and 1780's. It could only have been achieved by the emergence of interests in intellectual quests and moral and social values beyond the confines of the religious-oriented tradition. As society extricated itself from the traditional ties linking it to religious concepts of a predominantly Christian character, a way was opened for the Jew to enter. Still it is doubtful whether even this group can be called more than a semineutral society. In fact, even Mendelssohn's integration into non-Jewish society was incomplete. His exclusion as a Jew from Freemasonry is a case in point. Whereas his Christian friends Gotthold Ephraim Lessing, Friedrich Nicolai, and Christian Wilhelm Dohm and others were Freemasons, some of them even taking a leading part in the movement, and placing high hopes in its restorative spiritual force, Mendelssohn could not aspire to membership in a lodge. He did express some reservations about the high expectations his friend Lessing had of the Freemasons' influence.[17] Mendelssohn certainly could not concede the Freemasons' claim to exclusive spiritual perfection as he, a Jew, was excluded from a taste of it.

Mendelssohn remained aloof from some societies to which he would certainly have belonged had he not been a Jew. He was approached as early as 1762 by a Swiss writer, Isaak Iselin by name, to join a patriotic society whose object seems to have been to discuss political and social reform. Mendelssohn disqualified himself on the grounds of his being a Jew. "You know how little share my co-religionists have been given in all freedoms of the country (*Landesfreyheiten*). The civic oppression to which we are being condemned by the all too ingrained prejudice, lies like a dead load on the wings of the spirit and renders them incapable of ever attempting the high flight of the freeborn." [18] This is said less in self-deprecation than in resignation to the lot of the Jew who, while philosophizing on abstract problems, was excluded from suggesting practical social and political solutions. On another occasion the exclusion was the direct result of the low status occupied by the Jews in the estimate of the highest state authorities. The Academy of Science in Berlin elected Mendelssohn to membership in 1771. The election had to be endorsed by the king, the enlightened Frederick II, who refused and, on being approached a second time by the Academy, would not budge from his previous stand.[19]

The limited nature of the integration achieved by Mendelssohn and his group is best illustrated by the fact that the Gentile mind did not expect these enlightened Jews to continue remaining Jews. Some observers felt that the active participation of the Jew in the non-Jewish environment was a move toward Christianity. Although most Christians were able to reconcile their attachment to Christianity with their participation in the endeavors of the Enlightenment, they could not imagine a Jew making a similar adjustment. They expected, therefore, that the enlightened Jew would accept the natural consequences of his deviation from the customary Jewish way of life by joining the Christian churches. Some of Mendelssohn's Christian admirers were silently hoping for his conversion; others privately urged him to arrive at such a decision. Finally he was publicly approached by Johann Caspar Lavater, one of the important exponents of enlightened Christianity, and asked to clarify his position. Lavater dedicated to Mendelssohn a book (translated from the French) that contained proofs of the truth of Christianity and demanded that Mendelssohn disprove the argument or yield to its validity and accept Christianity.[20]

Mendelssohn did not take up this challenge. Affirming most solemnly his sincere conviction of the truth of Judaism, he declined to discuss the substance of his objections to Christianity. Instead, he taught his opponents a lesson in religious toleration. He asked to be left undisturbed as a Jew, as he himself was obliged not to disturb Christians.[21] By upholding the virtue of toleration, Mendelssohn claimed not only to conform with the dictates of reason and enlightenment but also to be in full harmony with the tenets of Judaism. As concerned toleration, he claimed that Judaism was on a higher level than Christianity, the missionary zeal of whose exponents he had himself experienced.[22]

His reticence on the controversial differences between Judaism and Christianity was not the result of any concession on his part; rather, it was dictated by an apprehension to discuss the religious tenets of the majority by a member of the still underprivileged minority. He was careful to apply to the church authorities, the Consistory, to be permitted to write on the subject. The permission was granted but with the understanding that Mendelssohn would himself know the limits to be observed. On the Jewish side, too, there were misgivings on the part of many who feared the results of a Jew's criticism of Christianity.[23] Thus Mendelssohn restricted his answer, and instead of discussing points of difference, he gave reasons for not discussing them. In this he was in accord with the spirit of the Enlightenment.

Lavater's public appeal to Mendelssohn was generally regarded as a tactless gesture; even more deplored by the general public was a subsequent literary molestation by one Balthasar Kölbele, who embellished his appeal for Mendelssohn's conversion with defamatory remarks of a personal and anti-Jewish nature. Mendelssohn had the sympathy of broad-minded Christians who felt that a man should not be publicly questioned about his convictions. But this did not mean that many of these Christians were not waiting for a spontaneous decision on his part.[24] The Jew who participated in the spiritual and social life of the enlightened and yet remained a professing Jew was too new a phenomenon to be taken for granted. Indeed, the Lavater affair was later repeated by another public appeal to Mendelssohn to convert. This happened during the last phase of his life, in 1782, when the first signs of change in the Jewish destiny appeared and Mendelssohn himself began to believe in the possibility of integration.

The appeal came anonymously in a pamphlet entitled *Das Forschen nach Licht und Recht*.[25] The mystification surrounding the authorship of this pamphlet is unclarified to this very day. The real author in the technical sense of the word seems to be August Friedrich Cranz, a pamphleteer and occasional ghost-writer. Cranz served the Jewish enlightened of Berlin in this capacity, in their fight against the conservatives and the rabbis. In the above-mentioned pamphlet, he turned against the master of the group and had good reason to conceal his authorship. He therefore attributed the work to a Viennese author by signing the pamphlet with the initial "S . . . ," spreading the word that it was Josef von Sonnenfels. Sonnenfels, of Jewish descent, was a professor of political science and Councillor to the Emperor who had attained social and intellectual eminence. Mendelssohn, taken in at first, felt obliged to answer the appeal of the respected Sonnenfels, one of the participants in preparing the Edict of Tolerance.

The pseudonymic author observed that Mendelssohn, in his statement on possible reform of the Jewish status, had mentioned that the coercive power of the Jewish community to control the religious behavior of its members was an anomaly and should be abolished. Being somewhat acquainted with Jewish sources, he said that Mendelssohn in this statement conceded the invalidity of an important feature of Jewish tradition that provided for the enforcement of Jewish law. This surrender of part of Jewish tradition, the author claimed, ought to lead to a total rejection in favor of Christianity.

In answer to this challenge, Mendelssohn wrote *Jerusalem*, his most comprehensive statement on the relationship between state and religion, the specific dogmatic content of Judaism, and the place of Judaism in the modern world. The details of this will be considered later. Here the concern is with the overall significance of this affair, which indicated the precarious situation of the enlightened Jews whose deviation from the traditional pattern of life and thought was easily interpreted as a halfway station on the way to Christianity.

Mendelssohn was not the only Jew to be annoyed by would-be missionaries. The same happened to Ephraim Kuh, the first German Jewish poet of some importance, and a great admirer of Mendelssohn. Kuh spent the years 1763–1768 in Berlin and frequented Mendelssohn's house. Then he traveled for three years in Holland, France, Italy, Switzerland, and southern Germany. Returning to his home town, Breslau, he found himself at variance with the traditionalists in the Jewish community. His Christian acquaintances took this as an indication that he was prepared to embrace Christianity. One zealous clergyman approached him publicly to take the decisive step. Kuh, who was a very sensitive and somewhat unstable type, was deeply hurt. His departure from the usual paths of traditional Jewish life was misinterpreted as an approach to Christianity — as had been done in the case of Mendelssohn.[26]

What did emerge, first of all, from the penetration of the Enlightenment into Jewish circles was not the inclusion of the enlightened Jews in the society of non-Jews. Instead, there came into being a particular Jewish variation of enlightened society that had some contact with their non-Jewish counterpart but, on the whole, remained socially aloof and also conceived of themselves as having a special social mission — namely, the spreading of enlightenment to the Jewish communities. Thus, enlightened Jews were working on two fronts: as writers, educators, and reformers they catered for their own brethren and pursued at the same time the culture of Enlightenment common to them and their non-Jewish counterparts, if possible in social communion with the non-Jew. Such communion existed but it can scarcely be said to have achieved the abstract model of a neutral society conceived by the propounders of Enlightenment. At most it can be said to have achieved the status of a semineutral society.[27] Faced with the marginal decomposition of both Jewish and non-Jewish society, it is no wonder that some favored an alliance between the uprooted of both sides on the basis of fusion of the religious symbols and tenets of both religions. This was attempted by the Order of the Asiatic Brethren, a kind of imitation, or travesty, of the Freemasons but never acknowledged by the latter. The Order was founded in 1781–1783 in Vienna and branched out to Prague, Berlin, Hamburg, and other German towns. The founders were impoverished aristocrats, bogus spiritualists, among them some Jews — one of them baptized — imbued with Jewish tradition and initiated in the love of Kabbala. The ideological foundations were accordingly a mixture of Christian and Jewish, especially kabbalistic, elements. The symbols used in rites and ceremonies were chosen from the traditions of both religions. Christian and Jewish members alike would encounter the familiar here and have to reconcile themselves to what they had always felt belonged to an alien religion. Interestingly enough, no small number of Christians — among them some from the upper strata of society — were attracted by the association, and some of the enlightened rich Jews joined as well. Here, at last, they found a society that openly declared its willingness to forego the exclusiveness that arose from the gulf that separated the two inimical religions.[28]

Absolute tolerance, however, did not last even in this extraordinary association. The Austrian authorities became suspicious of secret societies and the Order had to move its headquarters to Schleswig, where they found a protector in the person of Landgraf Karl von Hessen. The Landgraf was an enthusiast of secret lore, the Kabbala included, but he thought to find also in that a vindication for the Christian truth. Other members of the Order were similarly inclined. At the same time, the avowed tolerance toward Jews in the Order came under attack by Freemasons proper, who did not live up to the original principle of their founders. The leaders of the Order of Asiatic Brethren gave in and the Jewish members of the Order became the victims of discrimination. The brotherhood did not last for longer than a decade. By 1792 it was on the way out.[29] It was a product of the last days of the Old Regime when the process of decadence and social decomposition made all kinds of new experiments and combinations possible.

In a certain sense it is also owing to this atmosphere that there came into being the literary salons of the famous Jewesses Henriette Herz and Rachel Varnhagen in Berlin and that of Fanny von Arnstein in Vienna.[30] Their homes soon became the meeting places of celebrities, writers, intellectuals, officials, and statesmen. Among those who frequented the Berlin salons were the famous brothers von Humboldt, Wilhelm a humanist and statesman, Alexander, philosopher and scientist, and Friedrich Schleiermacher the theologian. In Vienna, Josef von Sonnenfels, the social reformer, and Theodore Körner mixed with many lesser lights whose claims to be admitted here were based on their capacity to contribute to the atmosphere of social ease and entertainment. The salons represented for the visitors — if not for their hostesses — the occasional adventure with the marginal character that could be overlooked by those who would otherwise perhaps have been more careful in their choice of social contact. As Henriette Herz herself observed: "The aristocracy was too far removed from the Jew in civic society to appear as his equals even when they mixed with them." [31] The Jewish salons were thus frequented by many who, nonetheless, retained reservations with regard to Jewish integration into state and society.

Although integration of Jews into non-Jewish society remained incomplete — even in the circles where, in fact, great changes occurred, its historical significance remains undisputed. Indeed, in the eyes of contemporaries, the partial disappearance of barriers between Jew and Gentile was hailed as a great social revolution. It looked as though segregation between Jews and non-Jews had been dispensed with. This impression contributed to the expectation of an impending change in all sections of society. The details of this hope were spelt out as a kind of social utopia where an entirely new relationship between Jews and Gentiles was visualized for the not-too-distant future.

V THE IMAGE OF THE FUTURE

The interrelation between change in social reality and in social thinking is too complicated to be neatly spelled out by the historian who seeks to establish the sequence of cause and effect. Sometimes, however, development on one of the two planes becomes so accelerated that it leaves the course of events on the other far behind. In the description given of the semineutral society that emerged in the last third of the eighteenth century in certain places in Germany, the concern was with the change that took place in social reality. This shift presupposes, of course, a corresponding change of attitude indicative of changing ideas. On the other hand, within the circle of the enlightened, ideas evolved that went far beyond the changes that had, until then, taken place in reality. For this change in reality pertained mostly to the social sphere; other fields, such as civil status or occupational distribution, as well as the traditional institutions of Jewish society, remained wholly or almost untouched. Enlightened social thinkers, Jews and non-Jews alike, had evolved conceptions in all these fields that transcended reality. They projected an image of the future in which everything pertaining to the Jews was to be radically different from that which had obtained up to that time.

Taking 1789, the year of the French Revolution, when social thinking received a mighty impetus from social action, it might be said that a complete program had by then already been fully elaborated. The principal exponents of these new propositions were Christian Wilhelm von Dohm[1] on the non-Jewish side and Moses Mendelssohn[2] and Naphtali Herz Wessely[3] on the Jewish side. Many others, especially on the non-Jewish side, participated in discussions, contributing by agreeing or dissenting. The proposals they made will be considered not by examining the work of each writer but as their ideas touch on the various areas of concern here.

It was clear to the promoters of the Jewish case that a radical turn in the destiny of the Jews depended upon their acceptance as citizens in their respective countries. A suggestion to this effect had already been put forward by a Jewish writer who, in 1753, argued that the naturalization of the Jews would benefit the country's economy.[4]

The idea reappeared occasionally in the 1770's, prompted by humanitarian or charitable Christian motives. Though the term "naturalization" was sometimes used, it had a different connotation from that appearing in the original English context. For the suggestion did not (as it did in England) concern the importation of foreign Jews, but rather those who lived in the country and were still regarded as aliens. In this at least the new suggestions represent a fresh angle. From now on the Jewish issue was no longer merely a question of being admitted; it was also one of being accepted as citizens. The issue of acceptance began to be discussed along with the question of admittance. As, however, the suggestions of acceptance appeared sporadically and were not part of a broader conception of the role of the Jew in state and society, they cannot be regarded as of great consequence.[5] Thus, the great merit of Christian Wilhelm von Dohm's *Über die bürgerliche Verbesserung der Juden* was that it considered the possible acceptance of the Jews by inquiring into conditions necessary for and the possible effects of such acceptance not only for the Jews but also for the accepting state and society.

Dohm's suggestions, like earlier ones, concerned Jews already settled in the country. He explicitly stated that, in the case of foreigners, non-Jews were to be preferred over Jews. Those Jews already admitted, however, should be given full civil rights and, in exchange, be obligated to fulfill all the duties of citizens. This, at least, was to be the ultimate result of the full implementation of the principle that religion and national origin should not play a part in the allotment of duties and distribution of benefits on behalf of the body politic. For the immediate future, however, Dohm still foresaw a restriction on Jewish rights. With respect to state officers, the indigenous inhabitants of the country should have preference over the newly admitted.[6] In this, as in his prejudice against foreign Jews, Dohm revealed that his thoughts moved along two different levels. On the level of theoretical expectations, he foresaw a state separated from the church and freed from the burden of established estates with their particular privileges. In a state founded upon the loyalty of free citizens under the law, Jews who would free themselves from their allegiance to their particular tradition and institutions would also be able to derive the full benefit of citizenship. For the time being, however, Dohm took into account the prerogatives of the established estates and, as will be seen later, the Jews' attachment to some of their institutions.[7] As he was himself an official of the Prussian state, which was based upon a strict division into estates with rights and duties, he did not wish to appear subversive or revolutionary. He suggested that the full measure of his *Judenreform* would be achieved when, exposed to the influence of reason and enlightenment, the privileged classes would voluntarily surrender their claim to any particular advantages.

Mendelssohn followed Dohm, but only on the more abstract level of his thinking. Mendelssohn relinquished his earlier position in which he, the Jew, resigned himself to the fate of the underprivileged: when signs of impending change appeared at the beginning of the 1780's, Mendelssohn, in contrast to his earlier passivity, became the outspoken interpreter of Jewish expectations.[8] More of a philosopher than Dohm and unhampered by official affiliation, he unreservedly put forward the principle of the separation of church and state.[9] The acceptance of Jews as equal citizens followed from this principle as a matter of course. Mendelssohn's justification for the separation of church and state was rational and well-defined. Since state and religion have different spheres of influence — the state that of action; religion that of *Gesinnung*, conviction and intention — a separation between them is both natural and feasible. Indeed, Mendelssohn continued, the combination of church and state in both Christian and Jewish history is an outrage to reason, and should be terminated as soon as possible.[10] Mendelssohn was unconcerned as to how this final termination was to be accomplished and relied on the ultimate victory of reason to fulfill his expectations; he merely pronounced his conviction that the aim would indeed be achieved.

Dohm assumed that the Jews, since they had become citizens, would take to all occupations, handicrafts and agriculture included, and that the anomaly of the castelike concentration in trade would cease. Only then would the benefit, inherent in the population increase — resulting from the acceptance of aliens — reveal itself. That the Jews, with changing conditions, would readily give up trade as their exclusive pursuit Dohm, like John Toland, fully expected because of his belief in the oneness of all human nature. Their one-sidedness he attributed to their traditional exclusion from most fields of human activity by the state and society in which they lived. Dohm agreed that the Jewish propensity to trade had been so conditioned historically and had become so ingrained that it could not be expected to change unless occupational choice was channeled by the state. This could be achieved by limiting the number of concessions granted to Jewish traders in a particular place and by releasing Jewish craftsmen from the payment of taxes. Such devices, however, would be necessary only as a beginning; in the course of time freedom of choice would lead to equal occupational distribution.

Dohm was not blind to the fact that the introduction of Jews into new fields of activity would necessitate more than the removal of legal restrictions; resistance on the part of those who traditionally occupied these fields would also have to be overcome. Here, once again, Dohm's thinking moved in two different lines. His ultimate expectation was that the craft guilds would altogether disappear and free competition prevail in this sphere as in that of trade. However, Dohm, warned by the abortive attempt to dispose of the guilds made by Anne Robert Jacques Turgot in France, was prepared to bide his time and was dissuaded from suggesting such a radical step. He recommended, instead, permission for Jewish craftsmen to work outside the guilds and regarded this as a wholesome measure by which the crippling influence of the guilds could be curbed.[11]

As might be expected, Mendelssohn fully concurred with Dohm in this recommendation for freedom of choice as regards occupation. But he did not share the assumption that the traditional occupations of the Jews were less important to the economy than handicrafts and agriculture. Not only the merchant, he claimed, contributed to the weal of the nation by transferring otherwise unattainable goods from country to country, but even the petty trader and peddler — the despised, most-Jewish pariah of the time — did the same on a smaller scale by bringing commodities to the customers' doorsteps. This claim, however, did not prevent Mendelssohn from hoping that Jews would relinquish their exclusive attachment to these fields. He was even more emphatic than Dohm in repudiating the charge that the occupational one-sidedness of the Jews was to be laid at their own door. The fault lay rather with non-Jewish society; in this connection Mendelssohn coined his famous phrase: "They bind our hands and then complain that we do not make use of them." [12]

The expectation that Jews would undertake manual occupations and venture into agriculture raised the further question of their ability to do so without coming into conflict with Jewish religious precepts. The same question arose with regard to the duties to the state that citizenship would impose upon the Jew. Would he be able to serve in the army when it entailed desecrating the Sabbath or violating the dietary laws? In agriculture a ban against working on the Sabbath would preclude the performance of urgent jobs that a peasant was called upon to do for his livestock or on the farm. The prohibition on pork, the cheapest food available, would penalize the Jewish peasant.[13] In other respects the role of religion in the life of the Jews, now recommended for full citizenship, had to be given some consideration. Should Jews retain their right to organize themselves into religious communities with apposite legal institutions and command a measure of control over the lives of their members? Interestingly enough, Dohm, the Gentile, was more willing to compromise on this point than was Mendelssohn, the Jew. Dohm saw no reason for compelling the Jews to constitute a community; they would have the right to do so if they wished and could exclude those who dissented from the defined tenets and practices. What is more, the Jewish community should be assisted in implementing its rules by the secular arm of the state in the same way as help was given to the Christian churches. Dohm also endorsed the prevailing practice of giving Jews the right to a choice of jurisdiction before Jewish courts and to be judged according to Jewish law even if their case came up before a non-Jewish court of appeal.[14] Mendelssohn, who himself had contributed to a compendium of Jewish law in German for the benefit of Gentile judges,[15] could not but assent to Dohm's endorsement of the practice. But he launched a spirited protest against Dohm's concession to the Jewish community to exclude dissenters even by force. This, he maintained, would amount to the condoning of an ecclesiastic ban; and as Mendelssohn allotted to religion only matters of conviction and spiritual exercise, it was only consistent to exclude any coercive measure.[16] In addition, his emphatic objections seem to reflect his own personal involvement in the issue. He himself was threatened with a ban, though not actually banned, because of his translation of the Pentateuch. He also witnessed repeatedly in his own lifetime the pronunciation of bans that could, at best, have been described as arbitrary.[17]

Mendelssohn could not but be aware of the difficulties the Jew would encounter upon entering into new social and occupational fields. He must also have felt the weight of the argument that citizenship could not easily be reconciled with some tenets of Jewish religion, for instance the dogma of an ultimate return to Palestine, which would conflict with a citizen's allegiance to his own country.[18] It is, however, doubtful whether he realized the extent, or spelled out the details, of these difficulties. With respect to the messianic belief, he maintained that it was no more than a simple formula appearing in the prayerbook and remarked — none too philosophically — that the repetition of such formulae would not greatly influence real behavior.[19] As to the conflicting practical demands of religion and citizenship, he restricted himself to the cryptic advice that in the new situation Jews should attempt to comply with the duties of both as well as they could.[20] Having

OUT OF THE GHETTO

himself found a personal solution to the problem of being faithful to the values of two worlds, he thought himself entitled to recommend it to others.

As an outsider Dohm could take a more detached view of the future of Jewish religion. In his recommendation for the immediate future he reckoned with Jewish religion, accepting what was customary at that time, and wished to exercise the principle of toleration toward it. But he clearly expected an eventual adaptation on the part of the individual and even a transformation of religious traditions. To the objection that Jews would be prevented from taking up certain occupations because of a conflict with religious obligations, he answered that, in the event of such conflict, enlightened self-interest would always gain the upper hand. The same would then apply to the fulfillment of civic duties, particularly military service. Should the Jews refuse to serve in the army because of such religious prescriptions as Sabbath and dietary laws, they would then lose their claim to citizenship, and it would not even be unjustified to expel them from the country. In fact, Dohm was sure not only that the individual Jew would give priority to his patriotic duty over his religious scruples, but that even the religious authorities would sanction such preference. He relied in this assessment on historical examples of Jews who had fought in the armies of ancient times as well as on reports of events not too long distant in which Dutch Jews fought on the Sabbath with the sanction of the Chief Rabbi of Amsterdam. But fundamentally Dohm's prediction rested upon his firm conviction that religious beliefs and observances would always give way to the needs and interests deriving from what he considered the more vital commitments of man.

A convinced deist at heart, Dohm could not attribute too much substantiality to the dogmas or precepts of any positive religion. He expected that the future would see the establishment of a denomination whose teachings would be limited to the religion of nature, that is, the self-understood conclusions of reason concerning the Supreme Cause and morality. In fact, he reckoned upon a substantial contingent for this denomination from those Jews who, with the amelioration of their social condition, would defect from their tradition altogether.[21] Here again Dohm envisaged a change in the status of the Jews as being connected with the transformation of society-at-large.

If Dohm's expectations of a sect of adherents to natural religion was never realized, his prediction concerning the variegations in religious tradition in the Jewish community turned out to be remarkably correct. According to his estimate, different attitudes would evolve. Some would reject the whole body of religious observances, retaining only the main tenets of the Jewish religion, which also conform to the religion of reason. Others would select from the ritual what seemed to conform to modern taste and conviction and reinterpret the whole body of tradition to adapt it to the needs of changing conditions.[22] This prediction disregarded the admonition of Mendelssohn to his brethren to adhere to the whole complex of the law to which they were bound by the covenant of Sinai. Mendelssohn identified Jewish teachings with the self-evident tenets of natural religion and thus Jewish law remained, in his theory, the only unique feature of Judaism.[23] Dohm assessed the prospective reaction to Mendelssohn's appeal in a crude but realistic estimate of human nature. He claimed that as the observance of Jewish law would, under changing conditions, become an impediment to economic and social advance, most Jews, unconcerned with the belief system underlying obligations, would simply drop observance altogether. Dohm predicted that even Mendelssohn's disciples would refuse to follow his lead on this point as it would run counter to their own feelings.[24]

The image of the future evolved by the enlightened touched not only on tradition and institutions; they expected the very character of the Jew to be transformed. This change was to be brought about through education, by which means the Jewish character had been molded hitherto. It was part and parcel of the weltanschauung of the Enlightenment to believe in the plasticity and perfectibility of man, and this principle was also applied in the case of the Jews.

According to the new expectation, the Jew was to be exposed

to the influence of the majority culture. This was first of all to be achieved by teaching him the language of his environment and encouraging him to drop his own vernacular, *Judendeutsch*. Mendelssohn's generation still used this language; he himself corresponded in it with his fiancée and later with others of his circle.[25] But the language was rapidly falling into discredit; it began to be regarded as crude and graceless. Indeed it was not considered a language at all but a corrupt form of German. Some of the German governments had already banned its use in business bookkeeping, thereby providing a strong practical incentive for learning German.[26] The newly emerging desire to come into social contact with and participate in the culture of the environment supplied the deeper, if less practical motivation. Mendelssohn's translation of the Pentateuch was an expression of this desire and became at the same time a tool for its realization. Young people who had been brought up in the institutions of traditional Jewish learning taught themselves German by using this new translation.[27]

Those who conceived of a new Jewish role in society began to realize that the old type of education was deficient.[28] The wealthy, who had always educated their children through private tutors and included secular subjects in the curriculum, now shifted the emphasis from the traditionally Jewish to these secular subjects. Mendelssohn's children were brought up in this fashion — with results that will be observed later — but the new preference was about to be shown by a larger public. Suggestions had already been made in 1761 and then in 1778 in Berlin for a new type of school, appropriate to the new condition, for the benefit of indigent Jews who could not educate their children without some kind of public support.[29] The launching of such a new institution tacitly assumed the validity of a new philosophy of Jewish education. The philosophy amounted to the principle that Jewish tradition was not the exclusive source for the values upon which the new generation of Jews should be nourished. Jewish teachings had to be complemented by the general knowledge man had accumulated or even deferred to a later stage. Precisely this program was now recommended by one who had been regarded as an enlightened but faithful follower of the Jewish tradition, Naphtali Herz Wessely.[30]

Wessely was a friend of Mendelssohn's and collaborated in the Hebrew commentary to the translation of the Pentateuch. Wessely's was a less sophisticated mind than Mendelssohn's; he was more a poet than a thinker and he easily reconciled the ideas of the Enlightenment with Jewish tradition. Wessely retained his allegiance to Hebrew, and Jewish society continued to be his reading public. Though writing poetry was somewhat new and though, too, his commentaries to some parts of the Bible and to the part of the Mishnah known as "The Ethics of the Fathers" promulgated some new ideas, he was still well received in traditional Jewish circles. His books were approved by leading rabbinical authorities.[31] It was perhaps just because of his warm reception in traditional circles and his own naiveté that he did not hesitate to put forward a kind of blueprint for Jewish education when the occasion arose.

The occasion was the Edict of Tolerance of Austria in 1781, which obliged Jews in the emperor's domain to erect schools of their own or send their children to Christian institutions. Both alternatives implied granting children a certain measure of secular education. Wessely surmised correctly that traditional-minded Jews would be alarmed and would regard the demand as an infringement on their religion. In order to allay such apprehensions, Wessely set out to write a pamphlet to prove that the emperor's suggestions were not only not detrimental to Judaism but might even become a means of enhancing it.[32] Of course, the underlying assumption of Wessely's thesis was that traditional Jewish education was inadequate and needed reform anyway, the emperor notwithstanding. His basic principle was that there were two sources of teaching: one, the Torah of God, and the second the Torah of Man. By the Torah of Man he meant teachings that could be developed through man's reason; by the Torah of God, the content of revelation that would otherwise have remained unknown. In concrete terms the Torah of Man would contain the secular knowledge evolved through human reason and research. The Torah of God would be the literary exposition of Jewish tradition. As a faithful Jew, Wessely could not but rank the Torah of God higher than the Torah of Man, but this was only a theoretical evaluation. In educational practice, the teaching of the divine Torah would be dependent upon a previous acquaintance with secular knowledge. For, as the theory ran, the divine Torah was a supplement, designed for the benefit of the Chosen People alone, which would be left without foundation if not based upon the knowledge that was obligatory for all mankind. For all practical purposes, this meant that in the first stages, the elements of general knowledge had to be acquired and only in the later stages was Jewish tradition to be added. Such a program obviously contradicted accepted practice. It even exceeded a conservative interpretation of the emperor's edict. This was reason enough for the traditionalists to decry the program and its author. An even more basic reason for the rejection was the underlying theory of Wessely that stripped Jewish teaching of any but its purely Jewish traditional objectives. Other objectives, including moral betterment through education, common to society at large, would be reached by acquiring general knowledge — that is, from a study of the Torah of Man. For traditional Jewish learning there remained only the secondary function of introducing the student to unique Jewish obligations and duties.[33]

For the inquiry here the case of Wessely has a special significance. He represents the divided spiritual allegiance of the enlightened Jew. The Torah of Man is a conception designating the common spiritual endeavor in which Jews and non-Jews are engaged; this could only be conceived by someone who felt himself to be part of a society that included both Jews and non-Jews. Wessely was not intimately associated with the non-Jewish Enlightenment, as was Mendelssohn; but he was aware of this possibility of social contact by his own casual experience and from what he observed in others. This was sufficient to turn non-Jewish society in his mind into what a sociologist would call "the reference group." He revealed his attachment to this outer group by accepting its evaluation of what his own group stood for. Wessely's writings reflect the Enlightenment's negative evaluation of traditional Jewish education as well as Jewish ethical standards. This is evident in his condemnation of the isolated Talmudic scholar, who is described by Wessely in most ungracious terms as a man utterly useless to any society. Thus Wessely is an example of a divided orientation that resulted from the penetration of Enlightenment into the closed Jewish world; this dualism could only have arisen in individuals who regarded themselves as belonging simultaneously to two different worlds.[34]

In a broader sense, the whole program of the Enlightenment of Jewish orientation was an educational one. The phrase "Civic Betterment" in the title of Dohm's book is indicative of this. The phrase implied the betterment of the Jews' status by the authorities but also, and especially, their own civil and moral self-improvement.[35] This improvement was to be achieved by granting them an opportunity to change over to more wholesome occupations, for their exclusive — if involuntary — addiction to trade (and particularly peddling) was held to be responsible, in part at least, for Jewish moral deficiencies. That the Jews were morally deficient and even corrupt (absolutely or relatively, depending on the critic) was assumed almost as a matter of course and was not contradicted by enlightened Jews like Wessely and Mendelssohn. They made some attempts to vindicate the Jews, as did Dohm and other well-meaning Gentiles, by attributing the reasons for Jewish deterioration to historical causes beyond the control of the Jews. But they did not doubt the diagnosis itself.[36] The negative judgment was obviously connected with a genuine criticism of the observable phenomena of ghetto life, the liberties taken by some Jews in dealing with their non-Jewish customers; this was aggravated by the ubiquitous itinerant peddler-schnorrer who plied his dubious trade among Jews and Gentiles alike. This could be ascribed to the moral double standard, arising from the Jews' isolation and has, in fact, been attributed to the deep mutual estrangement of Jew and Gentile.[37] Enlightened Jews and non-Jews who believed in the possibility of a remedy for these deficiencies by rectifying the basic situation that had produced them set out to do so with the passion of social and moral reformers. The image of the future contained not only a rectified political and social situation but also a refashioned Jewish type and a rehabilitated Jewish character.

Some features of the image of the future described here were not the invention of the Berlin circle but had already been anticipated by Jewish and non-Jewish writers elsewhere. It was John Toland who, as early as 1714, expressed his belief that the Jewish nature was no different from that of the rest of mankind.[38] The moral perfectibility of the Jew under appropriate circumstances was hinted at by Christian Fürchtegott Gellert and Ephraim Gotthold Lessing in 1746–1754. Both writers have depicted Jews (the first in one of his novels,[39] the second in his play *Der Jude*) who lived up to the standard of enlightened humanity. Both their heroes went out of their way to be unselfishly helpful to a non-Jew. In Lessing's treatment the Jew's actions were in striking contrast to those of his non-Jewish characters. Gellert implied, and Lessing said in so many words, that their literary figures did not represent any actual type of Jew but the type would emerge in the future under favorable conditions.[40] That bad conditions were responsible for Jewish cultural, social, as well as aesthetic and moral shortcomings was stressed by Isaac de Pinto in his polemic against Voltaire in 1762.[41] The Sephardim, of course, were ahead of the Ashkenazim in many respects, and it may well be that the Bordeaux Jews outdid the Berliners in reforming their education in a more radical way than was suggested by Wessely.[42]

Notwithstanding all this, it is the Berlin group that has to be credited with clearly visualizing what may be called "the image of the future." It was in Berlin and other Prussian cities that the ideas of change and transformation were not only expressed more or less casually by some individual but spelled out and propagated by a whole group. Indeed it was the commitment to the idea of change in Jewish society that bound the group together. The group centered, at first, around Mendelssohn but continued to exist after his death in 1786. The literary evidence of this was the appearance in Königsberg in 1784 (since 1786 in Berlin) of the Hebrew periodical *Hameasef*, dedicated to the ideas of enlightenment. The group had been recognized and evaluated as an avant-garde for social and cultural reform.[43] From Berlin the ideas of enlightenment spread. They could, of course, take root only where conditions were conducive and it may well be that in such places the ideas would have sprouted even without external stimulation. As the ideas were emanating from Berlin, however, the response to them was experienced as a reaction to a stimulus. Still within the lifetime of Mendelssohn, there arose recognizable groups of enlightened Jews in Königsberg, Breslau, Frankfurt an der Oder, Frankfurt am Main, Prague, Vienna, Amsterdam, Copenhagen, and Metz — to mention only the more conspicuous Jewish communities.

While the Jewish group in Berlin influenced their brethren in other places, Dohm's suggestion to rectify the Jewish status had a similar effect on Gentiles. Officials of states, philosophers, and social reformers took up the ideas of Dohm or discussed them. The suggested changes in the Jewish status met with a readiness to contemplate them owing to the general climate of opinion that penetrated states and society in Western and Middle Europe in the decades preceding the French Revolution. There was a widespread feeling that the status of the Jew, too, would have to be reconsidered. This is borne out by a coincidence, the Edict of Tolerance of the Emperor Joseph II, which was promulgated when Dohm's book was about to be published. Dohm was reading the proofs of his first volume when the news reached him that the Edict was about to be proclaimed and had the satisfaction of knowing that the ideas he had been contemplating were being taken up in high places.[44]

In fact, the original stimulus for Dohm's book had come when an appeal was made by Alsatian Jews to the French authorities to revise their status in accordance with enlightened ideas. The Jews of Alsace struggled against unscrupulous adversaries who were not particular in their choice of propaganda or of the nature of their accusations.[45] The champion of the Jews of Alsace, Cerf Berr, a rich court Jew and a great admirer of Mendelssohn approached the latter to compose a treatise stating the Jews' claim to fair treatment by the state. Mendelssohn turned over this task to Dohm, and from this appeal for benevolence toward the Jews of Alsace grew a more far-reaching plea to reconsider the status of the Jews in general. All this indicates that Dohm's appeal for reexamination of the Jews' status was a timely call corresponding to the feeling of the times. Therefore it had an excellent chance of being heeded. It became, indeed, the starting point for a prolonged discussion and directed opinions on the subject for more than two decades. The title of the book, *Civic Betterment*, lent the keyword to the problem — the word "emancipation" not as yet having been associated with the Jews.[46]

The complex of ideas summarized in this chapter expresses the trend toward reform of the Jews' status and of the whole Jewish social and cultural edifice. This trend manifested itself in the actual changes that occurred during the ensuing revolutionary period that began, as far as Jews were concerned, with the Edict of Tolerance in Austria in 1781–82 and closed with the decision of the Congress of Vienna in 1815. Geographically all the countries of Western Europe were drawn into the orbit of the trend of change, although not simultaneously. This development will be followed up in the description of what took place. Here emphasis will be placed on the fact that the actual changes in status as well as the corresponding inner adjustment were, if not prompted, then at least influenced by the ideas contained in what may be termed "The Image of the Future." It is not at all difficult to follow the imprints made by the revolutionary ideas of change expressed in literary compositions or in discussions preceding political enactments.

Four years before the French Revolution the Royal Society of Arts and Sciences in Metz announced a prize essay on the subject "Are there means of making the Jews happy and more useful in France." Nine manuscripts were received. Seven accepted the basic assumption that Jews could be made happy and useful; however, the arguments submitted in all cases were found to be incomplete and the suggestions for reform lacking in precision. Four of the authors then reworked their original opus and three of them were finally in 1788 jointly awarded the prize and their books printed. The three represent different sections of the population. Adolphe Thiéry, an advocate from Nancy, Henri Gregoire, village priest in Lorrain, and Zalkind Hourwitz, a Polish Jew working as librarian at the Royal Library in Paris. The three, as well as the other four whose work remained unpublished, agreed on the basic principle that Jews were capable of moral regeneration and civic betterment: "Les juifs sont hommes comme nous et, à ce titre, susceptible d'être Français" was the conclusion of one of the participants.[47] The concession that Jews were, after all, "human beings" indicates that the inclusion of Jews in the family of man was a kind of novelty. Grégoire expressed himself similarly, stating that "they were men like ourselves before they were Jews." [48] Faith in the basic goodness of human nature guaranteed, in the eyes of Thiéry, the ultimate success of Jewish rehabilitation. He did not close his eyes to the impediments to rehabilitation but thought that these were the results of prejudice that would disappear when confronted with an enlightening philosophy. Thus Thiéry envisaged the Jews, though at the time civilly excluded, morally wanting, and religiously estranged, as future citizens of France who would take part in all economic and civic endeavors and be reconciled with the adherents of other religions.[49]

Grégoire concurred in all this with one qualification: being a theologian with a millennial background, he could not give up the hope that, ultimately, Jewish rehabilitation would lead to Christianity.[50] In Grégoire's mind the hope for Jewish conversion and the humanistic ideas of enlightenment became one, and both of them induced him to speak up for the Jews.[51] His contemporaries, however, seized on the rationalistic points in his arguments while managing to overlook the expectations of the millennarian. To those who conceived of religion as a residue of the dark past, destined to disappear, the possible religious conversion of the Jews was of little importance. Zalkind Hourwitz, the Jew, was of this type and he concluded his arguments with the remark to Christian theologians that if they were so interested in the conversion of the Jews, it would be to their advantage to grant equality of rights as the best possible means of ensuring it. Hourwitz represented the radically enlightened among the Jews who were intransigent toward all manifestations of prejudice irrespective of its source, Jewish or Christian. He pleaded the cause of his brethren energetically, attributing all their faults and shortcomings to the eroding effects of maltreatment by Christians. He declared his conviction that, given status and opportunity, the Jews would cease to be different as to customs, occupations, and morality.[52]

The literary discourse of Metz on the Jewish problem is clearly a continuation of the controversy that took place in Berlin a decade before. Grégoire and Hourwitz referred to Michaelis, whose contribution to the Berlin controversy will be treated later. The French champions of the Jews were fully aware of the arguments put forward by Dohm and Mendelssohn.[53] These ideas were also shared by many admirers of Mendelssohn among Alsatian Jews eager for a better future for their community.[54] Prospects for betterment seemed to have arrived when all parts of the French population were requested to present their grievances to the Estates General convened for the spring of 1789. Not yet recognized as subjects of the king, Jews were not among those included. Still, after much effort and lobbying, they were permitted to state their wishes in a memorandum directed to the appropriate authorities.[55] Like most Frenchmen, who anticipated a reform from above rather than a revolution from below, they pleaded for a removal of legal restrictions and the enlargement of their economic opportunities. In the memorandum of the Jews of Metz, however, inspired by Isaiah Berr Bing, a stout champion of Jewish rights, was contained a real vision of the future where Bing imagined his community as an economically unfettered and a socially accepted and culturally advanced group.[56]

Finally it was the revolution that presented the forum where the ideas of reform could be put to the test. Grégoire is the link between this new scene and the prologue where the ideas were spelled out. As a member of the National Assembly, Grégoire found the opportunity to present his ideas along with other members who came to similar conclusions though not always by the same route.[57]

The legislative deliberations of the National Assembly that led ultimately to the granting of citizenship to all the Jews of France were governed by various considerations that will be discussed later.[58] Here the concern is focused on the ideas that served the Jews' advocates in promoting their cause during the public debates. These were essentially identical with those that had been aired previously in Berlin and Metz. "The *lettres patentes* of French Jews are to be found in nature and the seal of nature is worth more than the seal of all the chanceries of Europe," [59] said Abbé Bertolio on January 30, 1790, in the National Assembly. All the objections against acceptance of the Jews as equal citizens were declared to be the result of prejudices and as such to be uprooted and expunged. "Raison" and "Humanité," were the key words in the arguments in favor of the underprivileged. In the atmosphere of optimism that accepted nothing less than the complete regeneration of mankind, the lofty ideals for the rehabilitation of Jewry could ultimately not go unheeded.

The ideas on reform spread from France in the wake of French conquest and domination. Holland was one of the first countries where the French occupation brought about a social revolution as well. The new Batavian republic had, among other matters, to reconsider the position of the Jews. Although most Jews were conservative and not unmindful of the benefits bestowed by the Royal House, they were nonetheless eager to become citizens of the New Republic and to share in whatever advantages arose from the new status. This had, in fact, to be wrested from the Dutch National Assembly in the face of strong opposition on the part of the indigenous burgher and competitor of the Jews. The fight for acceptance was based here, too, on the great ideas of equality for all human beings. "Who will contest that the Jews are human beings and that they and the non-Jews are brethren in nature in the full sense of the word." These were the words of Jacob George Hieronymus Hahn, one of the outstanding members of the Dutch National Assembly, on August 1, 1796. The task of the Assembly is "to make (the Jews) happy by the elevation to the full dignity of man and citizens and to arouse in the heart of the Dutch Jews a genuine national enthusiasm." [60] Citizenship was granted not because of an appreciation of the Jews' quality but because of the general principle that included them in the category of man and roused the expectation of their eventually acquiring the necessary attributes of the enlightened man and citizen.

The ideas of reform arose first in Germany but the impetus for their practical implementation came from France. The Jews of the western provinces of Germany, conquered by the French or ruled by French-oriented kings and princes, were the first to receive their citizenship. The communities of Bonn and Mayence belonged by 1801 (the Peace of Luneville) to France and their Jews automatically became free citizens. The Jews of Frankfurt acquired citizenship in the year 1808 and those of the newly created State of Westphalia in the same year. The immediate causes of this development were of a political nature but nonetheless they were widely regarded as a realization of the ideas of enlightenment. The philosophical component was, of course, specially stressed by the spokesmen of the Jews who were interested in an ideological justification of their achievements. Far from disdaining the weapons of political pressure secured by the economic influence they wielded, the Jewish leadership was only too happy to make use of them while at the same time ensuring that they were accompanied by a kind of spiritual vindication. The case of the Jews in Westphalia and Frankfurt and later also in Prussia was pleaded inter alia by Israel Jacobson, originally a court Jew but one who exceeded the dimensions of his class in mentality as well as in the scope of his economic undertakings. Jacobson acquired immense wealth during the wars and revolutionary upheavals in western Germany that made him independent and, at the same time, an indispensable partner for states and statesmen who faced financial problems in consequence of the political throes. Jacobson was a convinced adherent of the philosophy of enlightenment and an energetic advocate of Jewish rights. In exercising his influence in negotiating for the rights of the Jews as citizens in the respective countries, he acted on his own firm conviction. He had no doubts that by pleading the cause of the Jews he was fulfilling the mission of enlightened humanity.[61] The same is true for his contemporary David Friedländer, an ardent disciple of Mendelssohn, who played a leading part in the Berlin community while the negotiations on the new legislation for Prussian Jews were conducted.[62]

These negotiations had been under way ever since the ideas of reform were publicly propagated. The representatives of the Jewish community repeatedly petitioned the authorities for reform and their requests were supported by the enlightened officials of the king. Serious and detailed discussion of the matter started only in 1808 when, in the wake of the Prussian defeat (at Jena in 1806) a general reorganization of the Prussian state was initiated. The deliberations conducted by the king, his ministers, and officials of the state, led to the Edict of 1812 that granted citizenship — with some qualifications — to Prussia's 33,000 Jews.[63] The connection between the granting of citizenship and political events is obvious. But this does not mean that the ideas of the Enlightenment did not play their part in promoting and justifying the decisions taken. Indeed, the ideas and ideals of reform kept recurring in the reiterated appeals made by Jews — among them the more radical exponents like David Friedländer and Israel Jacobson. Furthermore, some of the high officials drew at least some of their inspiration from the notions of natural rights, the belief in the perfectibility of man, when recommending the extrication of the Jews from their ghettolike isolation and their integration into state and society.[64] One of the participants in the deliberations, Wilhelm von Humboldt, entered more deeply into the problem and conceived a solution that was at the same time more radical and more realistic.

Wilhelm, and his brother, Alexander von Humboldt, have already been encountered as frequenters of the Jewish salons in Berlin.[65] Von Humboldt knew the Jews of his time and formed a judgment on their role in history. He found three characteristic features in their collective mentality: (1) A mobility, imposed or natural to them because of a nomadic origin, but leading in any event to the relinquishing of self-rule and the acceptance of outside domination. (2) The development of a quasi-ecclesiastical political constitution in which religion — that is, what religion meant for the semirationalistic, semiromantic Humboldt — is almost entirely submerged. (3) Attachment to a system of prescriptions best exemplified by circumcision, a rite that created a physical mark distinguishing Jews from those among whom they lived. Humboldt added the observation that the Jews excelled in clinging tenaciously to their ancient customs (*Ursitte*) and possessed a remarkable capacity for passive resistance. These qualities in their national character manifested themselves in the course of history that inextricably bound Judaism and Christianity. Judaism, according to Christian concepts, is on the one hand in the same category as Christianity, namely, the religion of the Biblical revelation. On the other hand Judaism is its counterpart, its denial. Through this association with Christianity, "the Jewish people who were at the time (of the emergence of Christianity) already quite insignificant gained an importance quite disproportionate." [66]

Although specifying the national and historical characteristics of the Jewish people, Humboldt, as one of the first thinkers to leave behind the rationalistic conception of human nature and the history of man, was well aware of the limited validity of such analysis.[67] Appropriately, it was Humboldt's contention that reform had to be conceived independently of the qualities ascribed to the objects thereof. In this, too, Humboldt was ahead of his contemporaries. He doubted the ability and the right of the state to guide and educate people according to a preconceived plan on the basis of a diagnosis of their moral quality and cultural achievements. The state has only to act passively, that is, to remove the hindrances to the free development of its citizens. Consequently, it is not the business of the state to strive for the betterment of the Jews nor teach their adversaries to appreciate them. The state should only "reverse the inhuman and prejudiced way of thinking that judges a man not according to his individual characteristics but according to his origin and religion and conceives of him — in contradistinction to all notions of human dignity — not as an individual but as belonging to a race and sharing certain of its characteristics as of necessity." How can the state accomplish this revolution in the way that people think?

"By declaring in no uncertain terms that the State will no longer recognise any difference between Jews and Christians." [68]

On the basis of this conception, Humboldt recommended what later became known as full emancipation, that is, complete disregard by the state for the religious affiliations of its citizens. He expected from this swift and decisive step the best possible results, an ultimate integration of the Jews into the surrounding society. Jews would adapt themselves to the requirements of all the occupations open to them. The much-lamented immorality conditioned by discrimination would disappear and so would the cultural gap between them and their neighbors. The only remaining difference would be that of religion, which did not concern the state. The state should accordingly refrain from any positive step to reform Jewish religion or strengthen the existing hierarchy by, for instance, the nomination of a Chief Rabbi. Humboldt's guess was that, left to itself, organized Jewish religion would deteriorate, Jewish individuals would turn away from Jewish observances, denouncing them as not being of a religious nature. The Jew, "driven by the innate human need for a loftier faith," would turn inevitably to Christianity. But this was a view of the future. At the time Humboldt had reservations about the converted Jew who was prepared to leave his deprived and indigent brethren. Once Jews as a collective body were integrated, the abandoning of the Jewish faith by individuals would be "desirable, gratifying and beneficial." [69]

Here one of the best representatives of the humanistically-minded Christians paints his image of the future — true, in a memorandum not intended for publication. The basic feature of his vision is the removal of all restrictions hampering the freedom of Jewish individuals but it was also combined with the expectation that the individual would eventually find his way to Christianity. This expectation was shared by many, although certainly not by all those who recommended or even fought for Jewish integration. Jews, on the other hand, welcomed their new status, convinced that somehow they would be able to retain their allegiance to Judaism even under the new conditions.[70] The different anticipations harbored by donor and recipient of Jewish emancipation are perhaps not unnatural, but the fact that this social contract is accompanied by conflicting hopes on the part of both participants augurs ill for a smooth implementation.

VI GENTILE OBJECTIONS

The inclusion of some Jews into non-Jewish circles and the recommendation for the universal acceptance of Jews into state and
society elicited a flood of doubts and protests on the part of those
who did not share the assumptions on which the changing attitudes were based. The idea of Jews mixing freely with non-Jews
ran against custom. From the tolerant Berlin of Mendelssohn's
time comes the amusing anecdote that Solomon Maimon, the
philosopher, upon attending a public house with a Christian
artist, was told by the proprietor that he himself was always welcome but that the customers objected to his "Jewish company," a
compliment the Christian artist no doubt appreciated.[1] Some
years later an innkeeper near Hamburg announced in a newspaper that pressure from his customers compelled him to refuse
entry to Jews.[2] To the rank and file it was generally not necessary
to give special reasons for excluding Jews. Such resistance was
self-evident to them as the continuation of a tradition.

It was different when the resistance was manifested by those
who had themselves broken loose from some of the traditional
bonds and were engaged in creating new social groups, as for instance the Freemasons and all those who claimed to be rationalist
and enlightened. They were, according to their own constitutions
or the principles of their institutions, bound to disregard the religion of their companions. However, moral postulates are all very
well but are not always followed by practical implementation.
No amount of logic and ethics could do battle with the age-old
and deeply ingrained prejudice against social contact with Jews.
The ideological background to this prejudice will be explored
later. But there can be no doubt that the prejudice was fed by the
actual appearance and behavior of the average Jew.

The common type, especially of Ashkenazi Jew, was conspicuous by his appearance, his strange raiment, his beard, his speech.

Even if he spoke the language of his environment, German, French, Dutch, or English, his pronunciation usually retained the traces of his mother tongue, Yiddish. Yiddish developed out of Middle High German. It absorbed several hundred words from Hebrew and Aramaic, key words in the ancient religious Jewish culture. Later generations have learned to appreciate Yiddish as a complete and independent language of an elastic and original kind, but in the second part of the eighteenth century, when High German was about to be installed as the model language at the expense of the local dialects, Yiddish came to be regarded as a laughable jargon, a debasement of the correct German tongue.[3] To the deprecation of the dialect there was added, in the case of Yiddish, a further derogation of all things Jewish. Gentiles seemed to recoil instinctively from any unnecessary contact with this alien type.

A revealing description of the common Jew as seen by an enlightened Gentile who, in other respects, had come a long way from the traditional view of state and society can be found in the writings of Baron Adolf von Knigge, one of the brilliant figures of the German Enlightenment. Stemming from an impoverished aristocratic background, Knigge dreamed of social reform and became an ardent Freemason and even joined the radical order of the Illuminati.[4] Knigge's lasting literary fame rests on his *Über den Umgang mit Menschen*, a kind of manual of correct behavior of the well-educated toward people in all walks of life. One chapter of the book is called "On Jews and how to treat them." [5] Knigge remarked, in 1788, that there were Jews in Berlin as well as in some foreign countries, in Holland or in America, for instance, who did not differ in their way of life from people of other religions; what he set out to do was to teach men how to behave with the ordinary Jew. Even with respect to this type, Knigge feels obliged to make two conciliatory remarks: first, that the blame for the Jews' social and moral shortcomings must be laid, to a great extent, at the door of the Gentiles who suppressed them and gave them only limited space to live in. Second, even under the oppressive conditions, there existed among the Jews "noble, good-willed, generous people." [6] These are rational reflections of the

enlightened author, a kind lip service to the humanistic philosophy then in vogue. But as he himself states, his task as guide was
not to dwell on what had led to the characteristics of the Jews nor
to spell out the possible future variations of these, but to advise
his reader on how to treat the Jew he would encounter if compelled to do business with him. He describes the Jewish character
as perceived by him, that is, as reflected in the consciousness of
the inimical majority.

The Jew is the ubiquitous businessman, ever-present when opportunity might offer a likely profit. He displays boundless
efficiency — partly because of objective circumstances, partly because of innate capacity. Jews command international connections and can rely on the cooperation of their brethren everywhere. Jews are tireless in their efforts to achieve their aim,
making what is almost impossible, possible. More important than
that, the Jew is unhampered in his endeavor by any consideration of ethics, gain being his sole objective. The Gentile who has
to do business with the Jew has to reckon with these attributes of
the Jew and try to use them for his own advantage. It is worthwhile for him to pay the Jew well and to fulfill punctually the obligations toward him. The Jew must be convinced that his customer is economically not unsound and otherwise reliable and
that the association with him will, in the long run, be a profitable
one. Once convinced of this, he will render excellent service also
in emergencies. But woe to the Gentile whose weakness has been
revealed to the Jew! He will fall an easy prey to the cunning
mind of the Jew and his situation will be exploited remorselessly.
In this description Knigge has in mind the rich Jew or banker to
whom the needy aristocrat or Gentile burgher would resort when
compelled by unavoidable circumstances. Knigge does not forget
a warning against the Jewish peddler and petty trader to whom
the Gentile would sell his old clothes or with whom he would
have some petty business transaction. These small fry will reveal
the same traits in plying their trade as the banker in his big business transactions. The Jewish peddler will use cunning and effort
to secure his small profit just as his rich brother will in order to
make a fortune.[7]

The Jew appears here as the symbol of cupidity involuntarily addicted to the pursuit of money. "It is mightily hard for the Jew to part from money"; "ready money is very dear to their hearts"; these qualities, as Knigge declares in his concluding paragraph, are deeply ingrained in the nature of the Jew: "Something quite characteristic for this nation . . . in everything . . . Listen to their music in their temples and the altogether original way in which they perform this. Watch them dancing. Observe the ornaments that even the richest old Jews have in their homes. Is there not always present something of knobs (Knäufe) of the temple of Solomon, something of the ornamentation of the Ark of the Covenant, the scarlet the rosy-red the silk twist." In his last remark Knigge connects, not altogether disparagingly, the special traits of the Jews with their ancient culture. But Jews are considered a species apart, certainly not one the Gentile would seek out for contact, except of a purely business and necessary nature. It is true that Knigge excepted from his description those "who (perhaps not by adding to their happiness) had refashioned themselves according to the manner of Christians." [8] But unless the Jew succeeded in proving that he was one of the exceptions, he was automatically identified with the preconceived image of the Jew which carried with it all the old traditional prejudices.

The attempts of rationalism and the Enlightenment to substitute another image for the old one was a formidable task. A Jew who wished to be accepted in non-Jewish society had to dispel the notions clinging to the idea of the Jew, to prove through his behavior that he was an exception. Candidates for Freemasons or for the learned societies or for literary circles were of course of the new type who tried to adopt the accepted patterns of behavior in non-Jewish environments in speech and conduct. The process of self-adaptation was, however, not an easy one. It was smoother for Sephardim, who were less embedded in a special Jewish culture. Isaac de Pinto asserted in his polemic against Voltaire that the common prejudice against Jews might be valid against Ashkenazim but certainly did not hold for Sephardim.[9] The ability to adapt themselves with greater ease to the culture of their neighbors may explain why Jews — usually Sephardim — managed to join the Freemasons in England, Holland, and France when Ashkenazi Jews in Germany were having their difficulties.[10] Ashkenazi women, for that matter, found it easier to adopt the cultural pattern of the Gentile environment. Jewish traditional society was perpetuated through the institutions of traditional education (the heder, a kind of elementary school, and the yeshiva, a talmudic academy). It was by means of these institutions that much of the traditional culture was transmitted from generation to generation; the traditional Jewish type was fashioned in this way. Once formal Jewish education was completed, business training followed, directing the Jewish "type" into a circumscribed channel. Women, according to religious tradition, were exempted and excluded from studying the law, the main component of the Jewish traditional curriculum. Women did not usually attend school; they had hardly any formal education but absorbed what they could from their surroundings. When enlightenment and secular education penetrated into Jewish society, it had to compete with the study of the Torah that had come traditionally to occupy the whole of a man's free time. This was not so in the case of women. Thus the daughters of the well-to-do families in the ghetto were the first to benefit from the new opportunities. They were the first to learn the language of their neighbors, to acquire a familiarity with foreign languages and literature. They were also the ones to acquire the social graces that enabled them to move easily in a society not limited to Jews. Men found it more difficult. It is on record from the time of the literary salons that some of those men, whose wives were the life and soul of social gatherings, were too embarrassed to put in an appearance.[11]

Even where great efforts were made by individual Jews to shed the more conspicuous features of their Jewishness, the observer would still be able to detect the traits that gave them away. The Jewish members of the Order of the Asiatic Brethren in Vienna and Hamburg certainly adapted themselves to the demands of their environment but nevertheless were mocked by their critics and described by them as boorish and uneducated.[12] When the Order was openly attacked by the Freemasons for accepting

Jews, one member felt obliged to defend the principle of universal acceptance irrespective of the applicants' religion. But at the same time he gave a most unsympathetic description of the type of Jew who aspired to membership: "Perhaps the nation of the German Israelites itself contributed not a little to the fact that many people cannot yet entirely free themselves from prejudice against them." German Jews, according to him, lagged behind their coreligionists in the Western countries of England, France, and Italy. The German Jews cling to "many superstitious opinions, to many useless and ridiculous customs" invented for expedience by numerous rabbis and "that is the main reason for the isolated lives they lead among us." Even if one found some Jews, he intimated, who had acquired enlightenment, this did not make them more sociable. They stuck selfishly to their particular objectives; they despised other less educated and more indigent Jews while they themselves differed only outwardly from their despised fellows. Mentally they are occupied with the same business matters — with bills of exchange, with pledges and mortgages and the interest to be collected in due course. Finally they will always be recognized by their "Sington" (intonation) "in the German dialect of the Israelites, their inclination (Hang) to stand out as a distinctive crowd." There are therefore many reasons "why the German Christian recoils from social intercourse with the Israelites not welcoming them as friends or brethren — as Masons." [13]

Here is the portrait of a Jew by one who declared himself to be willing to accept him on principle. What then can be expected from those who objected expressly to such acceptance? Karl Wilhelm Friedrich Grattenauer was one of these and he published one of the first anti-Jewish treatises as a reaction against the social advances made by the enlightened Jews. Grattenauer was first of all indignant about what he regarded as the economic ascendancy of Jews over Christians, especially in the great towns of Berlin, Vienna, and Prague. He therefore protested against the suggested concessions of political rights to Jews. But at the same time he deplored their unwarranted social advancement. Unwillingly does he concede that some Jews had acquired culture and enlightenment. But then, he continues, they had ceased to be Jews.[14] In general he mocked the attempts of Jews, especially Jewish women, to emulate the manners prevalent in high society. "Their dress, however splendid it may be, has nevertheless retained certain Jewish traits as has their physiognomy. Their language is still the wretched stammering jargon which, though they try to modernise it in conversation with Christians, they still use among themselves; filth and uncleanliness prevails among them and they cannot cover it with their great pomp — that they are in Vienna and Berlin complaisant towards Christians and even attempt some gallantry, is done for gain, for they have here their opportunity to ingratiate themselves with the great and what Moses does not obtain by subservience and flattery from his gracious Lordship, his pretty daughter Rachel, prattling in French, conversant with romances and herself not averse to a little romancing, does." [15] These remarks, vitriolic as they are, are still based on observation of what was happening to the Jewish social climber of the day, who, unready for the step, tried at a bound to bridge the gap between his aspiration and his real social status. This Jewish variation of the social parvenu later became a permanent figure on the stage, much laughed at by Gentiles and resented by Jews.[16]

A famous actor in Berlin, Albert Aloys Ferdinand Wurm by name, excelled in representing Jewish characters not only on the stage but in the houses of the Berlin burghers. His favorite piece was his imitation of a Jewish woman who wished to entertain her guests by rendering one of the well-known poems from the German classics. The Jewess makes a tremendous effort to sustain the standard of High German in pronunciation and intonation. At the beginning she does indeed succeed. In the process of the performance, however, she gets carried away and reverts to the common Judendeutsch she has been trying so hard to avoid. The whole business becomes a farce — in fact, a very profitable one for Wurm, who became much sought after for this particular ability as the Berlin burghers, who had perforce to show some respect for the enlightened and rich Jews, could take their revenge making fun of them in private.[17]

The immediate revulsion from the real or imagined type of Jew is one of the main reasons for the reluctance to admit Jews into society or to accept them as citizens. But the revulsion itself would scarcely have withstood the attack of rationalism and enlightenment which, by their very nature, demanded that such ingrained bias be overcome. Those, therefore, who were loath to part with their prejudices were prompted to formulate an ideological justification for their attitudes. The rejection of the Jew was to be made to appear not as wanton reaction springing from irrational drives, but as a well-considered attitude deriving from logical principles.

These ideologies of rejection, as they may be called, followed two different lines of reasoning. The one revolved around the Christian character of European society and maintained, more or less explicitly, that the process of secularization did not fundamentally change this fact, ergo: if the Christian character of society is established, Jews cannot belong to it. The other line — more inimical to Jews — pointed to Jewish religion, morality, tradition, or else to Jewish mentality in general as setting Jews apart and making their integration into non-Jewish society an undesirable and altogether illusory expectation.

The first approach, relying on the Christian character of European society even after the breakthrough of rationalism, could bring forward some facts to sustain the argument. The attacks on Christian churches and the criticism of Christian tenets and teaching did not uproot Christian ideas and symbols permeating European culture in thought and expression. Some of the most severe critics of Christianity retained allegiance to Christian notions and doctrines, of course reducing and reinterpreting them, in the light of a more or less explicit weltanschauung. For the purpose of excluding Jews, it did not make much difference how watered down these Christian notions were. As long as they retained some resemblance to the original Christian concepts, they served to exclude or could be used as a means for excluding Jews from being a part of Christian society.

This attachment to Christianity was repeatedly used by the adversaries of Jewish integration along with their direct rejection of Judaism. Grattenauer, who did not lack other arguments against Jewish advancements, started his polemics with a personal declaration: "I am a Christian, not in name but from true conviction." This sounds like a confession of faith with everything it stands for in dogma and mystery. But the reader is very soon undeceived when the reason for the author's loyalty to Christianity is stated. "My reason tells me that Christian morality is in exact harmony with my vocation as a human being and its exercise makes me happy and satisfied." [18] Grattenauer, with this explanation, reveals himself as a rationalist, reason being the criterion for accepting or rejecting certain principles. His Christianity is exhausted by his allegiance to Christian morals or what he considers as such. But this was sufficient background for rejecting Jews whose morality he regarded as the very opposite of what he conceived of as Christian ethics.

An even more striking example of a formal adherence to Christianity, serving as starting point for anti-Jewish arguments, is the case of Johann Heinrich Schulz. Schulz was an odd figure, a Protestant pastor who confessed to outright atheism, maintaining that Jesus himself was not and did not intend to be taken for more than a teacher of enlightened morality based upon human reason. This was too much even for the tolerant climate of German Enlightenment when rationalistic reinterpretation of Christianity was in vogue. Schulz was persecuted by his superiors and dismissed from his post. This naturally did not, in his eyes, disprove the correctness of his assumptions.[19] He clung to them and used them also to substantiate his savage accusations against Jews and Judaism.

The occasion for his attack on the Jews was a polemic against Mendelssohn who, although a champion of toleration, made an exception of atheists. People without a belief in God could not be tolerated since they were responsible to none for their deeds.[20] Schulz was outraged by the denial of his basic principle, especially as the denial came from a Jew, for Schulz had a most derogative opinion of Jewish morality; atheism, he was convinced, was better able to foster moral conduct than false beliefs. While Schulz's attack on Judaism was made essentially in the name of a consistent atheism, formally it was still presented as a continuation of the old conflict between Christianity and Judiasm. Schulz kept to the notion that Jesus himself was no more than a rationalistic moralist. He preached his anti-Judaism, so to speak, in the name of his atheistic Jesus. He rejected the social and political integration of the Jews, unless they would renounce Judaism altogether and accept either Christianity or rather the atheistic morality he thought to be identical with the original teaching of Christ.[21]

The permeation of European culture by the residues of Christianity was not the idiosyncrasy of an individual. That this was quite general is clear from the study of the history of Jewish integration in its political and social aspects. Freemasons, for example, in principle made eligibility independent of the candidate's allegiance to any particular denomination. In actual practice, however, Masons retained Christian symbols deriving from Masonry's prehistory. Although these were not introduced to exclude the Jew, it nevertheless became a stumbling block in the way of the Jew unless he had become completely callous about his religious background.[22]

The linking of society and Christianity raised problems whenever Jews wished to belong to a social unit, not excluding the larger one of the state. If the state is to be termed "Christian" because this is the religion of the majority of its inhabitants or by reason of its historic connection with Christianity or for any other reason, Jews would, by definition, find themselves excluded. In the early stages under consideration, such contentions turned up only occasionally and, unaccompanied by systematic arguments, they were of little effect.

The Protestant preacher Schwager, a participant in the Dohm controversy, reminded his opponent that "as long as our State will remain a Christian State as it ought to," Jews will have to be limited in some respects. The learned Orientalist Johann David Michaelis objected to the idea of installing Jews as civil servants on the plea that this should be the prerogative of those belonging to the religion of the majority.[23] One of the participants of the Metz symposium, a Catholic priest, even went so far as to say that any improvement made by the state in the status of the Jews would deprive the church of one of its cherished proofs for the Christian truths, namely, the eternal prostration and rejection of its adversaries, the Jews.[24] This was of course merely a repetition of the ancient theory of the Middle Ages, clearly on the wane at the time. Even the less injurious claim of Schwager and Michaelis that the state had to reckon with Christian religion was out of tune with the general trend of thought. Dohm commented on Schwager's remark: "This designation, 'Christian and Mahomedan States,' general as it may be, seems to me to contradict the correct ideas of the nature of *bürgerliche Gesellschaft*. This may embrace many religious groups, [and] subjects them to its aims and reconciles itself with them. But none of them belongs to the essence of the State and the idea of a religious society . . . must never be merged (gemischt) with that of a civic one." [25]

Dohm, without doubt, spoke here for his contemporaries. The secularization of the state was one of the great principles of the Enlightenment that led, ultimately, to the inclusion of Jews as citizens. It is true that later, in the nineteenth century, the idea of the Christian state reemerged and, bolstered by philosophical argumentation, served as a mighty deterrent to the full emancipation of Jews.[26] But this is another story. In the period under consideration, that is, in the last decades of the eighteenth and the beginning of the nineteenth century, the idea of the secular state was on the ascendant. Most of the Jews' adversaries were willing to concede the principle. One of the first and most radical opponents to Jewish aspirations, Friedrich Traugott Hartmann, opens his thesis on the subject of the Jews with a remark to this effect: "A hundred different religions and denominations, however one calls them, may therefore live together in one State and constitute its membership without their particular opinions hindering them from being good citizens or stopping them from fulfilling their physical and moral obligations that are necessary for the harmony, for maintaining and for developing the whole." [27]

But even those who were not committed to the complete indifference of the state toward religion denied religion's claim in being decisive for shaping the state's destiny. The welfare of the state and furthering of its interests should be the only considerations guiding the government's decisions. But it was just from this standpoint that Jews were found wanting, for it was maintained that the acceptance of Jews as citizens would conflict with these interests of the state and society. Thus Jews and Judaism were excluded from the principle of religious tolerance upheld by the participants — at least in abstracto.

The criticism of Jews and Judaism that led to their rejection as citizens were of varying degrees of harshness and varied also as to their ideological justification. The first rebuff came from the scholar introduced previously, Johann David Michaelis from Göttingen, an authority on matters Jewish. His fame rested on his *Mosaiches Recht* and his contributions to the periodical *Orientalische und exegetische Bibliothek*, of which he was the editor.[28] In this periodical he had repeatedly taken a stand on contemporary matters. It was here that he published his review on Dohm's book, revealing some sympathy for the plight of the Jews but rejecting the basic suggestion for its alleviation. Michaelis declared Jews unfit for citizenship, claiming that their religious prescriptions would hinder them from ever merging with another nation or fulfilling the obligations a citizen owes to the state. "As long as Jews keep the laws of Moses, as long as for instance they do not take their meals with us and at mealtimes or with simple folk over a glass of beer are not able to make friends they will never (I do not speak of individuals but of the greater part) fuse with us like Catholics and Lutherans, Germans, Italians (Wende) and Frenchmen living in the same State." Thus the dietary laws preclude fraternization and intermingling; these same laws and observance of the Sabbath would hinder Jews from rendering the citizen's duty of protecting his country in times of war. For how can a Jew join the army if he is unable to eat soldier's food and feels religiously obliged to stop all work on Saturdays? Michaelis knew that there were Jews who did not adhere to the prescriptions of their religion "who are Jews merely in name and by birth but who believe nothing of Jewish religion and are what people call Deists or not even that," but then Michaelis does not wish this type to increase nor does he believe that this type will supersede the observant traditional Jew. It was the strict observance of the law that preserved the Jews "as a separate people in their dispersion for 1700 years in contrast to what we observe of other people." [29] Michaelis thinks that this situation will continue and from this he concludes that Jews were neither fit nor entitled to become citizens of a non-Jewish state.

Another consideration leads Michaelis to the same conclusion — Jews will never be able to regard the country in which they live as more than a temporary abode "which they hope one day to leave, to their great happiness, and return to Palestine . . . A people that has such hopes will never entirely feel at home or have patriotic love for the paternal soil." [30] It is well to remember here that some 120 years earlier when Jews applied to Cromwell for readmission to England, their spokesman, Rabbi Menasseh Ben Israel, could argue that according to Biblical prognostication the Jewish people would have to disperse all over the world before the age of redemption arrived that would initiate the regeneration of all mankind.[31] Jewish messianism, far from contradicting Jewish claims, could be used as an argument in their favor. But times changed and, with them, the nature of Jewish claims. Jewish aspirations had gone beyond mere residence to naturalization, that is, a desire to become permanent and legitimate citizens. This desire elicited the argument that unless there was undivided attachment to the chosen home, there could be no citizenship. The messianic expectation to return to Palestine was found to be in conflict with this required loyalty. In fact, the possibility of conflict between these sentiments — the desire for citizenship and the messianic belief — was seized upon as an important argument with which to combat Jewish demands.[32] Interestingly enough, it began to be used only when the question of Jewish citizenship became a serious matter for discussion.

The incompatibility between a citizen's duties and sentiments and the prescriptions and messianic doctrine of Jewish religion concerned basic principles. To this Michaelis added some objections of a practical nature. Would not the naturalization of Jews artificially increase the number of those competing for sources of livelihood to the detriment of the indigenous population? More than that — the number of Jewish beggars, vagabonds, and miscreants which, in Michaelis's estimation, exceeded the German by twenty-five to one, would make life intolerable for the citizens of the country. Michaelis conceded to Dohm that the loose morals of indigent Jews stemmed neither from propensity nor were they prompted by the tenets of Judaism. On this point, as on others, Michaelis rejected the anti-Jewish point of view represented by the *Entdecktes Judentum* of Eisenmenger. Michaelis attributed the faulty behavior of Jews to their social deprivation. The well-to-do among them were not lacking in morality and were, in his experience, on a par with their Christian neighbors. An amelioration in the social condition of indigent Jews would result in an improvement of their moral standard. But Michaelis regarded the possible improvement as, at best, a slow process, and meanwhile the liberty gained by naturalization would only encourage the unsavory elements among Jews to take advantage of the situation. Any improvement in the condition of the Jews would therefore only be possible at the expense of the Gentiles.[33] The rights of the indigenous Gentiles being unassailable while those of the alien Jews remained questionable, Michaelis did not want to injure the former to benefit the Jews.

Michaelis was one of the first as well as one of the foremost rationalists in Germany. Nevertheless, born in 1717, he belonged to a generation for whom enlightenment served as a means of rationalist explanation of phenomena rather than as an instrument for changing social or political reality. As his arguments against Dohm's suggestions reveal, he regarded prevailing social conditions as well as the structure of society at large as lasting and not liable to change. In the same way did he conceive of the traditional type of Jew as being immutable and a direct result of his adherence to the permanent patterns of Jewish religious observances and doctrines. Thus the suggested changes in Jewish status in state and society appeared to him as an isolated deviation from the customary and, as such, likely to create an incongruous situation. No wonder then that he rejected it — his prejudice against Jews playing only a secondary part in his motivation.

It was different with Friedrich Traugott Hartmann, who advocated the absolute indifference of the state toward the religion of its citizens. Jewish religion, however, represented in his mind a definite and justified exception. Hartmann's reasons for withholding citizenship from the Jew were partly identical with those held by Michaelis, with whose publications he was probably familiar. But Hartmann, overflowing with resentment against everything Jewish, detected additional obstacles, partly real ones and partly imaginary, that Jews would encounter in their attempts at integrating into non-Jewish society. Jews would not be able to fulfill the obligations of a citizen toward the city or even perform the tasks of an ordinary member of civic society. Jewish religion would hinder the Jews not only from becoming soldiers but also from becoming peasants or craftsmen. The loss of time caused by Jewish festivals — whose number Hartmann ludicrously exaggerated — and the absolute ban on any work on the Sabbath would prohibit Jews from taking up these occupations. As the prosperity of a peasant or craftsman depended on reciprocal help between neighbors and relatives, Jews would be handicapped at the start because of religious restrictions and because they would have no family connections in the neighborhood. Dohm made little of the social cleavage between Jews and Gentiles and classed it with the kind of differences that are bound to exist between groups. Hartmann, however, considered the separation caused by religion as belonging to a special category. "All the divisions that exist between the burgher, peasant and nobleman, city-dweller and countryman, warriors and unarmed scholars . . . are not divisions that can be compared with those existing between Christians and Jews.[34]

Hartmann, of course, repeated the charge of moral unreliability but did not limit it to destitute Jews; he also included the wealthy in his indictment. Even perjury against Gentiles is common amongst Jews, Hartmann argued, and he had no doubt that the accusations of the notorious Eisenmenger were well founded.[35] No loyalty could be expected from a Jew. Messianism would keep him from acquiring a lasting commitment to any country. "More than this is unnecessary in order to be able to state that the greater part of the Jews . . . will never be able to settle as citizens (einbürgern) and will never be as loyal to the homeland as others who have no article of faith compelling them to flee when an imposter gives the danger signal." Thus the image of a false Messiah was conjured up to give substance to the concept of the Jew as the eternal alien.

Hartmann would have liked all the citizens of the state to have the same spirit and mentality. This, he thought, could be achieved by subjecting all citizens to the same laws. Jews paid allegiance to a special system of law administered by rabbinical courts. The privilege to continue this had been claimed even by Mendelssohn and acquiesced in by Dohm. Hartmann saw in this separate legal institution a confirmation of his thesis that Jews were spiritually as well as morally a group apart.

Like Michaelis, Hartmann saw in the Jewish religion the real cause of Jewish exclusiveness and the corresponding Gentile reaction. Jews are indeed hated by the nations but with reason. "Never can a community be hated by every nation unless it has earned this hatred." As religion is at the root of this hatred and the cause of the hiatus between Jews and Gentiles, only the removal of the cause can provide a remedy. Hartmann, though far from being a Christian in any dogmatic or ecclesiastical sense of the word, nevertheless recommends conversion — not so much because the act of conversion was important but because of the political and social adaptations it would entail. "It is not the baptism that counts but that the Jew, by saying 'Baptize me,' says at the same time: I obey the laws of the country, I submit myself to the institution you have created, I fulfill all the obligations laid upon me at all times." [36] Here, for the first time, the conversion of the Jew to Christianity is demanded not because of the alleged truth of Christianity but because political and social by-products would be gained.

Jewish religion is deprecated even more in the description of Johann Heinrich Schulz, the atheist who felt entitled to exclude Jews from the benefit of general toleration because he thought Jewish religion to be a paradigm of intolerance. Schulz adduced the — historically correct — fact that ancient polytheistic nations knew no religious intolerance and accused the Jews of having introduced it to the history of mankind. This is the consequence of the Jewish delusion of being the Chosen People of God. This led to the Biblical prescription to avoid making friends with other nations but to preserve themselves as a separate nation and regard other people as unworthy and to be hated for this reason. This belief made Jews suspect in the eyes of all nations and the various steps and measures taken against them were in the nature of justified self-defense. There is no reason to forego these measures "so long as the Jews of the present insist so emphatically on preserving unchanged the dividing wall that their religion has erected between them and other peoples . . . it is impossible that there should arise in the other citizens of the State a trust in the Jews and the willingness to allow the sons of Jacob an equal part in the rights and advantages of society." [37]

Representing the Jew and his beliefs as repulsive and threatening to Gentiles was not of course an invention of these writers. It relied on time-honored tradition. Historical analysis could trace some of the elements of the stereotype to Christian and even pre-Christian times. For the purpose here it is sufficient to mention the two authors in whose works two different versions of the anti-Jewish tradition found expression. One of these was Johann Andreas Eisenmenger, whose *Entdecktes Judentum* — printed in 1700 [38] — contained a mass of quotations from post-Biblical Jewish sources that reflected Jewish views and beliefs concerning all possible subjects, but especially Jewish attitudes toward peoples of other origins and religions. It was Eisenmenger's intention to show that Jewish religion, as interpreted by the rabbis, was a narrow, intolerant, and immoral system. He quoted chapter and verse to prove that the rabbis permitted the Jew to cheat, perjure, and even kill the Gentile. More, he set out to show that the latter was not even regarded as a human being by the rabbis. Eisenmenger was a man of enormous erudition. He only seldom misread his Hebrew and Aramaic sources but twisted, distorted, and misrepresented them almost continuously. The method of interpretation applied by Eisenmenger was neither a historical one nor the scholastic-juridical one used by the rabbis, but a kind of travesty of the latter. Thus, his conclusions based on the sources were seldom identical with those the sources conveyed to a Jew. Still, the massive erudition of Eisenmenger so overwhelmed his readers that they were prepared to accept his allegations. His book, more than any other single factor, helped to maintain the repulsive image of the Jew and Judaism — in spite of protests and corrections by those who were competent to judge. Michaelis, who was an Orientalist of no less a stature than Eisenmenger, made light of his allegations, stating that by applying the same approach to Christian sources an *Entdecktes Christentum* could be written.[39] But Hartmann, scarcely competent to judge, quoted Eisenmenger with admiration.[40] Hartmann had nothing of the Christian zeal of Eisenmenger, whose aim was, ultimately, to convince the Jews of the foolishness of their religion and persuade them to relinquish it in favor of Christianity.[41] The emotional as well as the intellectual elements of Eisenmenger's thesis continued to affect people long after the theological conceptions on which they had been based had lost their force.

The second author who fed the anti-Jewish propensities of the opposers of integration — but with arguments of a different nature — was Voltaire. In contradistinction to Eisenmenger, Voltaire drew his evidence for the inhuman tendencies of Jewish religion not from the writings of the rabbis but directly from the Old Testament.[42] It has been argued, not without good reason, that Voltaire's main objective in attacking the Bible was not Judaism but the destruction of Christianity.[43] If he could shatter the belief in the genuineness of the Biblical narrative, he would undermine the trust in the records on which the authority of the church rested. Similarly, if the immorality of Biblical figures and even that of the Biblical God could be demonstrated, the whole idea of supernatural revelation would be discredited. But although Voltaire's anti-Christian intentions are obvious, his anti-Jewish sorties are by no means a mere by-product of his fight against the church. The defamation of the Jewish character — whether the starting point was the Biblical figures or contemporary Jewry — became an objective in itself. Whether personal experiences or idiosyncrasies influenced Voltaire's anti-Jewish sentiments has been much debated by historians, but in fact this is not of much importance. For it is beyond doubt that Voltaire's anti-Jewish tendencies owed much to the philosophical school, the rationalistic deism, he belonged to.[44] Deism rejected most emphatically any religion based on revelation, rites, observances, and ceremonies. All these came under the heading of superstition. Biblical Judaism could easily be taken for a prototype of this kind of religion, and the full contempt reserved for superstition directed against it. Biblical rather than rabbinical Judaism, was chosen as the target for the attack so that Christianity, too, would be affected. But rabbinical Judaism as practiced by contemporary Jews was not less derided. The resentment against rabbinical Judaism was fed from two sources: a former pupil of the Jesuits, Voltaire's justification for his contempt of Judaism was probably inspired by the traditional Christian doctrines; this was now reinforced and justified by rationalistic deism. To be sure, not all the deists revealed this anti-Jewish trend based on rationalistic philosophy; some of them, for example John Toland, became on the contrary not only defenders of contemporary Jews but also vindicators of ancient Judaism while severely criticizing Christianity.[45]

But the mainstream of deistic thought was that represented by Voltaire and combined the anti-Jewish resentment with rationalistic criticism of Christianity. The Biblical narrative was declared to be the saga of an underdeveloped tribe, reflecting their irrational and primitive customs which led to the Jews' attitude of exclusiveness and disrespect for the rights of any but their own kin. For the Jews were said to be addicted to the tribal zeal, reflected in the story of the Bible which, in the light shed by the idea of humanistic philosophy, became more contemptible than ever. The rationalistic critic of Judaism discovered an ancient source of anti-Jewish criticism in the writings of the classics. Cicero, Tacitus, and others had accused the Jews of narrow-mindedness, bigotry, and inhumanity to all outside their own nation.[46] Rationalists of the eighteenth century combined all these sources and used them indiscriminately while they served their ideological purpose.

The polemic literature that grew from public discussion on the future status of the Jews duly reflected these notions developed by rationalistic anti-Jewish writers. Schulz, as the most outspoken follower of radical rationalism, adopted the Voltairian argument against religion in general and against Judaism in particular.[47] Hartmann perhaps did not directly rely upon Voltaire but was certainly influenced by the deistic trend he represented. Traces of the rationalistic evaluation of Judaism can be found in the writings of all those who took a stand against Jews and Judaism at this time.

The adversaries of the Jews at this juncture did not however simply repeat the arguments of Voltaire's school. While the reflections of Voltaire often sound like historical dissertations, the reasoning of the disputants we are concerned with here had a clearly conceived objective, namely, to prove the incapacity and unworthiness of the Jews for citizenship. This can be recognized from the way in which they marshaled their arguments, which are clearly directed toward a definite aim.

That a new phase began in the development of anti-Jewish argumentation can best be demonstrated by the appearance of a new slogan: "State within the State." Schulz was one of the first to use this expression against the Jews.[48] The formula itself had been coined to discredit the Huguenots after the Edict of Nantes in 1598 when they remained a tightly organized community not devoid of real political power. Later, when the centralized state set out to strike at all vestiges of autonomy in organizations — that of the Huguenots was annihilated with the revocation of the Edict of Nantes in 1685 — it was used also against the Jesuits, the Freemasons, and even against the guilds and craftsmen's associations. At this time the term had not yet come to be used against the Jews, probably because though they were organized in communities not unsimilar to the corporations, they were not considered a part of the body politic at all. They were not a state within a state but — at best — on the periphery. When the idea of giving citizenship to the Jews arose, the question was asked whether they would lose themselves among the other inhabitants or continue to exist as an ethnic and cultural social unit and constitute a state within a state. The formula stuck. Johann Gottlieb

Fichte, the philosopher, used it in 1793 in his famous treatise on the justification of the French Revolution. He applied the formula to all the social units that constituted compact subgroups in the state: the aristocrats, the church, the army, the craft guilds, and especially to the Jews. Against the latter the philosopher applied the formula in a most derogatory manner, describing them as a "mighty and hostilely disposed State that is permanently engaged in war with all the others" [49] in Europe. The faults, shortcomings, and moral defects that Fichte lays at the door of the Jews are reminiscent of the accusations made by Schulz, whom he followed also by using the expression "State within the State." But while Schulz was an oddity and his book very soon forgotten, Fichte's remarks on the Jews — endowed, so to speak, with the authority of philosophy — gained currency. It became a kind of locus classicus in anti-Semitic literature.

The first phase of the struggle for Jewish emancipation took a third of a century, that is, 1780–1814; thus anti-Jewish sentiments had enough time to come to the fore. The incompatibility of Jewish religion and mentality with the obligations of citizenship is the main theme of the arguments brought forward. The adversaries of Jewish citizenship in the National Assembly during the Revolution used the current arguments against Jews. Abbé Maury defined Jews as being "not a sect but a nation having laws that it has always followed and that it wished to follow." "Jews have traversed seventeen centuries and not mixed with other nations." Quoting Voltaire, he accuses the kings of the Middle Ages of allowing themselves to be guided by their cupidity in admitting Jews — to the detriment of posterity. Jews would not be able to serve in the army, nor do useful work in agriculture and industry. Their religion and their indolence would hinder them. The occupations the Jews excelled in were finance and commerce and they did so at the expense of those who earned their bread by the sweat of their brow.[50] Similar charges, if perhaps less demagogically worded, were brought against the Jews during the deliberations in 1806–1808 in France when Napoleon revised the status of the Jews once more and curtailed the rights of citizenship granted during the Revolution. The expression "état dans l'état" recurs in the article of Louis Gabriel Ambroise de Bonald in the *Mercure de France* in February 1806 summing up the reasons for the Jews' inability to hold full citizenship in a country of Christians.[51] De Bonald combined the traditional Christian objections against Jews with the reflections of the deists and rationalists.

Ideological reservations concerning the Jewish character also played their part in the considerations preceding the reform of the Jewish status in Prussia in 1812.[52] As early as 1803–1805, fearing a possible radical reform in the status of Jews, anti-Jewish writers embarked on a most violent defamatory campaign against them. The anti-Jewish ideologics evolved twenty years previously now crystallized and were definitely more virulent in character. "Judaism is in contradiction with naturalisation or rather destroys the civic constitution and without disadvantage to or the decline of the citizens, it is impossible to grant them the privileges of citizens. The essential points of Judaism undermine sociability. They bring about a State within the State and aim at gaining for the Jews domination and turning the rest of the citizens into their slaves." These words were written by Christian Ludwig Paalzov.[53]

In the same year Grattenauer reappeared with his second book *Wider die Juden*, which carried the subtitle, "A Word of Warning to all our Christian Co-citizens." The book contains selected passages from Eisenmenger to prove that Jews are permitted by their religion to cheat and rob Christians and take false oath against them. The warning mentioned in the subtitle was to prevent Christians from granting citizenship to Jews.

"Grant the Jews full right of citizenship . . . they will reward you royally, for
   you will stand and tend the flocks of the Jews;
   your sons and daughters will become the slaves and handmaidens
   of the Jews; you will work in the sweat of your brow, but
   the Chosen People of God will enjoy the fruits and live grandly!!!

This prophesy is written in the Talmud; allow it to happen, so that the prophesies of the rabbis will come true."[54]

Anti-Jewish agitation reached a peak of vulgar expression in Grattenauer's second book. Few perhaps were prepared to follow him there. But a basic anti-Jewish attitude is quite common. It penetrated into the ranks of the high officials of the Prussian state who were reluctant to go along with the planned reform under discussion since the death of Mendelssohn at the end of the reign of Frederic II in 1786. Baron Schroetter, serving in the Prussian cabinet in 1804, took up a stand when certain Jews sought a remedy for their grievances, for he regarded them as economically harmful and morally uninhibited: "for the greatest capital sums are in the hands of the Jews; for to the Jews all means are the same in order to attain their objective." [55] Derogatory opinions such as these were often expressed in high official circles during the course of deliberations on reforming the Jewish status and some reservations against them were harbored even by those who recommended and finally implemented the reform of 1812.[56]

The basic differences of opinion between the promoters of the reform and its opponents did not lie in their appraisal of Jewish character on which, more or less, they agreed. The issue concerned the future. The shattering political events — Prussia's defeat in 1806 by the French army — gave rise to a pervading spirit of reform and revision that took in its stride also the more optimistic trend in favor of the Jews. In 1808 Schroetter once again gave an unflattering portrait of the Jews. "As the tendency of their spiritual makeup is trade and its aim, money . . . from the richest to the poorest [this] has become a national matter . . ." But his conclusion, based on this characteristic, was now that the Jew must be given a new constitution "to undermine their nationality, destroy it, and thus gradually induce them no longer to aim at forming a 'State within a State.' " [57] This is a cruder version of the Image of the Future with which Wilhelm von Humboldt accompanied his recommendation of unreserved emancipation.[58] In the background of both conceptions there hovers the sinister figure of the Jew as he lived in the popular imagination for centuries. The analysis of the process of integration reveals to us that this unsavory image accompanied the Jew on his entry into European society via the highway of political and social reform.

VII THE DEFECTING FRINGE

The resistance of the conservative Gentile to Jewish integration threatened to blunt the optimism conveyed by the image of the future envisaged by enlightened Jews and Gentiles. True, the support for Jewish equality and integration was much more in harmony with the spirit of the age than the obstinate refusal to budge from the position that Jews were forever doomed to inadequacy and exclusion. On the other hand, the optimistic recommendations held at best a promise for the future without rectifying Jewish grievances. These continued to burden the life of the Jews, for nowhere was the image of the future given a practical expression that anticipated its political and social implications. Even where political equality had been granted, as in France during the Revolution, this did not imply complete social acceptance, and politically, too, the Jews suffered a setback at the height of Napoleon's regime.[1] In other countries even political equality was slow to materialize, and its arrival was not always complete and certainly did not entail equality in other spheres. The expectation of future equality could in no way substitute for the shortcomings of the present. On the contrary, some of the peculiar laws appertaining to Jews — as for instance the "Leibzoll," the toll a Jew had to pay when going from one country to another, and the "collective responsibility," where the community was responsible for taxes imposed by the authorities and debts resulting from bankruptcy incurred by any member, and the like[2] — were resented not only for the financial burden they imposed but for the stigma they represented. They symbolized the exceptional and inferior status of the Jews. As long as traditional notions on Jewish fate and destiny prevailed, these hardships were accepted as part of the Jewish burden-in-exile. With the emergence of the image of the future and all that this entailed in expectation and reevaluation, the ideological basis or justification for these evils disappeared and they, along with the other aggravations that formed part of Jewish life, seemed unbearable.

For the individual Jew, of course, there always remained one way of extricating himself from the Jewish predicament — by joining one of the Christian churches. It is a characteristic feature of this time that many a Jew sought this solution.

As noted earlier, conversions to Christianity were not unheard of even in traditional society. But at that time conversions occurred mostly among individuals who were dejected socially and were culturally on a lower level.[3] This type of conversion, to be sure, also took place during the period of disintegration. The *Institutum Judaicum*[4] of Halle ceased functioning in 1791. But the missionary attitude did not disappear even among some of the leading figures of the Christian albeit enlightened society. It certainly persisted with the rank and file of the clergy, who thought that they were merely performing their duty by saving Jewish souls whenever they had the opportunity. From enlightened Berlin — true, already under the regime of the successor of Frederic the Great in 1798 — word was received of the conversion of three Jewish sisters aged eight, ten, and twelve who were baptized with the assistance of high dignitaries of the Lutheran and Reformed churches and under the auspices of royal authority. According to the semiofficial report, the children had heard the story of Jesus from Christian children and had been so captivated by it that they had insisted on baptism. Since the children were all under age and the parents — poor Jews, it seems — protested, the suspicion that the baptism was the work of some zealot missionary may not be unfounded.[5]

The authorities of Protestant Berlin as well as of Catholic Vienna concerned themselves with similar cases, the baptism of children without the consent of their parents presenting delicate problems of a legal and ecclesiastical nature. There was, for instance, the problem of determining at what age a child could take a decision that could be considered both responsible and valid. The zealous Empress Maria Theresa was prepared to accept the decision in favor of Christianity coming from a seven-year-old convert but her enlightened son, Joseph II, stipulated that the would-be convert be at least eighteen years old. There were differences of opinion on the attitude to be taken by the authorities to those whose desire for conversion was obviously prompted by ulterior motives. Pregnant Jewish maid servants who wanted to marry their lovers and unlicensed students and traders threatened with expulsion were often candidates for baptism and apparently met with little reluctance on the part of the clergy. The authorities, however, were on the alert for those who wished to circumvent the law in this way.[6]

These converts were however not the kind that were typical for this age. To determine the outstanding features of typical converts it is necessary to inquire into the process of conversion, its motivation and justification. In traditional times conversion, whether genuine or for ulterior motives, meant transferring one's social allegiance immediately from one group to the other. The psychological process leading to the decision might have been slow and cumulative; the execution had to be abrupt. As to the justification, this always had to be made in terms of Christian theology. If genuine, the conversion meant that the Jew had become convinced of the truth of Christianity. If feigned, the convert had to pretend to be convinced. There is a whole literature of confessions written, during the hundred years preceding the Enlightenment, by Jewish converts who tell the story of their conversion.[7] Some of them seem genuine, others bear the telltale signs of hypocrisy.[8] In these confessions the authors always declare their conviction that the Messiah the Hebrew prophets had spoken of was Jesus of Nazareth. Thus, a confession to a belief in the central tenet of Christianity was expected of the Jew by Christians and the converted Jew either did arrive or pretended to arrive at it. The acceptance of this article of faith made him a Christian and severed him from the Jewish fold.

It is the mark of the new era that the Jewish convert was no longer expected to arrive at the truth of the central tenets of Christianity. Enlightened Christians like Hartmann and Humboldt expected Jews to embrace Christianity either as a condition for their integration or as a result of it.[9] These enlightened Gentiles did not expect Jews to be convinced of the Christian dogmas. They themselves could be considered Christians less because they believed in the Christian dogmas than for accepting Christianity as the historical and cultural agency that had molded their intellectual and moral life. A similar attitude would, they felt, in the long run be assumed by Jews.

This shift from the theological truths of Christianity to its general cultural and moral content is evident in the intellectual history of the whole period of Enlightenment. No wonder that this made itself felt also with regard to the Jewish convert. A case in point is that of Moses Mendelssohn who, as will be remembered, was twice approached publicly to convert. The first time the offer came from Johann Caspar Lavater in 1770. Lavater combined an enthusiasm for the Christian millennium with the spirit of Enlightenment. According to a widely accepted version, the coming of the millennium was dependent upon the "return of the Jews," that is, their conversion to Christianity. It has been suggested by historians that Lavater sought to convert Mendelssohn, the leading Jewish philosopher in Berlin, not only to gain an important proselyte but to set in motion the process of conversion of all Jews which, in turn, would have cosmic repercussions.[10] For the purpose here it is more important to see by what means he hoped to convince Mendelssohn. As mentioned in an earlier chapter, he dedicated to Mendelssohn the translation of the book by Charles Bonnet *La Palingénésie Philosophique*. This book was a modern apologia of Christianity basing the proof for Christian teachings on the findings of biology and other sciences, thus wresting one of the weapons from the deprecators of religion and using it to vindicate religion in general and Christian religion in particular. Bonnet was steeped in the intellectual problems of his time; his intention was ultimately, however, to rehabilitate Christian teachings with everything this implied in terms of dogma and irrational tenets.[11] By dedicating Bonnet's book to him, Lavater hoped to fix Mendelssohn's attention on the proofs for Christian dogmas and mysteries.

Altogether different were the intellectual assumptions of the author, who appealed to Mendelssohn a second time in 1782 with the intention of converting him.[12] His attachment to Christianity was a formal one. He was an exponent of rationalism, seeing no contradiction between these tendencies and Christianity — provided that Christianity was correctly interpreted. Accordingly, in appealing to Mendelssohn to renounce Judaism for Christianity, he had more to say about the reasons for renouncing Judaism than about those for embracing Christianity. Judaism belonged to a more primitive stage of religious development when the worship of God was still bound up with the whole regalia of rites and ceremonies. The observance of the external forms of religions was controlled by the theocracy established by tyrannical priests. However, with the fall of the Jewish state, the foundation of Jewish theocracy crumbled. On the other hand, what was of value in Jewish religion, "veneration for the only God, obedience to the divine commandments given through Moses, and the assembling of the nations into one flock under the common sceptre of one Messiah whose coming had been announced by the words of the prophets," [13] had been salvaged by Christianity. Elsewhere the author describes Christianity as "a liberal system for the more reasonable worship of God" ("das Freiheitssistem des vernünftigern Gottesdienstes").[14] In short, it is a most diluted version of Christianity, only slightly reminiscent of Christian dogma, that is thus proffered to the Jew to replace his Judaism.

The old expectation of ultimate Jewish conversion was not abandoned, only the traditional method of achieving this objective. That proselytizing in the traditional manner for converts among the Jews had been discredited was said in so many words in 1790 by Wilhelm Friedrich Hezel, a theologian of note, Professor of Biblical and Oriental literature at the University of Giessen.[15] Hezel was a good Christian and believed in the christological interpretation of the Old Testament. Yet he despaired of convincing Jews of the correctness of the Christian reading of the Jewish scriptures. The history of Christian endeavors to convert Jews taught him his lesson: results did not in any way justify the amount of effort invested. Hezel therefore determined to find out the reason for the insensibility of Jews toward what seemed to him the obvious truths. He found it in their degenerate taste in literature, which he ascribed to their lack of education and culture. Hezel's recommendation was, therefore, to abandon the attempt to prevail upon the Jews by fruitless discussion of theological tenets and proofs of Christianity. Rather Jews should be given the opportunity to make the acquaintance of European culture and taught the subjects that would develop their literary taste; this educational process would ultimately achieve the longed-for goal, a mass conversion of Jews.[16] Reeducation then, according to Hezel, was also the only reasonable answer to the question of civic betterment suggested by Dohm a decade earlier and discussed at length since that time. Hezel concedes to the opponents of Dohm that serious handicaps debarred the Jews from being included in a Christian society. But once they have so far advanced as to be able to appreciate Christianity, their acceptance would represent no problem. The old objective must therefore be retained but the method of achieving it radically changed.

Although Hezel's assumptions are somewhat odd and scarcely representative, they are nonetheless indicative of what was generally held at the time. The theological approach to Jewish conversion was given up and, instead, emphasis placed on what would today be termed "acculturation." Hezel's optimism, even though naive, is still symptomatic of the time, and his distrust of the theological approach was certainly shared by many.

The new approach to conversion has a corresponding sequel in the type of convert that now appears. The actual passage from Judaism to Christianity as well as its ideological justification appear in a new light. Going from one community to the other no longer seems the hazardous leap over a gulf. This has been in some way breached by the semineutral society, referred to in Chapter IV, which erected the bridge for a gradual transition from one community to the other. On the other hand, the reinterpretation of Christianity and Judaism in terms of enlightened rationalism seemed to temper the conflict between the beliefs and tenets of the two religions. The step toward Christianity could more easily be vindicated — once the decision to convert was taken. The decision itself was made easier by the social and psychological climate, for the rapprochement between Jews and Christians on the one hand and Christianity and Judaism on the other pulled down the barricades behind which the ghetto Jew had hidden himself, a member of an excluded minority shielded from the temptation of the world of the majority.

This world of the majority could not, of course, be entirely ignored even by Jews who still lived behind the ghetto walls. The converts who left the ghetto for the outer world, though they interpreted their experience as a recognition of the Christian truths, can be said to have exchanged the narrow precincts of the ghetto for the larger and richer world of Christianity. Such a sociological explanation of Jewish conversion must assume a hidden and protracted process that will never be more than conjecture.

At the time of the dissolution of traditional society and traditional values there is a clear connection between the visible enticements displayed by non-Jewish society and the resultant Jewish conversions. Those belonging to the enlightened Jewish upper class were attracted by the splendor, the freedom, and the greater spiritual amplitude of Christian society. The children of court Jews, who had received some secular education and had the means to adopt the expensive habits of high society, were most likely to observe the discrepancy between their material affluence and their low social standing. With greater freedom for contact with Gentiles, these children became an easy prey to intermarriage and conversion. If the encounter with non-Jewish society ended in joining it, the convert had no difficulty in justifying his step.

There exists a letter of one of the sons of Adam Arnstein in Vienna who converted to Christianity but, nonetheless, hoped to overcome parental resentment for the step — this in itself representing a clear deviation from the traditional pattern according to which baptism severed all ties between the new Christian and his Jewish family. Written some years after the baptism, the letter expresses the hope that the parents would by then be prepared to reconcile themselves to the fateful decision made by their son. The writer assures his parents that he had taken his step not "for any ulterior motive, or a predilection for good living nor any wish for libertinism" but "because he found himself convinced that salvation and peace of mind was to be found in another way." The converted son does not appeal simply to the natural affections of the parents, who could, incidentally, be expected to leave behind a considerable estate on their decease. He tried to evoke the spirit of tolerance that had penetrated everywhere, not forgetting to mention that the parents themselves were benefiting from it under the enlightened regime of the Emperor Joseph II. The writer points especially to the conduct of one of his brothers and his sister-in-law Fanny, famous for her salon in Vienna, who, unbaptized, moved in the same Gentile society and were appreciated and loved by all. The difference between the religions was not insurmountable; the writer and his parents might have "different theoretical principles" but this was no reason for estrangement. The son goes so far as to quote the Jewish tenet according to which "no human being is damned forever." [17]

Such scraps of enlightened reasoning sufficed to set the mind of the convert at rest and even permitted him to take a stand on the desirable relations between different denominations. Other converts have evolved an even less elaborate ideology to vindicate the step taken. They, and especially women converts, just allowed themselves to be swept along with the social current. It was a shrewd observation of Karl Wilhelm Friedrich Grattenauer that women who had access to enlightened education and culture and developed a sensitivity toward their inferior status in society were the first to try and escape it by means of baptism and intermarriage. Jewish males, one supposes, were able to compensate for social inferiority by means of the economic power they wielded.[18] Men and women alike, once they had decided to convert, needed not much ideological justification for a change of religion that was merely part and parcel of the new social elevation that followed in the wake of new family attachments.

The family's control over their children's decision weakened, and desperate attempts on the part of some parents to exercise parental authority were of no avail. There are on record cases of parents who tried to obstruct their children's conversion by a threat to leave their possessions to those that remained within the faith. Such a case occupied the attention of Berlin courts and authorities during the lifetime of Mendelssohn when two baptized daughters of a testator contested the validity of a will that made this stipulation.[19] Curiously enough, one of the experts consulted by the authorities, the learned Olof Gerhard Tychsen, ventured the opinion that the clause stipulating that the inheritors could benefit only if they remained Jews had not been violated by the daughters' conversion. Relying formally on traditional Jewish sources, but in a sense keeping to the Christian tradition, he declared that a Jew though baptized did not cease to be a Jew.[20] Certainly more in line with the feeling of the time was the opinion of another expert who justified the claims of the baptized children on the ground that there was in effect no difference between the Jewish and Christian religions as both strived for the moral elevation of man. It would be absurd to penalize an individual by denying him his inheritance simply because he changed his religious convictions.[21]

In the attitude of the elder Arnstein and the father of the two girls in Berlin the traditional attitude toward the act of baptism is revealed — an abrupt severance of all connection. But this attitude no longer prevailed exclusively. In the young Arnstein's letter to his father it is learned that another brother and a sister-in-law had remained in touch with him; these were, of course, of the new type of the socially emancipated, who remained Jewish but displayed unqualified religious tolerance. Mrs. Arnstein the younger was, as shown, a shining light in the salon, where it was considered bad taste to pay attention to one's former or present religion. Mr. Arnstein himself, the husband of Fanny, is known to have been a member of the Order of the Asiatic Brethren, which attempted to overcome the differences between Judaism and Christianity through a kind of syncretism. Baptized Jews were, of course, welcome members here. Indeed one of them — Thomas von Schönfeld, who was one of the founders of the Order — was a convert of a very special type, an adherent of the Frankist sect that was a ramification of the Sabatian movement.[22] The members of this clandestine sect were alienated from Judaism, the more radical among them leaning toward absolute antinomianism and nihilism while outwardly preserving the guise of Judaism. On coming into contact with the world of Enlightenment, they defected easily from a Judaism that was already undermined in the religious double life practiced in the sects. Here, it seems, is a case of the well-known phenomenon that sectarianism, while antirationalist in nature, nonetheless bred candidates for the new movement of Enlightenment. For these Jewish sectarians the acceptance of Enlightenment meant abandoning Judaism in favor of the larger world of the Christians.

For baptized and unbaptized Jews to mingle freely became an accepted social phenomenon. The *Gesellschaft der Freunde* in Berlin, founded in 1792, was one of the first associations of enlightened Jews. Originally established by the enlightened to fight the traditionalists, especially on the issue of early burial (on which more shall be learned later), the association served, in effect, as a meeting ground for the new type of Jew. The question arose as to whether conversion disqualified Jews from membership. The members, however, decided that religious affiliation was irrelevant.[23]

The principle of toleration demanded that religion should be ignored in the social sphere. Thus the Jew felt obliged to apply this principle also to fellow Jews who chose to convert to Christianity. What was valid in the social sphere came to be accepted as the rule governing family relationships. Simon Veit tried with all his might to prevent his sons from following their mother, the romantic-minded Dorothea Mendelssohn, into the Christian fold but, once they, too, embraced Catholicism, he played down the differences between the two religions. "I shall not cease to love you both and to do my best for you even if we are not of the same opinion in regard to religion . . . My dear son, as long as we differ only in religion and are at one in our moral principles a division will never fall between us.[24]

The fact that the enlightened Jew could reconcile himself to the baptism of his friends and relatives points to a decomposition of the old system of values. The process of disintegration of traditional society is revealed in the acts of those who took the step of conversion but also by those who weighed the matter even though they refrained from taking the ultimate step. Many could now envisage the formal acceptance of Christianity without genuinely believing. The price did not seem as exorbitant as it had in former times. For the theory of rationalism undoubtedly suggested that all positive religions were only the outward variations of one essence — the religion of nature or reason. The Christian theologians themselves stressed the moral teachings of Christianity and explained its dogmas and symbols in the light of rational philosophy. It almost seemed as though the change from Judaism to Christianity would involve only the exchange of the trappings. For already during the lifetime of Mendelssohn a Berlin Jewish physician is reported to have said, in conversation with the enlightened theologian Johann Joachim Spalding, that if Christianity would be content with the tenet of Socinianism — that is, forego the dogma of the Trinity — he would gladly convert. In the doctor's opinion this could be said for most of the enlightened Jews of Berlin.[25] Ten years later two Christians made a similar estimate of the enlightened Jewish Berliner's inclinations. Two otherwise unknown men, Catter and von Hirschfeld, made an effort to bring Jews and Christians together by founding a Masonic lodge that, contrary to prevailing practice, would accept Jews and Christians alike. Not all Jews, of course, would qualify for acceptance; only those who already had a spiritual affinity for Christianity but were hindered by family considerations from following their inclinations and converting. Catter and von Hirschfeld quoted examples, giving the names of the two brothers Itzig, Dr. Marcus Herz, and the banker Levy.[26]

There is no doubt that the idea of conversion to Christianity fascinated many an enlightened Jew. But the remark of the anonymous doctor and the thoughts expressed by the two Christian Masons show that they were kept from taking the conclusive step by various inhibitions and reservations. These are illustrated in the story of Solomon Maimon, who also toyed with the idea of converting. Maimon came from Lithuania to Germany with a deep desire to complement his vast Jewish scholarship with a knowledge of modern philosophy, a subject to which he later made a significant contribution.[27] His undeniable gifts won him the support of enlightened Jews, among them men like Mendelssohn, but he succeeded in antagonizing even his benefactors by his radical skepticism, his rejection of religious conformity and, generally, by his undisciplined conduct. A true wandering Jew, he finally despaired of ever being given the opportunity to pursue his studies. At heart he was by this time indifferent to all forms of religion and was ready to accept Christianity, provided he was not required to confess to any dogma he could not believe in. In Hamburg he approached a Lutheran pastor and expressed his wish for baptism. He explained that, in the final analysis, his aim was the admirable one of acquiring perfection through the study of philosophy. As this could only be achieved within Christian society, he was prepared to accept this religion while at the same time retaining his reservations as to its truths and significance. This was a form of reasoning that the Lutheran pastor, not unnaturally perhaps, was unable to appreciate and the conversion came to nought. The pastor could not condone conversion without faith.[28]

The attempt of Solomon Maimon to persuade the church to compromise on a half-hearted conversion could be dismissed as the whim of an eccentric if it had not had a sequel in the notorious suggestion made by David Friedländer, one of the leading personalities in the enlightened Jewish society of Berlin, a member of the Jewish community's governing body, and accepted as the representative of Prussian Jewry by the state authorities.[29] The suggestion was contained in a pamphlet published in 1799 in Berlin in the name of "several Jewish households" and addressed to the Provost, Wilhelm Abraham Teller. It was an attempt to pave the way for the absorption of a part of the Jewish community into the Christian church. The Jews would join the Protestant church of which Teller was an enlightened representative; they would be duly baptized but as they had their reservations about Christian dogma, they asked to be allowed to confess only to the religion of nature.[30] The pamphlet appeared anonymously in Berlin but the author did not long remain a mystery. A disciple of Mendelssohn's, David Friedländer nevertheless drew conclusions from Mendelssohn's teachings far beyond what the master had contemplated. Mendelssohn, though he may be said to have identified Jewish teachings with what was taught by the religion of reason, still gave validity to traditional Jewish religious practice. David Friedländer maintained that the religion of reason was self-sufficient and needed no assistance whatsoever from religious practice.[31] Jewish religious practices were not only superfluous but harmful in that they prevented Jews from being accepted by non-Jewish society and were the main obstruction to their being given full rights as citizens. It did not seem unreasonable to wish to obtain these social and political objectives by abandoning observances that were in any event becoming obsolete.

Friedländer seems to have arrived at these conclusions at an early stage of his career — perhaps even while Mendelssohn still lived.[32] These ideas guided him when, shortly after the death of Mendelssohn, he undertook negotiations with the Prussian authorities to try and improve the status of Jews in Prussia. His stated objectives were not always the same. At times he negotiated for a basic reform that would alleviate the Jewish situation in Prussia; at others he made an appeal for exceptional citizenship on behalf of his own family and sometimes he spoke on behalf of his class, the rich and enlightened merchants of Berlin. Ultimately, he wished to destroy the whole fabric of the Jewish communal organization that tied the individual Jew to the community and bound Jewish communities together. The organization guaranteed the payment of taxes and undertook collective responsibility for the liabilities incurred by individuals. At the same time the organization secured for the rabbinate and for communal leaders the virtual control of the life and conduct of members of the Jewish community. This state of affairs seemed outdated to Friedländer, counter to the spirit of the times and therefore not to be borne.[33]

It is only fair to state that the wish to see the communal organization dissolved and its power for coercion destroyed could be deduced from Mendelssohn's theory about the different spheres of influence of state and religion. In this, at least, Friedländer could have boasted that he was only following where the Master had led. Yet, while Mendelssohn imagined a society where individual Jews would voluntarily keep together to devote themselves to the fulfillment of their religious obligations — even where there was no organization to coerce them — the disciple hoped that a removal of communal control would lead to the obliteration of everything typical of Jewish tradition in religion and custom.[34]

Friedländer sought to achieve his objectives by persuading the authorities that they would benefit the state no less than the Jews.[35] But the Prussian state was slow to move, and despite small changes, the ultimate objectives seemed as elusive as ever even after more than ten years of continued efforts on the part of the representatives of enlightened Jews. Friedländer and those who thought like him lost their patience and tried to escape what to them seemed the prison of their Judaism by making a deal with the representatives of Christianity.

The reaction to Friedländer's suggestion by Provost Teller, and by many others who felt they had to take a stand on it, reveals the attitude of Christian society to the would-be convert. Of course, no Christian who attributed any significance to the rites and dogmas of the church was prepared to replace them with the abstract tenets of natural religion. The orthodox theologians thus rejected Friedländer's suggestion as an audacity and demanded that the would-be convert accept Christianity in its entirety.[36] Teller himself, an exponent of the rationalistic school of theology, was committed to a critical attitude toward the dogmas of the church and consistently assured the new converts that they would be free to follow their own interpretations of the Christian teachings without jeopardizing their legitimate place in the church. But Christians they must be. That is, they had to accept the baptism and take the sacrament for the symbols of the religion founded by Christ.[37] This religion was superior to the Jewish faith and went beyond a mere submission to moral precepts. The special content of the Christian religion is left undefined but the manner of its achievement is clearly stated to be that of faith.

The comments of other theologians were in a similar vein.[38] Friedländer's plan did not stand a chance of being implemented. Even if Teller and the other theologians had been in sympathy with it, it would have been beyond their competence to adapt the rites of the church to the needs of a new type of convert. This was clearly seen and said by the most important participant in the controversy, Friedrich Schleiermacher:[39] "Herr Teller and our whole upper consistory are unable on their own authority to found a new sect or change the ancient customs of the ecclesiastic societies acknowledged hitherto." [40] But, in fact, they were far from being in sympathy with it. Schleiermacher, an inveterate attender of the Jewish salons in Berlin and a personal friend of Henriette Herz, closely followed the transformation of Jewish life and the attempts at integration into state and society. He was eager to see the Jews accepted as citizens by the state and resented the repeated slights the leaders of the Prussian Jewish communities were made to suffer at the hands of the authorities. But not less severely did he condemn the shortcut attempted by Friedländer, whose compromise would discredit both parties to it, the Jews and the church. Instead, Schleiermacher recommended the establishment of a reform sect in Judaism that would relinquish the traditional practices and tenets — especially the belief in the coming of the Messiah — that, he thought, conflicted with the obligations of citizens in a Christian state. Those who, like Friedländer, could with a good conscience concur in this, would then be acceptable subjects of the state and should be granted citizenship. Other Jews would have the choice of following them or of retaining their old status.[41]

Teller, it is true, wished to avoid the political aspects of the problem. Nevertheless, his advice was on similar lines. So long as Jews were not convinced of the truth of Christianity, the most commendable course for Jewish society was an adaptation to the way of life and moral standards of Christian society. The desirability of ultimate conversion was not questioned. That would have meant a repudiation of Christian principles. For the time being he recommended that both Jews and Christians should bide their time.[42] This, in a sense, was Teller's answer to Friedländer and it conformed with his remark on Mendelssohn made in private many years before: that it was better for Mendelssohn to remain a Jew and improve his community by his example.[43]

The unconvinced converts, who took the step from expedience, could scarcely hope for public approval. On the whole, however, they met with little difficulty when they demanded baptism, no matter with what mental reservations they approached the confession. True, there were some who warned of the dangers of accepting the half-convinced convert. Schleiermacher was one of those who sounded a warning at the time of Friedländer's appeal.[44] Such warnings had little effect and the doors of the church remained open.

Yet it would be a mistake to assume that all those who turned Christian did so with the consciousness, so to speak, of striking a social bargain. Although, objectively, the disintegrating Jewish community may have had its effect on the converts of the time, some may nevertheless have been spurred by genuine conviction. Jewish youths began attending non-Jewish educational institutions and absorbed the elements of Christian culture while their Jewish education was neglected or conducted in a way that could not compete with the Christian influence. Some of these students found themselves converted by the end of their studies almost as a matter of course. The conversion of David Mendel, later the famous church historian, August Neander, is a case in point. David completed his studies at the gymnasium in Hamburg in 1805 at a time when Jewish aspirations gained momentum from the prevalence of French revolutionary ideas. The director of the gymnasium, Johann Gottfried Gurlitt, a liberal writer and educator, had asked him to make a speech on Jewish emancipation at the leavetaking ceremonies. A year after leaving the school he converted — no doubt an act of conviction but not in the sense of religious experience; rather, an act of cultural adaptation. Only at a later stage of his development did Neander also become a Christian in the emotional and pietistic sense.[45]

But there were already at this time those whose conversion had been mainly prompted by the emotional component. Religious conversion was, for some, a kind of by-product of the disenchantment with a rationalism that was being superseded by the new wave of emotionalism and romanticism. This new movement returned to religion its emotional quality and its mystical depth. Friedrich Schleiermacher's *Speeches on Religion*, published shortly after he had taken a stand on the Jewish issue, did a great deal to rescue religion from its subordination to rationalism.[46] Religion to the romanticists meant the Christian religion, Judaism being explicitly or tacitly excluded from the definition. The reason for this was partly the old partisan definition of Judaism as a religion of law, that is, of observances and prohibitions. Traits of inwardness and spirituality in Jewish religion were either overlooked or discarded. This evaluation was strengthened by the statement made by Moses Mendelssohn — the accepted authority on Judaism — that the unique content of Judaism reposed in its law.[47] For those who were now seeking in religion an escape from rationalism, Jewish religion seemed an unpromising haven.

Such a wave of emotion swept the hostesses of the famous Jewish salons toward Christianity and all of them converted.[48] Henriette Herz tells us in her memoirs that the need for emotional satisfaction drove her to religion. In speaking of her father, she used the expressions "Andacht" and "Innbrunst" (devotion and fervor) to describe his prayers in time of distress. Reflecting on her father's virtues, she says that "he lived strictly within the Law of his faith, but had the gentleness and love of Christianity in his heart." When it comes to an ideological evaluation, she dismisses Jewish religion as a dull practice of mechanical observances.[49] The identification of romanticism with Christianity gave conversion an ideological cover that left aside the issue of dogmatism. The way to Christianity was thus paved also for Dorothea Mendelssohn, the daughter of the great man himself, the cause célèbre of romantic love. Dorothea had left her Jewish husband to live with Friedrich Schlegel, the romantic philosopher, preferring the elevation of the personality to the dull tread of duty. After some years she married Schlegel after having embraced the Protestant faith. Ultimately she found a safer haven in Catholicism, the religion that typified the requirements of the romantic spirit.[50]

No matter what the personal motivation of the different types of converts, all of them reveal the precarious state of the Jewish community they left behind. This knowledge may have affected the decision of many a Jew. If the Jewish community was in any case on the verge of disappearing, it was no reflection on the individual that he accelerated a process that seemed unavoidable.

The extent of defection during the period under consideration, that is, from the 1780's up to the end of the Napoleonic era, is difficult to assess. Statistics are lacking so that we have no exact numbers. Still, there are indications that — even as far as quantity is concerned — the loss to the Jewish community was considerable.

As early as 1790 the communal leaders of Berlin complained that many who inherited a fortune from their parents and could have materially assisted the community had gone over to Christianity, thus depriving the community of potential supporters.[51] Complaints of a similar nature are heard later as well. Friedländer, in his open letter to Teller, tells of the embitterment of Berlin Jewry against those who severed their connections with their community and escaped their obligation, which was a collective one.[52] The apprehensions of Christians like Schleiermacher, that the ungenuine converts might pervert the life of the church, makes it appear fairly certain that the number could not have been negligible.[53] On one occasion, at least, a reliable estimate of the numbers involved is available. David Friedländer, in a letter to Chancellor Hardenberg in 1811 on the eve of the Edict of 1812, usually referred to as the Act of Emancipation — once again with a view to showing what a great moral and financial loss the conversion represented to the Jewish community — enumerates the cases of baptism that occurred in Berlin during the preceding five to eight years. He collected 50 cases, all designated by name, some of them single, others parents with children — this out of a community of 405 established families. Friedländer estimated that the proportion would be about the same in the provincial cities, especially in Breslau and Königsberg.[54] Certainly the phenomenon was not limited to Berlin or Prussia alone. Heinrich Schnee registered the cases of baptism among the court Jews, some two-thirds of whose descendants converted during the time under consideration.[55] Perhaps the expression "mass conversion" employed by the historian Heinrich Grätz did not altogether deserve the strong criticism leveled at it by others.[56]

But more important than the number is the kind of person that converted during this time as compared with those who converted in the preceding period. The converts no longer stemmed from the margin of Jewish society but from its very core. Schleiermacher, writing in 1799, pointed to the difference between the converts of his time and those of twenty or thirty years earlier. "True, there were from time to time some proselytes but these were — except for lovers whom I exempt — only bad creatures of whom the Jewish communities were only too glad to be rid, those that were ruined and brought to despair . . . Everything is different now . . . These are a different kind of people altogether who are preoccupied with the idea of turning Christian, educated, well-to-do persons, well versed in all worldly things who wish to acquire rights and be accepted as citizens." [57]

The converts were from two leading groups, the rich and the intellectual. No wonder that at times it seemed as though the whole community was about to be dissolved and absorbed by the Christian church. A Protestant pastor, Ernst Gottfried Adolf Böckel, reveals that this had been the impression of Christians in Königsberg in his student days.[58] Königsberg was, of course, a stronghold of Jewish enlightenment in those days and the place where the family Friedländer originally had their residence.

Pastor Böckel's reminiscences were made in the 1840's, when the sanguine hopes of those in favor of mass conversion had long since disappeared. The defection from the Jewish community did not stop; neither did it become a landslide with an ever-mounting and accumulating effect. It turned into a social process with periodic fluctuations. The first wave was broken, it seems, with the granting of citizenship in most of the countries of Germany toward the end of the Napoleonic era — the Edict of 1812 of

OUT OF THE GHETTO

Prussia being one on the most important acts in this direction — when one of the strongest motives for conversion, that of belonging to a legally inferior and socially deprived group, if it had not disappeared entirely, at least had lost much of its weight.

It is not for the historian to speculate on how Gentile society would have reacted if the wave of conversion had continued to rise; but what has to be recorded is that baptism, from the beginning, was not universally welcomed. Already in the 1790's is heard the dissenting view of Grattenauer, who derided those Christians who rejoiced at Jewish conversion, as he was convinced of the utter corruption of Jewish character that no ceremonial immersion in baptismal water could ever cleanse.[59] Another author, less inimical to the Jews but still skeptical of the wholesome effect of baptism, warns the churches in 1799 that they should not hasten to accept every Jewish convert. He suggested six years' probation for every candidate so that he could prove his worthiness.[60] At the same time the warning of Schleiermacher is voiced, for he feared that an influx of Jews would result in the Judaization of the church — in his view, a dreadful prospect.[61] The absorption of converts into Christian society was not always an easy process. That the newcomer to Christian society met with reservations is self-evident. A Christian writer in Berlin in 1804 ascribes the following remark to a Jew who lived like a Gentile but still refrained from baptism: "What would I gain by this change; I would not lose the name of Jew but would be called X, the baptised Jew." [62] Had the wave of conversion swept all Jews in its wake, it is probable that the resistance would have increased proportionately. At any rate, the historical fact is that although at times the flow of Jews to the church seemed to endanger the very existence of the Jewish community, in the course of time it turned out that the organism, though it suffered a severe loss of blood, sustained no fatal consequences.

VIII A BLOW FOR REFORM

The disintegration that freed Jews from the bonds of traditional society resulted in the absorption of only a fraction of Jews by the non-Jewish environment. The reason for this lay not only in the nature and attitudes of that environment. The disintegration was a dialectic process, which, by its very nature, generated the forces that halted and reversed the tide of dissolution. This phenomenon has already been observed when Jews, having escaped from the traditional Jewish social unit, did not join non-Jewish circles but created new Jewish social entities with the declared purpose of furthering their newly accepted educational and religious objectives.

Education in the wider sense of the word and religious reform of a diffuse and unclarified nature were the two instruments with which the enlightened hoped to remodel Jewish life. The belief in the almost unlimited power of education was basic to the philosophy of rationalism, which regarded human nature as basically good and human character and temperament — of the individual as well as of the group — as undetermined by inborn qualities.[1] Enlightened Jews were especially disposed to accept this optimistic view as it opened a vista of improvement and advancement in their social position and political status. They displayed an affinity for the educational ideals of rationalism and its implied social improvements. It was the educational program of Naphtali Herz Wessely with which the movement of Enlightenment made its first public appearance and which brought about the division in Jewish society, separating protagonists from detractors. The educational program of Wessely, though seemingly directed at reconstructing the school curriculum, did in fact also envisage, as did the movement of Enlightenment, the remolding of Jewish attitudes and mentality.[2] The new education aimed to give the Jew a more realistic view of the world and a better understanding of his non-Jewish environment that would help to reconcile him with it. Similarly, the new education would lead to the adoption of a universalistic ethic and — perhaps not less important — lead Jews to develop a taste conforming to the aesthetic standard of the European world.[3]

The enlightened believed that all this could be achieved, firstly, by spreading their ideas on these subjects. This they did by publishing books and, especially, by launching a Hebrew periodical, the famous *Hameasef*. It was published in Königsberg in 1783 by young intellectuals who had established a society *Dorshe Sfat Ever* (Friends of the Hebrew Language) in Königsberg in that year. After two years they adopted the more appropriate German name *Die Gesellschaft zur Beförderung des Guten und Edlen* (The Society for Promoting the Good and the Noble). In 1786 the *Hameasef* moved to Berlin and appeared with interruptions until 1811 (occasionally it was printed in Altona and Dessau). Its language throughout this time remained Hebrew, but occasionally there were some German additions.[4] In 1806 a German periodical, the *Sulamith*, was started in Dessau, its purpose defined in its subtitle, "Periodical for promoting culture and humanism among the Jewish nation." This periodical continued to appear for the whole period here under review.[5]

The choice of Hebrew for *Hameasef* was dictated by its readers, who could be depended upon, by reason of their traditional education, to know Hebrew but not necessarily German. The new periodical went its own way also in the Hebrew it used. On the one hand it modernized the language to fit the subjects to be dealt with, on the other it resorted to Biblical Hebrew and demanded a grammatical excellence neglected by those who made do with the rabbinical dialect.[6] The preference of *Sulamith* for German showed what headway the language had made in the short space of less than one generation.

The main intention of the periodicals — whether they were written in Hebrew or in German — was to impart information and knowledge, to foster moral and aesthetic sensitivity, and generally to win the reader for the enlightened ideals of the promoters of these periodicals. *Hameasef* assumed a most militant attitude in its middle period between 1786–1790. *Sulamith*, though generally preserving its polite tone, was not less radical in criticizing traditional Jewish society and in recommending whatever appeared on the horizon to herald the new epoch. The circulation of the periodicals — and most likely their impact on their readers — had its ups and downs. The greatest influence seems to have been wielded by *Hameasef* during the first seven or eight years of its existence.[7] But at all times these periodicals served as a link among the enlightened. On the one hand there were the publishers, editors, and contributors who regarded themselves as an intellectual and moral elite, conscious of their mission, laboring and, if necessary, fighting for a worthwhile cause; on the other hand there were the subscribers, a loose social group that nevertheless stood apart from the bulk of the community who persisted in pursuing the well-worn path of tradition in life and thought.

The most extensive and conspicuous efforts of the enlightened were in the field of education in its more limited sense. The established educational institutions of the ghetto were rightly considered the channels through which the traditional mentality of the Jew was perpetuated. It was clear that any attempt at remolding the Jewish mentality would have to start with reforming the old institutions. Practical steps in this direction were taken even before Wessely appeared on the scene. The Sephardim of Bordeaux seem to have drawn some conclusions from rationalistic philosophy even as far back as 1778, for in that year Rabbi Hayyim Joseph David Azulai, the famous Palestinian traveler, found that the whole traditional text deriving from the oral law had been omitted and that only the text of the Pentateuch had been retained in their schools.[8] Plans for the establishment of a modern school for the children of the poor in Berlin were aired since the 1760's, and in 1781, one year before the appearance of Wessely's pamphlet, the famous *Freischule* was established by David Friedländer.[9] The expression *Freischule* means that the school was free and exacted no payment from the poor. The rich, of course, had the means to ensure an appropriate education for their children by employing private tutors, a method that had been used also in the days of traditional education when the poor had attended institutions provided by the community. When Enlightenment started making an inroad into accepted educational goals, it remained for the rich to change the content of the curriculum, giving preference to secular subjects over the religious. The poor continued attending communal institutions that were controlled by the more conservative elements. The enlightened, however, the rich and the intellectual, felt the children of the poor to be their responsibility; first, because this was in the nature of Enlightenment, second, because the new education would transform them into productive and respectable human beings capable of being included into the non-Jewish state and society. For it was clear to those who did not seek the way of individual escape by means of conversion that, as Jews, they would always be judged by the collective and it was to their advantage to see that the lowest type of Jew, who seemed to provide a model for the stereotype, should disappear altogether.[10]

The new schools were established by funds provided by wealthy Jews, served by enlightened intellectuals, and attended mostly by the children of the destitute. The example of Berlin was followed in Breslau, where a school was erected in 1791, in Dessau in 1799, and in Seesen in 1801. A special case is that of Wolfenbüttel, which only adopted the new program in 1807, for this was originally a traditional institution founded in 1786 by a pious benefactor. A year earlier the Philantropin of Frankfurt am Main was founded by Siegmund Geisenheimer, the enlightened head clerk of the Rothschilds, with some support from this rich house. In most places these schools were initiated by the enlightened but supported by the state; in Breslau the initiative came from the state authorities.[11] In Austria the educational program planned by the emperor provided for a measure of civic education to complement traditional education. The Jewish communities complied with this demand if not enthusiastically, then under necessity, but where there was a nucleus of the enlightened, as in Vienna, Prague, and later in Pressburg, the German ideals were followed and schools were established on the German model.[12]

These educational institutions differed in their aims, organization, methods, and curriculum. Some of them, such as the Austrian state-initiated schools, taught at the elementary level only. The Berlin school emphasized commercial subjects such as arithmetic and French. In Seesen the pupils were taught handicrafts while at the institution in Wolfenbüttel there was the opportunity to study classical subjects.[13] As to the methods, the Austrian schools followed the old-time method of repetition; most schools, however, were influenced by the Philantropinists, the educational exponents of rationalism, who put their hopes on rationalist psychology and had unlimited belief in the power of the intellect over the behavior of the individual. Some few had come across the methods of Johann Heinrich Pestalozzi, whose deeper understanding of the process of human growth was to supplant the pedagogy of the rationalists.[14] Occasionally the Jewish schools made some original contribution to educational practice — for instance, by publishing a German reader that served as a model in non-Jewish schools.[15]

Different as the new type of Jewish schools were, they all fulfilled the same historical function; they were instrumental in breaking the hold of the traditional program that concentrated on Jewish subjects and taught Pentateuch and Talmud to the exclusion of all else. Whereas during the reign of traditional education secular subjects could, at best, be taught only privately, now they found a place in public institutions where they complemented — and in some instances supplanted — the traditional subjects. In Bordeaux, Talmud and related subjects were altogether excluded. This was done also in Seesen. In Berlin, Breslau, and Dessau there was a compromise, allowing students to attend an old-type Talmudic school in their free time. Sometimes the schools themselves introduced a study of the Talmud in their curriculum to meet the demands of more conservative parents.

The shift from the traditionally Jewish to secular subjects indicated the greater importance attributed to the latter at the expense of Jewish subjects. Schools did take some responsibility for Jewish education and discharged it in accordance with what they thought worthwhile to transmit from the bulk of the Jewish inheritance. The Pentateuch continued, as it had always done, to serve as the child's introduction to learning, but the way in which it was transmitted to the child underwent a radical change and, instead of the wonted translation into the Yiddish vernacular, schools accepted Mendelssohn's newly completed translation into High German. At the same time, the eleventh century commentary of Rashi (Solomon Yishaki) was supplanted by the Biur, a commentary prepared by the coworkers of Mendelssohn.

Mendelssohn began his translation of the Pentateuch so that his children could absorb Jewish tradition in a language and form in harmony with the atmosphere in which they were being educated. Later he yielded to repeated requests from friends, among them his children's tutor, Solomon Dubno, to make the translation generally available. Dubno became his first coworker and undertook the Hebrew commentary of which he finally completed the first two books, Genesis and Exodus. For the other three books Mendelssohn had to depend on other friends, among them Naphtali Herz Wessely, who wrote the commentary on Leviticus.[16] It was only natural that Wessely should recommend the new translation when he publicly put forward his new educational program, and he did so enthusiastically.[17] The Mendelssohn translation was, indeed, hailed by all those who strove to lift the Jews out of their cultural backwater. The new schools were only too glad to introduce this translation.

The Mendelssohn translation as well as the running commentary Biur were conservative, clinging to the original text and not contradicting the traditional Jewish interpretation. Nevertheless, its application as a basic educational tool represented a revolutionary step with far-reaching consequences. The new translation introduced students to the language of their enlightened neighbors and edged out Yiddish, the language hitherto in use. The introduction of Biur to replace Rashi had another, not less significant, effect. The medieval commentary not only explained the Biblical text but also incorporated essential parts of rabbinical tradition. The new commentary, though not contradicting tradition, concentrated on the Biblical text and stressed the moral and aesthetic aspects of the Bible. Thus, by studying the

Bible, the student was not automatically initiated into Oral Law as had been the case while the old system of education prevailed. Enlightened educators took, to put it mildly, a rather selective attitude toward Talmudic tradition. By using the new commentary they were relieved from paying attention to many details of the tradition they preferred to ignore.[18]

Even if educators did not repudiate any part of the tradition, they still emphasized the doctrinal aspects — the belief in God, the immortality of the soul and Divine Providence — and moral teaching. This enjoined pupils to strict honesty and stressed, in particular, the universal character of ethics that did not differentiate between the members of one's own group and those of other groups. The strong tendency of Jewish sources to insist on the solidarity of the Jews and their special obligation toward each other was played down and a humanitarian, universal tinge given to Jewish teaching. The enlightened education stressed pureness of heart and religious feeling as the highest good. Very often these doctrinal and moral principles were formulated for use in the various manuals that very often replaced the classical Jewish text.[19]

The great emphasis laid on the universal aspect of the moral teachings of Judaism was a part of the preparation for the expected entrance of Jews into state and society toward which education was being directed. The obvious overemphasis of ethics and religious intention was meant to divert attention from the ritual and ceremonial aspects of Jewish religion, which came to be largely neglected. In the Seesen and Frankfurt schools, directed by the more radically-minded among the enlightened, some religious innovations were made: German songs took the place of the Hebrew prayer and organ music was introduced.[20] On the whole, however, enlightened educators did not openly recommend religious reform. Nor did most of them have a clear conception of what ought to be retained and what discarded of Jewish traditional practice. Instead of planned reform, they relied upon a natural process of selection that would relegate to oblivion whatever hampered the integration of the Jew into the economic, social, and political life of the non-Jew. This is some-

OUT OF THE GHETTO

times openly expressed and sometimes only inferred. In 1792 an anonymous writer described the immense difficulties a Jewish boy encountered while getting his training from a non-Jewish crafts-man. He could not partake of the meals of the non-Jewish house-hold, his day of rest was different, and his daily prayer interferred with his work. "So long, therefore, as the common man among the Jews is not prepared to listen to and accept reasons that make clear to him that this or that law, this or that ceremony do not belong at all to the essence of religion; so long as he cannot bring himself to see that the essence of religion suffers in no way from discarding many a law and many a custom; so long as he cannot understand that so many religious institutions are as unsuitable for our times as a costume of another climate and other time; so long can there be no hope for a general improvement." The writer knows that what he has in mind is nothing less than a thorough "reformation" and he is prompted to ask: "Where then is the reformation that has been undertaken on behalf of the Jew? Where are its reformers and its pedagogues? These latter must precede all else; most depends on them." [21] The educator has been allotted the task of enlightening the pupils in matters of religion and conveying to them the relative significance of Jewish observances so that they would be able to relinquish them in case of conflict with other obligations.

The teachers in the new schools, like other enlightened, while not completely discarding Jewish observances, did display laxity toward them. This was in clear contradiction to what the first promoters of enlightenment, Mendelssohn and Wessely contem-plated but what others, for instance Dohm, clearly foresaw.[22] A measure of nonconformity in religious behavior became, in the course of time, the shibboleth by which the enlightened could be told from the bulk of the Jewish community. The antagonism be-tween traditional and enlightened grew; the latter could neither be suppressed, as formerly, nor dismissed. Their number alone would have prevented this, apart from other reasons that will be touched on later.

Having assumed a positive function in Jewish society, espe-cially by founding and supporting new schools, the enlightened represented themselves as the exponents of a legitimate variation of Judaism which they believed belonged to the future. Lazarus Bendavid and Aaron Wolfssohn, two outstanding exponents of educational theory and practice,[23] divided Jews into types according to the extent of their adherence to religious observances and ceremonies.[24] The last, and in their view the only desirable type, was the Jew who altogether rejected religious observances. Among these were those who are either "adherents of the genuine natural religion or 'Moseiten' that is, followers of Mosaic Judaism cleansed of all ceremonies and customs as taught and expounded by the prophets." [25]

Many of the enlightened educators shared the hope of abrogating Jewish observance altogether. In view of the tenacity of ritualistic tradition in general and the addiction of conservatives to what would be called today the symbols of Jewish identity, such a hope had scarcely any chance of being realized. Most Jewish parents certainly did not wish to see their children diverted entirely from all Jewish religious practice. Educators had to accept, nolens volens, a selective approach toward Jewish tradition by including in the syllabus at least some of the more popular religious rites. The trouble, however, was that for such compromising half-measures it was difficult to find an ideological justification. The enlightened boasted of being the followers of Mendelssohn — rightly, as far as the identification of Jewish beliefs with the tenets of deism or natural religion went. Mendelssohn maintained that Judaism did not contain any revealed doctrines that could not be comprehended by human reason alone. But Mendelssohn did not repudiate the notion of revelation which, according to him, had the special function of conveying to the Jewish nation a system of law and religious observances which, owing to their inherent symbolism, would constantly remind those who practiced them of the eternal truths of the religious tenets. Jews were, in any event, bound to observe the revealed laws unless these were abrogated by divine revelation. Mendelssohn also argued that the world was not yet free of polytheistic ideas and other religious misconceptions and misuse — despite the spread of enlightenment. Therefore the Jews still had a special mission to safeguard the pure monotheistic religion symbolized by Jewish observances.[26] The whole of Jewish law had therefore consistently to be kept.

This stand could of course be contested, as it was by many, who maintained that in view of the progress made by the religion of reason amongst civilized nations, Jewish observances had lost their raison d'être. Some of the enlightened regarded this conclusion as inescapable and would not have been able to imagine that Mendelssohn could think differently. It was maintained by some of his disciples that the master himself was not in earnest about the observances and kept them only in order to conform and not to lose his influence over the Jewish community.[27] Such arguments could be used for abandoning the observances altogether and this is exactly what some educators, such as Lazarus Bendavid and Aaron Wolfssohn, managed to do. Most of them, however, clung to their former attitude, selecting what they pleased for observance and discarding the rest without a clear basis for such differentiation.

Such a basis could be secured only by reversing Mendelssohn's theory. Instead of identifying Jewish teachings and doctrines with the religion of reason and seeing in Jewish observances the peculiar feature of Judaism, the enlightened felt that Jewish teachings and doctrines should be elevated to first place as having something unique to offer while ritual and observances were given a secondary place. This reversal was to become the theoretical turning point from Enlightenment to the Reform movement proper. It was accomplished for the first time by Saul Ascher in his *Leviathan,* written six years after the death of Mendelssohn.[28] Very little is known about Ascher's life, origin, and background. He did not belong to the more or less organized group of Jewish enlightened but supported himself, it seems, by working for non-Jewish periodicals as a free-lance writer.[29] At any rate, he maintained not only his independence but also a strong individuality and did not hesitate to voice dissenting, original, or startling ideas. As he was an outsider, his ideas are not indicative of what was prevalent in Jewish thought and society but point, rather, to theoretical possibilities.[30]

Ascher retained the notion of revelation and evolved his definition of Judaism around it. But obviously he used this term, as he did other terms of a theological connotation, to characterize Judaism as belonging to a certain category of religions differing from the religion of nature and that of reason. Ascher did not concern himself with the historicity of Sinai relevation, which still served Mendelssohn as the criterion for the truth of Judaism. The validity of Judaism, as that of other religions, Ascher vaguely conceived as resting on the happy convergence of historical tradition with the psychological need of man. For, contrary to the rationalistic point of view, Ascher regarded the urge for religion as a genuinely psychological or, perhaps, even a metaphysical quality. This secured for religion a permanent place in the life of men. But at the same time, by relinquishing historical truth as a criterion for the validity of religion, he could accept the possibility of variations occurring in religion at different times. This, applied to the special case of Judaism, meant that Jewish religion is a basic element of the Jewish community but that its form was susceptible to change. The legitimacy of such change depended on whether it occurred in what was essential or only accidental to the religion.[31] This is the theory that lent justification to religious reform — or reformation, to use the Christian term Ascher employed.

The kind of reform that was contemplated was circumscribed by the historical situation — observance, still regarded even by Mendelssohn as the criterion for establishing a man's allegiance to the Jewish religion, was on the wane. "With every day that passes we see how religion declines among our co-religionists. Every day we see the numbers of apostates increasing." The law is "being neglected as neglected it deserves to be." There were two reasons for this neglect, one practical and the other spiritual. The Jew, partially integrated into non-Jewish society, is hampered in his social life and career by his obligation to Jewish observances. Then the "autonomy of personality" — a Kantian expression adopted by Ascher — demands that the individual act without being fettered by ritual imposed by an external authority.[32] Ascher, while sympathizing with the need of the individual to neglect the law, nevertheless considers such aberration undesirable, as ultimately it opens the door to conversion. The only remedy he could suggest was a redefinition of Judaism in a way that would free the individual from the obligation to observe the laws while still retaining his allegiance to the Jewish religion and the Jewish community.

This is the background to Ascher's outline of reform. It is, in short, a relegation of the law to the periphery and its replacement by the dogmas as the essence of the Jewish religion. Said Ascher: "According to our theory the dogmas form the essence of Judaism." Ascher does not recoil from using the much-reviled term "dogma," for it is his firm conviction that reason has to concede something to faith. As to the definition of the obligatory tenets of Judaism, Ascher has only tentative suggestions and leaves the final exposition of a system of Jewish beliefs to the theologians.[33] Yet his suggestions are indicative enough of what he has in mind. The belief in God and his revelation initiating the covenant with Israel is fundamental. But the laws revealed at the same time were only of passing significance, their purpose being purely educational. Of eternal validity was just the belief in God and his attributes, a God of Love, omniscience, and omnipotence. The covenant with Israel guaranteed also "redemption through the Messiah in this life or in the grave of those who will be deemed worthy of resurrection." [34] This is quite equivocal and avoids the issue of the national restoration of Israel.[35]

On the whole, however, Ascher is rather generous in preserving as much as possible of the traditional system of Jewish beliefs, expecting in return that the law would be relaxed or even revoked. He was prepared to retain some conspicuous parts of Jewish law such as the circumcision, the consecration of the Sabbath and the festivals, as mementos of the covenant and adequate expression of the religious tenets — of course, without insisting on the meticulous observance as laid down in the Halakah, that is, in rabbinical law. Although he does not expressly say so, Ascher was in fact altogether discarding rabbinical law and he assigned the place of "Halakhist" to theologians, those theoreticians whose task it was to expound Jewish teachings and their significance by inquiring into their sources.[36]

Ascher's position had the advantage over the simple demands for reform in that his suggestions were based on a carefully thought-out theory. In a way he anticipated what was later to become typical for the Reform movement, namely, reverence for Jewish teachings counterbalancing the disregard for the rigor of the law. But disregard alone, and even an ideological justification for it, was not enough. An innovation in religious practice, if it is to be acceptable to the community, must be not only rationally justified but also sanctioned by some kind of religious authority. The problem of Jewish religious reformers, therefore, was to find a respected religious institution that would command the allegiance of the Jewish community. True, many Jews were clamoring for innovations or, at least, for an adaptation of the law to the obvious needs of the times. The tenor of their demands was that the rabbis should use their authority to sanction the necessary changes. In 1796 there appeared in a newspaper in Hamburg an account that a synod of rabbis, meeting in Florence, had decided to transfer the weekly day of rest of the Jews from Saturday to Sunday, to alleviate the prescriptions for Sabbath observance, to relieve women from shaving their hair, to permit the use of a razor in shaving, and to allow the eating of pork. The intriguing news was then repeated in "all the gazettes" in Europe.[37] If the details reflect the wishful thinking of some of the Jewish reformers — who probably launched the news item — it is nonetheless revealing that they attributed these decisions to the important rabbis of the large communities of Rome, Mantua, Modena, and others. Be this as it may, the hoax was accepted as a challenge by contemporary rabbis. Baruch Jeitteles of Prague made inquiries in Mantua and published the answer in the Berlin *Hameasef*.[38] Raphael Cohen, the Rabbi of Hamburg-Altona, requested his Florentine colleagues to protest, and they did, indeed, publish a pamphlet to deny that any such synod had met and to affirm that no such decisions were contemplated. The protest was countersigned by the leaders of other Italian communities and the pamphlet republished in Hamburg.[39] According to the Palestinian Rabbi living in Livorno at the time, the famous Hayyim Joseph David Azulai, who was one of the signatories of the protest, the news had been fabricated in Altona for the purpose of inducing the state authorities in Germany to compel Jews to initiate similar reforms in Germany.[40] Whether this was the case is difficult to say, but the idea that the state should exercise its power to reeducate the recalcitrant, also in religious matters, was not inconceivable to either Jewish or non-Jewish rationalists.[41] Signs of restlessness and dissatisfaction with the contemporary state of affairs in Jewish religion were noticeable and the rabbis had cause for apprehension.

The next chapter will show why the conservative element in Jewish society, among them most of the rabbis, were unwilling to cooperate with those favoring reform. There are, in fact, only two instances where rabbis went out of their way to assist reform. The first is the case of Saul Berlin[42] and occurred during the period following Mendelssohn's death (1786), when spiritual confusion and social unrest among the enlightened reached a peak. Saul Berlin, the son of the Rabbi of Berlin, was the spiritual head of the community of Frankfurt an der Oder for some years from 1786 onward. Later he gave up his rabbinical post and lived in Berlin. He more or less openly joined what had by now become a party of innovators but lost none of his authority as a leading Talmudist. In 1793 he published a manuscript he had allegedly found on his travels in Italy containing the responsa of the famous fourteenth century Rabbi of Barcelona, Ascher ben Yehiel. The editor added his own comments to the basic text. These, as well as the basic text, contained rabbinical decisions with a clear tendency toward leniency. Relaxation was urged, for example, to allow Jews to partake of Gentile wine, regarding the shortening of the daily prayer, and on the question of early burial [43] — all matters on which the innovators and the conservatives were at variance. Very soon the suspicion arose that the supposedly medieval text was nothing but a forgery fabricated by the editor, who wished the support of an ancient authority for the innovations he favored. That Saul Berlin resorted to subterfuge to gain support for reform is perhaps only partly explained by the enigmatic and often erratic personality of the man. It may be ascribed also to the confusion and bewilderment that ensued as a result of the disintegration of accepted values.

The other instance of cooperation between rabbis and innovators is connected with the political activities of Israel Jacobson in Westphalia. When this state was established in the wake of the French conquest in 1807, Jacobson was appointed head of the consistory that had to regulate Jewish communal matters. Jacobson used the opportunity to impose his views on the none-too-willing communities. His innovations were not too far-reaching: they concerned decorum in the synagogue, the curtailment of the daily prayer, and the omission of some marginal part of the rituals on festivals.[44] Jacobson wished also to waive one restriction in the dietary laws of Passover that were particularly severe, especially in the Ashkenazi communities. To the Biblical prescription for unleavened bread was added in the Middle Ages the prohibition pertaining to rice and leguminous plants such as beans and peas. Jacobson, in common with others, no doubt wished to see all dietary laws discarded but made an issue out of this special law since it seemed as though permission to relinquish it might be obtained from the rabbis. Jacobson did succeed in obtaining the consent for this from the rabbinical commission heading the new consistory.[45] One member of the commission, Menahem Mendel Steinhardt, published a treatise defending the proposed change with Talmudic dialectic.[46] Halakah allowed for a certain measure of flexibility to meet changing situations throughout the ages. The Westphalian rabbis made use of these techniques without being particularly concerned with the motivation behind the demand for reform. Later this action earned them the scorn of other contemporary rabbis who sensed the danger inherent in a deviation from the customary even when covered by Halakah.

One thing was clear: whatever reform could have been achieved under the sheltering wing of the Halakah technique, fell far short of the expectations of the more radically-minded reformer. This was clearly felt by Ascher, who resolutely dismissed a "negative reformation," meaning piecemeal amendment of some details of the religious tradition. He demanded "positive reformation," where Judaism would be set on a new basis.[47] On what authority this was to be achieved still eluded him. Certainly it could not be attained within the terms of Halakah. On the contrary, this kind of reform meant the abandonment of Halakah, that is, the codification of the law and its continuous reinterpretation.

The reformers resorted at times to historical-rationalistic interpretations of the sources of Jewish religion to prove that originally they had a different meaning from the one ascribed to them by later authorities. Abraham Asch went to great lengths to demonstrate that Moses did not intend circumcision to be taken literally nor did he fix the day of the Sabbath unalterably. The Jews could therefore with a good conscience relinquish the practice of circumcision and transfer the day of rest to Sunday.[48] Although Asch lavishly used Talmudic sources to support his thesis, he could scarcely claim to be in accord with traditional interpretation. His method, a crude form of guesswork, was obviously a means of arbitrarily arriving at the desired conclusion. It certainly failed to carry conviction.[49] Such methods could never provide the authority needed to sanction the desired changes. Without such an authority, reform was doomed to failure from the start.

A method that did occur to some reformers was the convening of a rabbinical assembly that would assume the authority of a legislative body. The fiction of the synod meeting at Florence that took the initiative in reforming basic practices reflected the mood of the time for a rabbinical assembly that would have almost unlimited authority. The idea was certainly in the mind of Israel Jacobson who, upon learning of Napoleon's intention in 1805 to reopen the Jewish issue in Alsace, suggested to him in a letter that a Jewish council be established, which would be entitled to resolve all possible conflict between the obligations of a Jew to his religion and his state.[50] It stands to reason (as suggested by Jacob R. Marcus) that Jacobson's letter was among the factors moving Napoleon to convene the famous Paris Sanhedrin.

This would go some way toward explaining the strange fact that it was a non-Jewish agency that created the first authoritative body to initiate reforms.[51]

However this may be, it is a fact that the plan for convening a rabbinical convocation as a means to implement the desired changes were accepted by the emperor.[52] Lending an ear to the complaints of Alsatians that Jews still clung to the old attitudes in spite of their new status as citizens, Napoleon decided to tackle the problem at the root. He expected the Jewish population to adapt themselves to their new situation, to give up their unique institutions such as rabbinical jurisdiction, and to be ready for amalgamation with their environment even to the point of inter-marriage. This led him to convene an assembly of Jewish nota-bles from France, Italy, and French-occupied western Germany. Here laymen and rabbis discussed the issues put to them in the form of twelve questions on behalf of the emperor. The questions concerned the attitude of Jews toward their non-Jewish neigh-bors, their loyalty toward their adopted country, their business practices — especially the taking of interest and usury — and the authority of the rabbinical court. In the course of the delibera-tions Napoleon realized that whatever the decisions of the assem-bly, they would not be binding for the Jews unless they were sanctioned by a purely religious authority. This gave rise to the idea of calling a Sanhedrin consisting of religious leaders and rabbis. The assembly, however, turned out to be a rather con-servative body as far as its rabbinical members went and they alone counted in terms of religious authority.[53] In spite of radical demands by laymen who went as far as requesting permission for mixed marriages, the rabbinical authorities refused to yield. They did not admit to any alterations in the law beyond what they found justifiable according to the rules of Halakah they had been called upon to repudiate in the first place. They did endorse the Jews' allegiance to the country and the duty of the Jews to obey its laws, but for this they could easily adduce Talmudic sources. They refused, however, to sanction intermarriage — the only real challenge among Napoleon's demands. The only concession they made was a promise not to discriminate against a Jew who married a Gentile according to civil law.

The idea of the synod as an autonomous institution was on this occasion defeated by the tacit, if unspoken, opposition of the rabbis. Outwardly the Sanhedrin may have given the impression of being able to lay down laws. But when the committees met to formulate the answers to the emperor's questions, prior to having them endorsed by the Sanhedrin, they met with implacable rabbinical opposition. The rabbis felt committed to the Halakah and were prepared to put to the assembly only what could be squeezed, with a slight twist, from the Halakah. As a result even the most conservative rabbis could be satisfied with their colleagues who, even under pressure, had succeeded in defending the old system, conceding no more than could be substantiated within the terms of Halakah even under those particular circumstances.[54] What outwardly appeared to be an autonomous synod functioned in fact as the mouthpiece of the rabbis, approving only what the old methods of reinterpretation could yield. An institution for "positive reformation," such as was contemplated by Ascher and attempted by Napoleon, thus failed to materialize.

Though not obtaining any tangible results, the proponents of reform nevertheless drew some encouragement from the deliberations of the Sanhedrin. If this assembly did not live up to their expectations, another of its kind, functioning perhaps under other conditions and composed differently, could be expected to do so. For the idea of reform lingered on and sustained some Jews in their hope of seeing Judaism renewed and reinstated.

IX CONSERVATIVES IN A QUANDARY

Jewish society of the prerationalistic era was traditionalist by its very nature. In the realm of action, in thought and feeling, it relied on patterns transmitted from the past. Indeed loyalty to the ancient traditions lay at the very core of its philosophy. According to this philosophy the Jewish tradition could be transcended or discarded only at an undefined date in the future, namely, with the arrival of the Messiah, when the boundaries circumscribing Jewish existence — and perhaps also those known to all mankind — would suddenly and miraculously be transformed.[1] Meanwhile, faithfulness to the traditional way of life was the highest virtue, or rather, the precondition for all the virtues.

The actual changes that occurred in the lifetime of one or two generations — between 1770 and 1815 — seemed to challenge this whole conception. From the standpoint of those who remained loyal to tradition, changing events must have appeared like some kind of metaphysical debacle. The messianic expectation that Jewish exile would be terminated by a miraculous regathering in their ancient homeland was dealt a blow by the craving of Jews for citizenship in the countries where they lived. The defection of a minority of Jewish society from traditional life and, even more, their attempts to impose their own views on the whole Jewish society must have been confusing and revolting. There is ample historical evidence to show that traditionalists viewed the changes in Jewish and non-Jewish society as nothing short of catastrophic. Small wonder they were shocked into passivity at the beginning. It was some time before they could rally their forces sufficiently to present a systematic answer that took into account all the ingredients of the new reality and, despite them, maintained the validity of tradition. The readjustment of the traditional point of view was at last achieved, teaching the historian yet another lesson: that there is no ideological system so rigid that it cannot adapt itself when pressed by hard historical reality. The concern here is only with the incipient stages of their reaction when, from the standpoint of the traditionalist, his world seemed to dissolve into chaos.

In an earlier chapter the question was raised as to whether the crisis in Jewish society, which came to the fore in the last decades of the eighteenth century, had not been latent already some generations previously.[2] One thing is certain: that those who were later to regard the crisis as the ruin of their world had no inkling of what was happening, and no fears for the future of traditionalism disturbed the even tenor of their routine. The measure of unawareness can be gathered from the fact that men like Mendelssohn and Wessely, who were to usher in the new movement, were at the beginning of their careers honored both by the Jewish community and those that most jealously guarded its traditions. They may have been unusual in some respects but were still acceptable members of the community.

Upon visiting Hamburg in 1761 to see his future wife, Mendelssohn became acquainted with the famous rabbi there, Jonathan Eibeschütz, who gave him a diploma of sorts attesting to his erudition in Talmudic literature; only the unmarried state of his visitor prevented the rabbi from giving him rabbinical authorization. Rabbi Eibeschütz was full of praise also for Mendelssohn's proficiency in all branches of philosophy, adding that he had succeeded in achieving a harmony of philosophy and Jewish tradition.[3] Mendelssohn also corresponded with Rabbi Jacob Emden, the other great scholar in Hamburg-Altona, and during the Lavater controversy in 1770 the rabbi became a helpful consultant and clarified a point of Jewish teaching on which Mendelssohn wanted to make an authoritative statement.[4] Most probably Emden neither knew the reason for the inquiry nor grasped the significance of the issue, which concerned the position of "The Righteous Gentile" according to Jewish tradition.[5] This again proves that the emerging differences were still hidden, even from the participants themselves.

Even in 1772 Emden found it possible to appeal to Mendelssohn for help on behalf of the community of Mecklenburg-Schwerin, which was in conflict with the government on the question of early burial. This question, one that was to appear with unflagging regularity, here puts in an appearance for the first time.[6] Scientific or rather rationalistic medicine of the eighteenth century claimed to have found irrefutable proof for apparent death, or *Scheintod,* when a patient could still be alive despite all physical signs, that is, cessation of pulse and breathing to the contrary. To avoid making mistakes and burying people who were still alive, they recommended that the burial be postponed for a few days until death had been clearly determined. This was in any event the customary procedure among Christians. With Jews, on the contrary, it was the custom, as well as a religious duty, to bury the dead on the day of their decease. When the prevalence of this custom was brought to the attention of the Mecklenburg-Schwerin government — by the learned Orientalist Olof Gerhard Tychsen, whose attitude toward all things Jewish was ambivalent — the government felt duty bound to put an end to what it regarded as a barbaric rite. Traditional Jews, on the other hand, had no qualms and regarded the intervention of the authorities as interference with their religion and to be warded off by men of authority and influence. Thus the matter was brought before Rabbi Emden, who referred it to Mendelssohn, assuming that the latter would be best able to state the Jewish point of view in an appropriate manner. To the astonishment of the rabbi and certainly the community, Mendelssohn, although prepared to comply with the request, nevertheless made it clear that he regarded the Jewish custom as most questionable. He maintained that early burial was not a Jewish custom in Talmudic times and that contemporary Jews had every reason to accept the state regulation.[7]

Mendelssohn, it is certain, was not motivated primarily by the antiquated proofs he had unearthed from Talmudic sources. What influenced him mainly was a trust in the scientific basis of the regulation, for, as a rationalist, he accepted the results of rationalistic thought and observation. When these results conflicted with tradition, the latter would have to be discarded. The recovery of the Talmudic sources did however serve its purpose by providing legitimate reason for deviation from the customary. This is typical for the rationalistic, albeit not too radical, reformer. This stand could of course not be accepted by a traditionalist proper. It was indeed rejected — the suggestion and the learned justification — by Rabbi Emden as well as by later traditionalists. It was in the course of this correspondence that Emden, for the first time, mentioned the rumors that Mendelssohn was veering from the traditional. Still, the conflict between Mendelssohn and the traditionalists was kept within bounds and certainly led to no public scandal. Even his relations with Emden remained friendly and the correspondence continued.[8]

Wessely, like Mendelssohn, was well regarded in traditional circles. His works were duly approved by leading rabbis and widely studied by the traditional public. Though his works contained some harsh reflections on the old-type rabbi, who spent his time in intellectual isolation immersed in the study of the Talmud, these passed unnoticed by his readers until the polemic of 1782 suddenly showed them up for what they were — a harsh criticism of the entire system of traditional education.[9] Until then his observations had been either overlooked or else dismissed as exaggerations, the privilege of those engaged in preaching and homiletic. In fact, Wessely's books were not of the common run of homiletics; he commented on Biblical and Talmudic texts but did not use them, as did other preachers of the time, as mere starting points for the free association of ideas. On the contrary, he tried, by a methodological differentiation between synonyms, to arrive at the exact meaning of a text. This new approach had something refreshing about it and was, as such, warmly welcomed also by the traditionalists, who, despite its novelty, did not fear any repercussions for traditional beliefs and principles. Rabbi Yehezkel Landau of Prague, who authorized the publication of one of Wessely's books in 1775, said this in so many words.[10] Until the open clash of the 1780's traditional society allowed variation to this extent.

What was it then, at last, that brought traditionalists to perceive the alarming signs of revolution? There seem to be two factors: the accumulation of deviations and the claim of the transgressors that they were acting from conviction and therefore had the right to go their own ways. These two factors clearly influenced Rabbi Israel Baer in Amsterdam who, in 1772, composed a poem (unpublished) with the telling title "A New World." The rabbi enumerated the shortcomings of his generation. The Jew of Amsterdam, whether Ashkenazi or Sephardi, was dressed and curled to the height of the new fashions; men used razors to shave their beards; people went to the theater and to the opera; the daily prayer was neglected and cardplaying was the rage; the Sabbath was not strictly observed and some did not even fast on the ninth of Av, the day commemorating the destruction of the Temple; the sons of the rich attended universities and lived a life of dissipation.[11]

To all the details mentioned in this lamentation, a parallel could be found in the sermons of the moralists of earlier times.[12] It was the accumulation of these occurrences that drove this rabbi to see a new world resulting from them. In addition he also points to the ideological stand behind these incidents. He quotes the transgressors as saying that what they were doing was not aimed against Judaism proper, for they were only neglecting what was Oral Law and this was man-made and not obligatory.

Here is the expression of a new attitude that appeared first among the Sephardim in France and Holland and then, with the spread of rationalism, also reached the Ashkenazim. By the eighties this attitude had become general throughout Central Europe. Prague may be taken as an example, since there are records of sermons preached here by some of the great rabbis in the years immediately preceding and following 1780. From the tone and content of these public admonitions the extent to which traditionalists were aware of the turn events were taking can be gauged.

In earlier admonitions the themes deal with the usual neglect of religious observances, sometimes pointing to serious deviations. For instance, in the year 1769 ten male children in the Prague Jewish community were born out of wedlock; the number is known because they were duly circumcised in the community's synagogue.[13] The preachers deplored the deterioration of morals, but only in the traditional fashion of referring back to better days. No special group was as yet singled out for rebuke, except the Sabbatians, who remained the number one enemy even after the appearance of the new group of enlightened Jews.[14] In 1770 Rabbi Yehezkel Landau preached against the teachings of new-fangled philosophers — non-Jews it seems likely — who explained the functioning of the world in terms of purely mechanical self-perpetuation.[15] He may have been influenced by the apprehensions of non-Jewish authorities who at this time introduced censorship to suppress atheistic writings imported from abroad.[16] At any rate, such newfangled teachings were not held responsible for any deviations in the conduct of the Jewish community.

It was only in the wake of the Edict of Tolerance and the appeal of Wessely to implement in full its educational program that rebukes were directed against innovators and defectors. Just at this time Rabbi Eleazar Fleckeles returned to Prague from a post in Kojetein, a small Moravian town, where he had officiated as rabbi for a short period.[17] In Prague he became a preacher and later a leading rabbinical authority. While he was in Kojetein he preached on prevailing offenses and transgressions against Jewish prescription — the text used by most of the rabbis since time immemorial. In Prague, Fleckeles began to direct some part of his sermons against the liberties taken by the innovators and to criticize the new ideas, which he regarded as the source for those liberties. Of course there was the inevitable difference between the small town and the great city; but it was also a matter of the changing times. The preacher himself testifies to this change, as he often expresses his longing for the past when his sole task was to rebuke people for "old sins" like chattering in the synagogue and tale bearing. He characterizes his own time as the age of "new sins" like the public flaunting of dietary laws and the neglect of Torah study in favor of secular subjects. Not only had the transgression undergone change, but also the transgressor. The old-type sinner accepted rebuke and was prepared to make amends by repentence; the new type of sinner refused to repent.[18]

There were two new facts which caused the rabbis of that time to despair. First, they observed the growing laxity or even the neglect of religious observances. According to Jewish tradition the community was, in the eyes of God, responsible for the conduct of its members; thus the behavior of the deviants could not be a matter of indifference. This religious tradition was doubtlessly strengthened by the closely knit community organization of ghetto Jewry and by its responsibility toward the non-Jewish world in moral and even legal matters for every one of its members. Thus, the leaders of the community, both lay and rabbinic, were only in tune with tradition and custom when they attempted to control the behavior of individuals. Their right to do so was taken for granted and the means for implementing that right were built into the organization of the community. The means of control, however, were gradually being weakened as the state increasingly tended to limit Jewish communal autonomy. The Jewish community's right of ban was repealed by the state authorities or limited by them. But even where this right was formally still upheld, it became discredited by enlightened public opinion so that it could hardly be imposed. When Raphael Cohen, the revered Rabbi of Hamburg, used the ban against a member of his community in 1780 because the latter publicly desecrated the Sabbath, the Rabbi was maligned for it by both Jews and Gentiles alike.[19]

It was just this open defiance of their authority by part of the enlightened that must have bewildered the rabbis. To be sure, a rabbi very often had to contend even in the traditional community with recalcitrant members or competing lay leaders. But these vexations could not undermine the acknowledged spiritual and religious authority of rabbinical leaders. It was to them that the community turned for guidance on points of Talmudic law as well as on points of dogma. When differences of opinion arose there remained the appeal to higher rabbinical authorities whose decision rested on their reputation for greater erudition and wisdom. No book destined for the Jewish public could be published without the approbation of usually more than one famous rabbi. Very often the approval was a mere formality aimed at protecting the copyright of the author, rather a kind of recommendation and not real censorship.[20] Nevertheless it signified the uncontested control by the rabbis over the intellectual pursuits of Jewish society.

It is against this background that the resentment of the rabbis at the enlightened laymen who presumed to take a stand on questions that had hitherto been the exclusive province of the established leaders must be viewed. In the polemic against Wessely, objections were voiced against his educational program; but his incensed rabbinical opponents resented the very fact that Wessely took a stand on a public issue and intended to put him in his proper place. They held that Wessely, who was not a Talmudic scholar but only a poet and exegete, had no right to interpret the emperor's edict and advise the entire House of Israel on how to conduct its spiritual affairs.[21] Only gradually did it dawn on the old leaders that they had now come across a new kind of antagonist who, relying on a new system of values, would not accept judgments made on the basis of established authority alone. Mendelssohn refused to take the well-meant advice that he ask for rabbinic approbation for his translation of the Pentateuch, even though the work was intended for Jews, was printed in Hebrew characters, and provided with a running Hebrew commentary. His waiving of the customary approval was a slight but conscious defiance of rabbinical authority and it was no doubt registered as such in the appropriate quarters.[22] The Mendelssohn translation preceded the scandal caused by Wessely's pamphlet by two years. Genesis appeared in 1780. The publication of the work had been announced as early as 1778 when samples of the translation and the commentary, prefaced by an introduction written by Mendelssohn's first coworker, Solomon Dubno, were distributed. Dubno was an uncontested authority in his field and well thought of also in rabbinical circles. Nonetheless, the work was regarded with some suspicion because of its novelty and because of the feelings its author had managed, by this time, to evoke in rabbinical breasts.[23] Still, it took some years before it was publicly denounced in Prague, in the fall of 1783, by Rabbi Fleckeles, who quoted Chief Rabbi Landau as an authority for his objections.[24] Rabbi Landau later stated his objections to the translation.[25] These were not of a dogmatic nature. He objected because the translation, unlike the traditional Yiddish used in schools to facilitate understanding of the Hebrew text, could be read as an independent version. The high level of the German used in the translation was also objected to, for it was considered beyond the grasp of the ordinary Jewish student. Mendelssohn's critics anticipated what, in fact, was later to happen: the German translation would serve as a textbook for studying German rather than for understanding the Bible. Fleckeles, it is true, accused — incorrectly as it turned out — the translator of ignoring the traditional interpretation based on Oral Law and translating literally from the text.[26] Still, the work would probably still have passed the rabbis' test had there not been other signs of deviations from the traditional to antagonize them.

The turning point in the relation between the old and the new was the controversy that raged over Wessely's "Words of Peace and Truth." Here for the first time the clash became public. Reaction to the pamphlet came from as far as Lissa, Prague, Frankfurt, Trieste, and other Italian towns.[27] All community leaders with the exception of the Italian were opposed, some even vitriolically, to Wessely's suggestions. The new educational program and Mendelssohn's translation came to be linked together and from this time stemmed the estrangement between the rabbis and the Berlin circle.[28] Both Mendelssohn and Wessely continued, however, to maintain an urbane and courteous standard in their relationships with rabbinical authorities. Wessely committed a slip of the tongue when he applied a strong Talmudic phrase "a man of knowledge but no sense" to describe the type that represented contemporary rabbinical scholars.[29] But he subsequently took it back and apologized for this lapse. The younger generation of enlightened Jews was not so considerate. A member of Mendelssohn's immediate entourage, Dr. Marcus Herz, wrote a fierce attack against the rabbis on the thorny question of early burial just one year after the master's death, with Rabbi Landau, still living in Prague, as his main target.[30] The tone was only equaled by the rabbis themselves in their attacks on innovators.

The hiatus between old and new was widening.

The division between the two camps was however not clear-cut. Many of the enlightened who were prepared to support some innovations, such as educational reform, remained definitely conservative with regard to other issues. Thus Salomon Pappenheim in Breslau, a contributor to the philosophies of the day in Hebrew as well as in German, enlarged in his more popular Hebrew works on the symbolic meaning of Jewish observances and in this way lent them some philosophical protection.[31] On the issue of early burial he was staunchly on the side of tradition, ridiculing the lifesaving zeal of the rationalists in several pamphlets written in German.[32] A similar attitude is displayed by Baruch Jeitteles in Prague, a Talmudist of the first rank, a supporter of enlightened education, but otherwise conservative,[33] and Wolf Heidenheim in Frankfurt, critical editor of the prayerbook and other classical and contemporary texts — among them the Apology of the Westphalian Rabbis.[34] These works clearly reflect his intermediate stand. To this type Wessely also belonged. He had come into conflict with the rabbis quite unintentionally and later manifested his full attachment to Jewish tradition.

Such conciliatory types notwithstanding, the post-Mendelssohnian generation is characterized by deepening mistrust between the innovators and the traditionalists. The concern here is with the reaction of traditionalist to actual and suggested changes. This was sometimes expressed by a kind of passive resistance against the demands of the innovators and, at others, took the form of active protest. The Berlin Burial Society, a voluntary organization of a kind ubiquitous in all Jewish communities, refused to comply with the wishes of the rationalists to defer burial. Finally the Jewish enlightened appealed to the authorities and were able to enforce a compromise whereby the burial society allowed the enlightened free choice in the matter as far as their own dead were concerned. The members of the burial society, however, could not be prevailed upon to give their usual voluntary assistance; the enlightened had to make their own arrangements for the funeral, which they did by hiring the poorer members of the burial society.[35]

Educational reform met with resistance from traditional parents. This was illustrated in Breslau where the modern reformed type of school had been established on the initiative of the state authorities, and attendance was therefore obligatory for all members of the community, even for the children of those who were unwilling to concede that the Talmud could be taught in a way other than the traditional and by teachers that did not have the approval of the local rabbi. The conflict ended in compromise. The school was opened in 1791 but the teachers of Talmud remained under rabbinical control.[36] Such clashes were common in many communities, and not only in the field of education. When Israel Jacobson as head of the consistory of Westphalen wished to shorten the prayer in the synagogue and imposed a fine on those who insisted in adhering to the "piutim" added to the prayer by medieval poets, the greater part of the Halberstadt community arranged a private service, the richer Jews vying with one another to pay the required fine in order to preserve the traditional service.[37]

Though the conservatives' powers of passive resistance were remarkable, they gained no more than a weapon with which the progress of their opponents could be delayed. They were at a great disadvantage. Unable to impose the old standards by the customary coercive means, they were slowly learning new methods of persuasion and compromise. They continued to preach and condemn. An unconscious adaptation is perhaps to be seen in their use of ridicule, an indication that they were accepting the situation despite mental reservation. Ridicule was not a weapon discovered by the conservatives. On the contrary, it was first used by enlightened writers who developed a whole new genre of parody and satire written in Hebrew and in Yiddish.[38] The conservatives tried in their homilies to emulate the example set by these writers. They were clearly at a disadvantage in being limited to the only form known to them, namely their sermons, which had to be adapted to this new form of art. Their method was to hold the innovators to scorn and show that their conduct made a travesty of the basic notions of tradition. According to the dictum of the Talmud nothing could be worse than a man who had studied the Torah and then ceased to do so. Rabbi Zvi Hirsch Horowitz of Frankfurt, preaching to his community in 1807, told them that apparently they wished to guard their children from committing this particular sin and therefore did not even allow them to begin studying the Talmud. He quoted another Talmudic saying that even an ignorant Jew would not tell an untruth on the Sabbath. How times had changed! Learned Jews were repeating the morning prayer on the Sabbath: "And the Children of Israel observe the Sabbath in all their generations," and then would calmly go off to their business and later in the afternoon leave the Jewish quarter to seek their pleasure in ways contrary to the spirit of the Sabbath. Not only was their conduct a desecration of the Sabbath but it contradicted the morning prayer and, in addition, gave the lie to the Talmud's confidence in the integrity of the Jew.[39]

Such jibes, and the sermons of Rabbi Horowitz are full of them, are an expression of the prevailing feeling that tenet and reality were moving further and further apart. Subjectively the rabbi was condemning the reality and this was his method of chastening the community. But it is somewhat doubtful if the method achieved its purpose with those against whom it was directed. The very fact that the rabbis used this method was an admission that the concepts of tradition had lost touch with reality and become the ghosts of a living past.

Rabbi Horowitz of Frankfurt ascended to the high position of Chief Rabbi as the heir of a famous father in 1806 when the French conquest was beginning to pave the way for the realization of dreams the Jewish enlightened had cherished for over a generation. Rabbi Horowitz preached his sermons during the years the Jewish community was fighting for full citizenship and when many Jews were ready to move out of the ghetto.[40] In 1806 the Philantropin School, representing the new trends in education, was founded by enlightened Jews and a year later the Jewish Freemasons established their special lodge l'Aurore Naissante.[41] Community discipline and the religious unity it guaranteed was at an end. Individuals did as they pleased, some observed the dietary laws, others did not; some came to synagogue every day, others only on the Sabbath, and some of these, paid lip service and then took up their ordinary pursuits.[42] To be at the head of such a community was a new and bewildering experience for a rabbi who, according to the accepted pattern, was responsible for the religious conduct of his flock. The fashion in which Rabbi Horowitz addressed his community was tantamount to an admission of defeat in the face of deviation that had become a common phenomenon. Exposing the rebels to ridicule was the rabbi's way of gaining an alibi for himself rather than the means for herding them back to the fold. In this way the rabbis and those who opposed the newfangled ideas dissociated themselves from the miscreants. And this was the most they could do.

Indeed the reaction of the old guard may be characterized more as flight than as open combat. In some cases the flight is literally just that. Rabbi Moses Sofer, a former Frankfurter and a disciple of the saintly Rabbi Nathan Adler, tells in a letter in 1803 of the perturbed arrival of another of Rabbi Nathan's disciples. This man left Frankfurt for Mattersdorf, western Hungary, where Rabbi Sofer officiated at that time, because he feared the corruption of his offspring from the polluted atmosphere reigning in the German communities.[43] A similar story is told by Nahman Berlin about some German conservatives who, disturbed by the disintegration of the old pattern of life, left Berlin for the eastern communities of Poland. Berlin himself left for Lissa.[44] Another story concerns the Polish-born daughter-in-law of Rabbi Yehezkel Landau in Prague. After trying fruitlessly to convince her husband to leave for Poland where her children would get a more God-fearing education than was possible in Prague, she demanded a divorce, obtained it, and left for Poland with her two children.[45]

It was some time before the traditionalists learned how to react adequately to the new situation. However there were deeper reasons than lack of time for adjustment to account for their initial inadequacy. Their attitude was the result of unresolved conflicts, for although they condemned the symptoms of disintegration they could not help but concede that some aspects of the change would benefit the Jewish community. They could not but welcome a change that promised to relieve Jews from the legal restrictions that had so painfully burdened them. The abolition of the body tax *(Leibzoll)*, unrestricted permission for residence, greater opportunity in the choice of occupation, and certainly the granting of full citizenship not only elevated the Jew socially but increased his chances of making a good living — an advantage not even a conservative could ignore. The rabbis deplored the way in which their communities suddenly spread out beyond the confines of the Jewish quarters, for it made attendance at synagogue more difficult. At the same time the spontaneous control which the closely-knit Jewish community tended to exercise over its members also ceased. Clearly the removal of physical as well as legal restrictions furthered the social contact with Gentiles and increased the danger of straying from Jewish observance. Still, such unhappy results could not undo the benefits obtained from new social accessibility. Thus the conservatives, while fighting some of the effects, were disinclined to totally reject the change, which entailed many beneficial consequences. It is true that the promoters of social and political aspiration came from the ranks of enlightened Jews, mainly because they were the ones who foresaw what was to be gained and had a common language with the Gentile authorities. But at least post factum the conservatives had to approve of what had been secured. The Edict of Tolerance of Joseph II was hailed by Rabbi Yehezkel Landau in Prague as a gracious act of the emperor "who removed from us the stigma of slavery," [46] although the rabbi was not unaware of the implications of the new freedom gained by the Jews for traditional patterns of life.

The only case known of resistance of conservatives against the implementation of political change is that of the community leaders of Amsterdam, who were less than enthusiastic about the revolution that ousted the House of Orange, under whose patronage they had enjoyed a comparatively passable existence. The revolution was likely to change the structure of the community and introduce reforms that might threaten those holding leading positions. Their objections to the changes were sometimes couched in terms of religious scruples, for instance, when they rejected a request to read out a declaration of the Rights of Man in the synagogue.[47] In fact it was more of a struggle for power eliciting an ideological smoke screen. The behavior of the traditionalists can also be explained as a reaction to the overzealousness of the innovators, who were here a small but militant group, and it may be that the conservatives judged them to be opportunists who wished to take advantage of the revolutionary situation for their own ends. In any case, it is difficult to regard the Amsterdam case as anything more than just the exception that proved the general rule that conservatives were prepared to acquiesce to the impending change without putting up a real fight.

The traditionalists, having conceded either explicitly or tacitly that political, social, and economic change was inevitable, were faced with the task of sorting out their traditional precepts and saving what they could from the collision between tradition and the new functions they were called upon to assume. To be sure, the issue was seldom spelled out, but it hovered nevertheless over the lamentations about the good old world that was disappearing before their eyes. The attitude of the traditionalists could furthermore be gauged from their complaints that were mostly directed to those Jews who failed to live up to the standard of religious and moral behavior set by their forebears. The authorities of the state, who were, after all, instrumental in bringing down one by one the pillars that supported the edifice of the old society, came in for hardly any criticism. The annulment of the rabbinical court as the competent institution for dispensing justice in legal matters concerning Jews — an event that took place in most Western countries during this time — passed without public reaction on the part of the rabbis. They did (and an instance is their resistance to immediate burial) try and avert infringement of their customs but, once legal steps had been taken by the authorities, they abided by the inevitable, and made their peace with it unless some way could be found to circumvent the law.[48] When Napoleon demanded that the rabbis of the Sanhedrin adapt the Halakah to pave the way for the merging of the Jewish community with the French nation, even if this meant giving sanction to intermarriage, the rabbis — as already mentioned — found a way to appease Napoleon without making any real concessions.[49] One rabbi, according to the minutes of the Sanhedrin, did object to this and declared that "truth must be told no matter what the consequences" [50] and that the assembly should frankly declare intermarriage forbidden. Such a heroic stand, however, was the exception. The assembly, directed by the conservative Rabbi David Sinzheim, learned to couch resolutions based substantially on Halakah in a manner that met the authorities at least halfway. This method was warmly applauded by Rabbi Moses Sofer of Pressburg, who afterward became the champion of conservatism.[51]

One reason why the traditionalists could not cope with the situation was the lack of a common language both literally and figuratively with the European environment in which they lived, though separated from it by the walls of the ghetto. They lived intellectually and emotionally in the world of Jewish tradition, using its rich, but involved and very special system of thought and expression that could not be communicated to anyone not as steeped in it as they were. One of the tasks the enlightened Jews set themselves — and there were some as religiously observant as any rabbi — was to extricate Jewish society from its cultural isolation by reformulating Jewish teachings in the idiom of European Enlightenment. This was at the back of Mendelssohn's mind when he started rendering the Pentateuch into German so that his children and students generally might absorb Jewish tradition in a European garb. But it was just this divesting of tradition of its wonted guise from which traditionalists recoiled. Most of the rabbis did this instinctively; others, like Rabbi Moses Sofer, consciously.

It was clear to Moses Sofer that reformulating Jewish tradition in a European idiom meant also exposing it to rationalistic examination. Thus tradition would be brought before the tribunal of reason and called upon to vindicate its truths. It would have to be prepared then to accept the judgments of its investigators, whose method would lead to selective acceptance and rejection. That the result would not be an acceptance on the whole tradition was only too clear to those who knew the conduct and propaganda of the innovators. Sofer wanted to evade the danger of dissection. He wished his contemporaries to have the choice of accepting Jewish tradition in full or not at all. He rejected Mendelssohn's translation and wished, indeed, to avoid any rendering of Jewish tradition in terms of another system of thought.[52] The necessity for such rendering might very well arise, as it did at the Sanhedrin, but in that case it would have to be done by outstanding exponents of Jewish tradition who would be able to think on two different levels simultaneously — that of tradition proper and its translation into a foreign idiom. What the actual substance of Jewish teaching was would have to be carefully ascertained according to tradition and its wonted method of interpretation; only afterward could an attempt be made to present the finding to others in a form they would be able to understand. Sinzheim had, in the opinion of Sofer, performed this task in exemplary fashion and deserved the highest praise. But Sinzheim had to perform a task for the special needs of the Sanhedrin, an occasion that was exceptional. For the day-to-day life of the Jewish community and the education of its children such a translation of traditional teachings and its rationalistic appraisal were condemned. According to Sofer, Jewish tradition had to be preserved in its totality, not only as far as its contents were concerned, but also with respect to its form, its system of thought, and its linguistic expression. That this could only be done at the price of continued social and cultural isolation was clear to Rabbi Sofer and he was prepared to pay the price.[53]

Perhaps Sofer could have reached this conclusion and implemented it only because he was somewhat removed from the main scene of the social struggle, living as he did since 1806 in Pressburg, a town situated on the outskirts of the main Western Jewish communities. Rabbi Sofer succeeded in preserving the traditional structure of his communities and even in giving them a new infusion of life. He founded a new type of yeshiva that was even more demanding than the old, exacting complete dedication to the study of the Torah and excluding the study of all else and, especially, of what could lead to rationalistic enlightenment.

Students became more emotionally attached to their master, who was not only their teacher, but acted also as their spiritual guide. In his community, too, a strong commitment to the ideal of absolute attachment to tradition was demanded — at least from those who wished to become followers of the rabbi. Within this circle Sofer assumed the role of leader and exercised a spell over his community quite in excess of what was expected of a rabbi. He became the oracle and undisputed authority on matters not generally falling under a rabbi's jurisdiction. Formally based on the authority of Halakah (religious law), his influence bore the clear mark of charisma.[54] This may have been owing to his deeply religious personality but was also linked to his single-minded attachment to a religious ideal, that is, the dedication of life to the study of the holy law and an absolute submission to its behests. As such, the charisma could be transmitted to others as it was through the founding of a whole school made up of disciples of Moses Sofer. The growth of the school and a full evolvement of the system he initiated belongs to the later period of Sofer's life (he died in 1839) but the main ingredients of the system and the beginnings of the school emerged before 1815. The insistence of Rabbi Sofer on keeping traditional teachings absolutely intact was already illustrated when he commented on the procedure at the Sanhedrin. That the practice of religion in all its details must remain sacrosanct had been expressed by him at an earlier date when news of the innovation of the Westphalian consistory reached him. On this occasion he was approached by traditional rabbis from Germany and asked to join them in publicly condemning the trend of reform and, especially, as it concerned the dietary laws of Passover.[55] This Sofer declined to do because of tactical reasons but in his own community he took the strongest stand against the infringement of the customs, although fully aware that the permission of the Westphalian rabbis could halakically be vindicated. Sofer evolved a theory to substantiate why no distinction should be made between different religious obligations. According to him all parts of the tradition are of equal importance and should not be trimmed by reformers on the pretext of practical need or theoretical differentiation. The theory demanded an unequivocal and unqualified commitment to tradition in its entirety.[56]

Understandably, the whole community could not be expected to follow these far-reaching demands and Sofer was aware that by putting his standards as high as he did he would antagonize at least a minority of his community as well as many other Jews in other communities. He was prepared to accept the consequences of his system. He gave practical proof for this when a group of enlightened in his community decided to establish a school of the type already described. The idea of such a school ran directly counter to his ideas of Jewish education — that is, preservation not only of the traditional content but also of the age-old method of teaching, and only just tolerating secular knowledge without attributing any educational significance to it. The new school, on the contrary, wanted to replace the old compromise. He publicly condemned the new institution and attacked the instigator in language clearly intended to give offense. Sofer declared the innovators to have severed their ties with the Jewish community — indeed, to have divested themselves from the insignia of any religion.[57] The sermon preached on this occasion in 1811 is one of the first signs of the schism between the orthodox and the reform to which Moses Sofer contributed more than any other traditionalist.

X LEGAL STEPPINGSTONES

Looking back on the three or four decades before the close of the Napoleonic era, cultural, educational, and religious changes and shifts in social relations may be discerned. All these transformations may be considered as being interconnected. As Jews adopted the cultural patterns of their non-Jewish environment, social relations between individuals of the two camps became possible, and the prospect of social acceptance in non-Jewish circles served as a motivation for cultural adaptation. Social acceptance and the accompanying absorption of new ideas gave Jews a new yardstick for evaluating their own inner Jewish world and led, sometimes, to criticism of it. This criticism eventually led to a dissociation from tradition and provided a stimulus for those seeking new roads in education and urged them toward religious reform. But here the causation of events did not work exclusively in that order; cause and effect at times followed in reversed sequence. Religious criticism could have been the wedge that caused a crack in the traditional structure and created the motivation for subsequent cultural adaptation and social aspirations.

Whatever the configuration of motivations and events, a lasting effect of the changes could be expected only if the new trend were effectively supported by legislation. In fact legislation did not lag far behind social and cultural changes. In Berlin, Christian Wilhelm von Dohm, who in June 1781 had just sent to press the pamphlet on "The Civic Betterment of the Jews," containing his far-reaching recommendations, was gratified to hear of the contemplated "Edict of Tolerance" that was about to be promulgated by the Emperor Joseph II in Austria. According to rumors "the Jews of The Imperial and Royal State would be vested with the rights of other citizens." [1] This assured Dohm that his reflections had not been mere fancies. However, the actual content of the edict was not as far-reaching as rumor would have had it. But even so it revealed the tendency to extricate the Jews from their singular position. As such it can serve as proof that the trend toward change began to affect the realm of practical politics and that of theoretical conceptions simultaneously.

No wonder that contemporaries, Jews as well as their Gentile well-wishers, hailed the edict as an act of deliverance. In Vienna they celebrated with poetic exuberance assisted by writers who made up in enthusiasm what they lacked in talent. In Prague, Chief Rabbi Landau, praising the gracious act of the emperor, felt duty bound to warn his congregants not to let their enthusiasm carry them and blind them to the respect due those he still considered the indigenous masters of the land. In more remote Berlin the exponents of Enlightenment, Mendelssohn and Wessely, looked upon the edict as realizing many of their hopes[2] and their Christian friend concurred in this feeling. The German poet Friedrich Gottlieb Klopstock, later an open sympathizer with the French Revolution, celebrated this event, too, with an Ode to the Emperor, Joseph II.[3]

The Edict of Tolerance concerned the Jews of Lower Austria including Vienna, Bohemia, Moravia, Silesia, and Hungary. The competent authorities of these countries were consulted by the emperor and then the edict promulgated for each of them separately between October 1781 and March 1782. [4] Although the acts varied somewhat for each country, in essence the content was the same. All the versions contained the prescription that Jewish communities had to establish schools for their children's civic education and, where this was unfeasible, Christian schools were obliged to take in Jewish pupils. Institutions for secondary schooling and higher learning had to be open to Jews but they would be spared contact with religious teaching. The special emblem of the Jew and the particular Jewish dress could now be discarded; the body tax Jews had to pay on going from one place to another was abolished. A Jew would be permitted to learn handicrafts and encouraged to open factories. Jews were free to seek apprenticeships with Christian masters if they wished, but the guilds retained their rights to exclude Jews, and Jewish artisans would therefore have to work on their own. In Bohemia, Jews were also allowed to take a lease on land for twenty years but, in order to acquire it, they had to become Christians.

These are, without doubt, ameliorating measures on behalf of the Jews. The enthusiastic welcome accorded the edict is however no measure of its legal significance. The question to be asked is whether the Edict of Tolerance altered the legal status of Jews. The wording of the edict is evasive, even contradictory on this point. The opening paragraph speaks of the emperor's wish to see all his "subjects without distinction of nation and religion, as soon as they are accepted or tolerated in our states, take part together in the common weal . . . enjoy a legal freedom." [5] This seems to include the Jews among his majesty's subjects. But in many respects the position of the Jews remained unchanged. They were still not permitted to settle where they liked nor, as clearly stated in the edict, were they permitted to increase their number, a control that in Bohemia and Moravia was exercised by limiting the number of marriages permitted. Despite the law, they continued to pay their special taxes. In Bohemia and Moravia these were collected by the community organizations; in Vienna, where no communal organization was permitted, every "tolerated" Jew had to pay his own dues.

The contradictory features call for an explanation. The Edict of Tolerance did not concern Jews alone but attempted a general reform. The emperor intended to transform the state, based until then on local particularism and class privileges, into a centralized and unified entity. The non-Catholic denominations would enjoy religious freedom — with some limitations — while in civic matters the state was to maintain a strict neutrality.[6] Jews, too, would be generously included among the beneficiaries of the new tolerance. Guided by abstract principles, the emperor and his advisers were unable to be consistent when it came to their practical implementation. The Catholic church and the traditionally established estates were too deeply enmeshed in the fabric of state and society to be disentangled by the magic of an edict. The emperor, while the edict was being discussed in council, recoiled from many of the suggestions made with regard to reforms concerning Jews.[7] That explains the uneven character of the edict.

The emperor's officials seemed to have interpreted the intention of the edict concerning Jewish status in several ways, one contradicting the other. In Bohemia the local authorities found it necessary to confirm anew the old privileges of the Jew on which their stay in the country rested — an indication that the edict did not affect Jewish status. In Moravia the authorities declared such approval unnecessary.[8] The edict seemed, in their opinion, to have superseded the old privileges.

In point of legislative niceties the significance of the edict could be debated. Seen in a general perspective, however, it certainly indicated one underlying intention, namely, to oblige the Jews to step out of their occupational, social, and cultural isolation, thus opening a new vista of the future.

The liberal policy of Joseph II was continued during the short reign of his brother Leopold (1790–1792). A change occurred, however, under Leopold's successor, Francis II. In Vienna permission for Jews to settle or stay for business purposes was granted most parsimoniously, although their role in the economic sphere was steadily gaining significance. The measures employed to keep an eye on the Jews in Vienna were reminiscent of the methods used in the pre-Josephian era. In the provinces, too, Jews, instead of enjoying greater liberty, were given less freedom.[9] The practice of prohibiting marriage, by which means the number of Jews in every province and every locality was to be kept constant, was kept up and was enforced most rigorously by the authorities.

The Edict of Tolerance was, however, not revoked. The clauses concerning education were implemented; more important from our point of view, the Jew emerges at all times, even in the context of legislation that set him back practically, not only as a permanent resident but also as a legally acknowledged citizen or subject — albeit of a very special kind. In the fifth year of his rule, in 1797, Francis promulgated a new *Judenpatent* for the Jews of Bohemia, intended to regulate their lives. This patent contained the ungracious prescription for controlling Jewish marriages as well as rules severely restricting the Jew's choice of occupation. Nevertheless, this ruling opened with the resounding preamble that indicated its ultimate purpose: "In order to bring Bohemian Jewry closer to their civic destination for the benefit of the State and themselves in accordance with the accepted principles of Tolerance so that legislation may finally altogether abolish the difference that it has been compelled to maintain between Jewish and Christian subjects." [10] In fact, their obligation to serve in the army was the only recognizable sign that they and their Christian neighbors enjoyed equality of status. Already under Joseph II, Jews were drafted for transport service, and in the first year of the reign of Francis, in 1793, Jews were obligated to serve in the army unless like some Christians they could buy their release. Army service for Jews was compulsory for "every citizen, irrespective of religion, estate or birth, was due to serve." [11]

This privilege of serving in the Austrian army — not always appreciated by his majesty's new subjects[12] — was the only one to mark the equality so grandiloquently promised by the preamble to the law. For the rest, the discrepancy between the declared intention and the details of the law was only too glaringly apparent. Nevertheless, the preamble should not be dismissed as mere hypocrisy. The author may have felt that the Catholic state made a great concession by granting Jews what the regulations set out. The fact that they included Jews among the subjects of the emperor and held out hopes for future equality shows that these notions were inescapable as an integral part of public opinion and could not altogether be ignored. Indeed, the idea to include the Jews in the state had gained almost universal acceptance. It is an exception if the Municipal Council of Prague, in rejecting the Jews' request for some changes in the patent of 1797, says that "Jews are a nation tolerated only under certain restrictions." [13] This was not the usual language used by the imperial authorities. These designate Jews as citizens of the state and although of limited rights, they are not sui generis. They are regarded as subjects of a special kind, who, for religious or other reasons, enjoy fewer rights than others. As the state was known to make exceptions for reasons such as religion and estate, also in respect of non-Jewish subjects, the special standing of the Jew did not exclude him from being a citizen. For the Jews themselves the classification "fellow-citizen" [14] was a starting point for the claim and hope that the distinctions would eventually be abolished.

The Edict of Tolerance and the legislation that followed in Austria may be designated as a reform, that is, the implementation of social and political changes within the legal authority of existing institutions. Later changes of a revolutionary nature will be treated. The aims and objectives of reform were well defined and clear and dictated the means for their implementation. No overall change was contemplated. Reform was a congenial way to deal with the problems in the enlightened absolute state of Joseph II and has been used in all states where enlightened absolutism had persisted for any length of time. It was followed in Württemberg,[15] Baden,[16] and Bavaria[17] in the years 1808, 1809, and 1813 respectively. Reform was implemented either by promulgating a set of laws or by the release of particular decisions concerning Jews. In either case the result was a radical change in Jewish status. Tacitly, as in Austria, or explicitly as in Baden,[18] Jews were acknowledged as subjects of the state.

The urge to educate was even more evident in countries other than Austria. In Baden, for instance, the right of residence was granted by law to Jewish subjects only if they chose occupations other than the traditionally Jewish ones of peddling and petty trade. The Jew had to become either a peasant or a craftsman. If he still wanted to become a tradesman he had to prove his qualifications, indicate what his speciality was, and undertake to remain stationary.[19] Diverting Jews from their traditional occupations became a major objective of legislation. The final goal of the state was to turn Jews into full-scale citizens but, for the time being, they were still treated as a special group with special obligations, though the body tax had been repealed everywhere[20] and they were now obliged to serve in the army.[21]

Reform in every country followed the Austrian pattern, urging Jews to adapt themselves culturally to their surroundings. The state-controlled schools were established to further this aim. Religious freedom was guaranteed everywhere but it was expected that a conflict between religious obligations and the duties of citizenship would be resolved in favor of the latter. In one of the states, Mecklenburg-Schwerin, this was expressly stated. Jews were permitted to continue to observe their Sabbath, but the regulations of 1812 stated clearly that "Jewish soldiers, apprentices or craftsmen with Christian masters viz. Jews serving in public Christian offices, and all Jews in general who enter into relations with Christians, are not permitted to use customs that cannot be reconciled with this as pretexts for evading obligations undertaken." [22] Where civil marriage had been introduced, as in France, Jews had of course to comply with it.[23] Divorce was universally subjected to the jurisdiction of civil courts. Jewish couples who wanted a religious divorce could approach the rabbinical court only after the divorce had been granted by civil courts. In the Mecklenburg-Schwerin regulations referred to previously, even this was forbidden: "the Jewish divorce . . . must be sought from competent judges . . . But there was no need for a Letter of Divorce which should therefore not be executed." [24] The Baden regulations indicated that the state would respect Jewish religion as far as the Mosaic laws were concerned but not as regards the Talmudic enlargements.[25]

As is well known, France in the period preceding the Revolution attempted to solve its problems by means of reform in a legitimate constitutional fashion. Among the problems attacked in this way was the issue of the Alsatian Jewish communities, whose legal and cultural status resembled that of German Jewry. Inquiries into the grievance of the Alsatian Jews and complaints voiced against them by the local Gentile population resulted in 1784 in a new set of regulations that resembled the reforms introduced first in Austria and later in some German states. The body tax was abolished, Jewish initiative in industry encouraged, but the Jewish population limited through strict control of marriages.[26] The effect of this legislation on Jewish status could never be assessed, for the attempts at reform were swept away in the current revolution, which diverted the Jewish issue into new channels. The Declaration of the Rights of Man did not automatically grant Jews the rights of citizenship, for it applied only to those whose right to be called French — of whatever estate — was uncontested. This did not apply to Jews.[27] But at least the Jewish issue was now thrown into sharp focus and it was clearly felt that their old position could not be allowed to continue in the new circumstances. As long as society was built on the lines of estates and privileged groups the Jews, though their position was unique, were still a category that fell into place in the general structure. With the disappearance of this whole structure of privileged groups the Jews became more of an anomaly than they had ever been. Only two radical solutions were conceivable: either to grant the Jews citizenship by special act of legislation or expel them. The first course was the one ultimately implemented after prolonged discussion in the National Assembly, during which all possible arguments for and against naturalization and possible assimilation were rehearsed. The Sephardim received their citizenship in January 1790 and in September 1791 the Ashkenazim were given similar rights.[28]

Thus, for the first time in European history, a Jewish group acquired unqualified citizenship. As French rule was expanding in the wake of the Revolution and Napoleonic wars to Belgium, the German countries west of the Rhine, and later to Holland and Northern Germany and some parts of Germany east of the Rhine, the principle of equal citizenship was introduced in all these places. French rule and the revolutionary principles of the day may have carried all before it or the local institutions simply yielded to the revolutionary trend and, among other radical changes, granted civil equality to Jews. In the newly created State of Westphalia, for instance, the new regent, Napoleon's brother Jerome, based his rule on a constitution after the French pattern and Jews automatically acquired citizenship.[29] In Holland, then the Batavian Republic, the National Assembly granted citizenship to Jews after having thrashed out the matter even more thoroughly than had been done during the Revolution in France.[30] Whatever variations local conditions insinuated into the discussions, the result was predetermined by French hegemony. The law granted Dutch Jews their citizenship in 1796. In Frankfurt, occupied by the French since 1806, the Jews re-

ceived full citizenship from the Grand Duke Dalberg, an appointee of Napoleon who still retained a shadow of independence. The Jews of Frankfurt paid an indemnity of 240,000
gulden, the equivalent of what they would have paid to the municipality in special taxes for twenty years if not for the act of enfranchisement.[31]

To round out the picture it must be noted that the Act of
1790–91 in France was not the last word on the Jewish issue. In
response to complaints from Alsace, Napoleon resorted in 1808 to
regulations that are reminiscent of those encountered in countries
where reform and not revolution was responsible for change. He
restricted the rights of Jewish residents and tried to limit their
choice of occupation. Worse than that, the Jew lost his full legal
standing to the extent that on presenting a bill he had first to
prove its validity and that the transaction had actually taken
place. These discriminatory measures were aimed at diverting
Jews from moneylending and petty trade and forcing them to
take up agriculture or become artisans — the aim of reform everywhere, but here supported by the strong arm of the police
state. All the legislation was to be reviewed after ten years and if
the result justified repeal, Jews would be reinstituted to full citizenship. When the time came, however, Napoleon's day was over
and in spite of the efforts made by adversaries of Jews in Alsace,
the restored regime of the Bourbons allowed the restrictive regulations to lapse.[32] These restrictive regulations, by the way, applied also to German territories under French administration
and there they remained in force even after they expired in
France.[33]

Besides the two patterns of reform and revolution there was a
third that evolved in Prussia. It may be characterized as a combination of the two, for it was legalistic in form and revolutionary
in content. Prussia was defeated by Napoleon in 1806. It lost a
good deal of territory but retained its independence at least so far
as internal affairs were concerned. Out of the great humiliation
arose the will for rehabilitation. This led to far-reaching reforms
through legislation instituted by the Prussians to attain a level of
civic freedom and social adjustment that in France was gained

by the Revolution. The abolition of serfs, the dissolution of the craft guilds, and the acceptance of Jews as citizens were some of the main reforms initiated. The Jewish issue, as has been mentioned repeatedly, had been under consideration ever since the death of Frederick II in 1786. Comprehensive reform had been contemplated but never completed — conflicting views on the Jews' desirability and perfectibility running rampant in the administration. Only partial remedies had been found, such as the abolition of the body tax (1788) and of collective responsibility for theft and the like (1801). Then, during the era of the great reforms, the Jewish issue was also tackled in a more radical fashion, resulting in the Edict of 1812, which elevated the Jew to his new status. Jews became citizens of the state, their particular privileges such as special jurisdiction and exemption from military service abolished and their special contributions, such as taxes and the like, revoked. They were granted free choice of residence and occupation. Government posts were meanwhile denied them, the ultimate decision on this point being deferred.[34]

The political integration of Prussian Jewry, the culturally most advanced community of Jews in Western Europe, was considered a great achievement and a turning point in the history of German Jewry. Far more significance was given the event here than elsewhere in other Jewish communities. Not since the Edict of Tolerance had any legislation concerning Jews elicited such enthusiasm.[35] The common feature of all legislation, revolutionary or constitutional, was that it acknowledged Jews as part of the population, perhaps in need of improvement and correction, but still not aliens who could be expelled at will. They all accepted a measure of responsibility for Jews residing in the respective states. If this did not include the granting of full citizenship, it held out a promise at the end of an unstipulated time, and at least acknowledged Jews born in the country as citizens. What emerged as the sentiment of the various legislative acts was that each state was prepared to put up with the Jews who happened to live within its borders at the time of the reform or the revolution.

All the states took into account the possible desire of Jews from other countries to emigrate and some, as for instance the Prussian edict, made provision for transactions of business and for marriage between Jews of different states. Visits of foreign Jews on business were naturally countenanced but the infiltration of foreign Jews was viewed with suspicion. There were strict regulations in some states against this possibility.[36] It was tacitly assumed that each state would absorb its Jewish community into the larger population, thus dissolving the tenuous links that bound different Jewish communities together.

By conceding citizenship to Jews, the state did not immediately resolve all problems with regard to the Jews. It might have gone a longer way toward doing so if the concession to the Jews had followed on the acceptance of the principle of separating church and state. On the basis of this principle the state could simply have ignored the religion of its citizens and the Jews would have been left to their own devices, to maintain their religious institutions, or not, as they wished. In France such a state of affairs had come to pass in the wake of the Revolution, and the state, while granting citizenship, had at the same time — at least theoretically — divested itself of all interest in religious matters while guaranteeing freedom of worship. During the Reign of Terror all religions were proscribed and worshippers, Jews included, were molested and even persecuted.[37] This state of affairs was reversed when the Reign of Terror came to an end and the cooperation of state and church was again the order of the day. It depended solely on the Jewish communities whether they kept up their synagogues and maintained the rabbinate, and individuals could join the communities and avail themselves of these institutions at will. For example: the Jew could content himself with the civil marriage required by the state. If, in addition, he wanted a religious sanctification he could obtain this from the rabbi. But no rabbi was able to perform the religious ceremony without ascertaining whether the obligatory civil marriage had taken place.[38] At most the state recognized the existence of religious institutions but, as far as the Jewish ones were concerned, did not contribute anything toward their support. The communities could only be sustained on a voluntary basis under the new circumstances, a procedure for which there was no precedent as

European Jews had been accustomed to compulsory participation in community finances and affairs. No wonder they ran into difficulties.[39]

This situation, however, did not last. Napoleon, realizing the part religion continued to play in the life of Frenchmen, sought a modus vivendi with the church. In 1801 a concordat was contracted formalizing relations between the Catholic church and Napoleon's government. According to this, the state acquired an important hold on the church, for it had the right to choose the bishops while the church only had the right to confirm the choice. Napoleon sought similar agreements with other Christian churches as well.[40] The Jews were, of course, only a small minority in France but their affairs were of concern to the French authorities — including the emperor — as has already been observed in connection with the convening of the Sanhedrin. The main result of these deliberations on the status of the Jews of France was the establishment of the *Consistoire,* an organization to which all Jews had to belong.

Formally the establishment of the consistoire was the decision of the assembly of Jewish notables who met in 1806, preceding the Sanhedrin. It could therefore be regarded as an organization created voluntarily by the Jews.[41] In fact, however, it was the imperial officials who worked out the details for establishing the organization and later, in 1808, the Constitution was sanctioned by a decree of the emperor. Indeed, the consistoire could exercise its power only because it relied on the state, from which it derived its legal authority.

According to law, Jews living in a particular department or in several departments where the number of Jewish citizens warranted this, had to unite to form the consistoire, an organization that revolved around the synagogue. The consistoire had lay members and elected the rabbis who, together, were responsible for the administration and the welfare of the community. All consistoires were affiliated to a central one, situated in Paris, composed once again of Jewish notables and the Grand Rabbin. The function of the central consistoire was to supervise and control the work of the local organizations.[42]

There is some similarity between the consistoires and the country-wide organizations that, in prerevolutionary times, linked together Jewish communities in certain countries[43] — though not in France. At that time, however, the organization catered for every aspect of Jewish life, whether religious, juridical, or even economic. Now that French Jews were subject to law like all citizens of the state, their special organization linked them together only qua adherents of the Jewish religion and not qua the citizens they had become. By establishing the organization, the state recognized the Jewish religion along with the other religions with whose organizations it maintained formal relations. Nonetheless, there were some discriminatory features. While the dignitaries of the Christian churches received their salaries from the state, the rabbis had to be remunerated from the coffers of the Jewish communities. Furthermore the consistoire, although conforming to other religious organizations, was obliged to concern itself with the civic behavior of its members. One of its main functions was to control Jews in their locality and ensure that they did not engage in unlicensed occupations and that their members fulfilled their military obligations.[44] This reflected the prevailing attitude that Jews were still on trial and had to be taught, if necessary by compulsion, what it meant to be a citizen of the state and a member of society.

A similar spirit dictated the constitution of the Consistoire of Westphalia, established under the regime of Jerome Napoleon in 1808. It admitted to a double purpose, that of granting Jews free exercise of their religion and controlling their moral and civic behavior.[45] Even more far-reaching was the responsibility of the *Oberrat,* the executive body of Baden's Jewish communities. Not only had it to supervise the moral conduct of Jews but also to direct the occupational distribution of Jewish youth,[46] for it had been conceived as an instrument for the reeducation of Jews. This was the tendency of the legislation introduced in all countries where the idea of Jewish integration had been accepted provided the Jews would conform to the demand of the state and society. If certain states still withheld some rights from the Jews, it was done with the hope that their eventual progress in adaptation would obviate the necessity for such restrictions. And the acceptance of the Jewish religion as one of the acknowledged denominations was implied in this attitude. It is true that this was not tantamount to granting organized Jewish religion equal status with the established church or churches of the country. This status was dependent on the extent of the state's involvement with the Christian church. For instance, in Vienna the government, although deliberating the possible integration of Jews, did not permit them to form a community[47] — obviously because such permission would have been interpreted as an infringement of the supreme position occupied by the Catholic church. In Bohemia the regulations of 1797 granted free exercise of the Jewish religion but did not provide for the establishment of full-scale communities, so that the appointment of a rabbi was possible only through the voluntary contribution made by Jews for this purpose.[48] In Moravia the situation was different. These Jews had for centuries had their own country-wide organization headed by a Chief Rabbi and this they continued to maintain also when emancipation was already achieved.[49]

The exact nature of the status Jewish religion would occupy once Jews were granted citizenship was not explicitly stated. In Prussia the Edict of 1812, although far-reaching and detailed with regard to the granting of civil rights, left the issue of the legal status of the Jewish religion and its organization undefined. The last paragraph of the edict promised that the matter would be dealt with later.[50] For the time being an older definition from 1788 remained valid. According to this only the three Christian churches, the Reform, Lutheran, and Roman Catholic, were protected by the state. Others, among them the Jewish, were in the category of "publicly tolerated" religions. How the definition could be applied in practice was not clear. In the ensuing years there arose legal doubts as to whether all Jews had to become members of the organizations of the Jewish communities and whether a Jewish community could take its own decision regarding deviations from the traditional service.[51]

Naturalization did not automatically secure for the Jew the same rights that were enjoyed by more fortunate citizens. In some places even his civil rights were restricted; in others his religion was not given the legal status accorded to others. Nonetheless, the history of Jews and Judaism took a decisive turn in the period between 1780 and 1814, for during this time the old legal edifice on which Jewish status rested trembled in the balance as though waiting to be supplanted by the absolute equality envisaged by the enlightened. At least the stage had been set for the struggle for full equality.

XI THE FUTILE FLIGHT FROM JEWISH PROFESSIONS

The advocates of Jewish integration persistently predicted that Jewish integration would have its effect on the nature of the occupations Jews were engaged in. Jews, granted free choice, would make ample use of it and their age-old addiction to trade and other occupations depending on the investment of money — especially usury — would disappear.[1] Occupational change was also envisaged by the legislators who turned Jews, more or less explicitly, into citizens. The expected change, it is true, could not always be provided for in terms of legislation; the revolutionary type of legislation, exemplified by the decisions of the National Assembly in France, granted Jews citizenship unconditionally. The wording could not even hint at the expected change. However, during deliberations preceding the decision, the prospective transformation of Jews into "normal" citizens, as far as their occupations were concerned, had been thoroughly discussed and it had been tacitly agreed that the political step would not be justified unless it gave rise to the expected economic redistribution.[2] Where Jewish citizenship was gained by reform, this condition was embodied in the legislation. Starting from the Edict of Tolerance in Austria in 1781 and ending with the Edict of Bavaria in 1813, all the acts carried clauses to divert Jews from their traditional occupations toward becoming agriculturists and handicraftsmen.[3] Less explicit, but nevertheless indicated, was the expectation that under the new conditions Jews would no longer choose to crowd together in their ghettos and Jewish quarters would cease making themselves conspicuous by their adhesiveness to the group.[4] Jews had been compelled by the laws of the Old Order to confine themselves to their particular quarters but, once exempted from this necessity, it was thought logical that they would spread out among their neighbors.

To what extent these expectations were realized in the ensuing period is a point that must now be considered. As the period under consideration here ends in 1814 and many of the legislative acts — especially those in Prussia and Bavaria — came into force only shortly before this date, the terrain is limited. Still, the tendencies that were later to become dominant can already be detected in the history of the countries where free choice of occupation — in a greater or limited measure — was already creating the laboratory that would indicate the trends inherent in the situation.

First an examination of what happened in the provinces or countries where for a substantial period the law allowed complete mobility and complete freedom as to choice of occupation will be made. These are France between 1791 and 1806, Holland between 1796 and 1813, the Rhine cities at about the same time as in Holland, Hamburg and vicinity between 1810 and 1813, and Frankfurt for the short time from 1808 to 1813. The relevant data is not always available for these places. The best-known and best-explored case is that of France, especially Alsace.

Nowhere had Jews been more criticized and attacked for their manner of earning a livelihood than in Alsace. The Jewish population, from an occupational standpoint, can be divided into three categories. There existed a small layer of capitalists who acted as purveyors for the army and performed other transactions such as the import of victuals and other commodities on a grand scale. Then came the well-to-do middle class that used its capital to do business with the peasantry, providing for loans, advancing money on crops, and buying up — and selling at a profit — property and whatever chance put in their way. The third group was made up of peddlers and paupers who roamed the countryside offering their wares and looking for bargains in the by-products of agriculture, in feathers, hides, and whatever could be bought up. Criticism was leveled particularly against the two lower ranks. The business transactions that occupied the middle class were characterized as "usury" and the distress of the peasantry laid at their door.[5] Peddling, too, was regarded as obnoxious as it allegedly enticed the peasant to spend more than he could afford on fripperies.[6]

It is difficult, even in historical retrospect, to ascertain the economic significance of the role played by the Jews in prerevolutionary Alsace. They certainly intensified the economic life of the district, thereby benefiting some of its inhabitants and harming the interests of others.[7] It is however beyond doubt that the Jewish occupations — like the Jewish living quarters in the ghettos — were overcrowded with too many persons attempting to eke out a living from the same source. Thus competition among those engaged in these transactions — and they were not the prerogative of Jews only — became severe. The Jewish answer to the complaints against the one-sidedness of their business activities was of course that all other avenues of fruitful endeavor were closed to them.[8] It was only reasonable to expect that the removal of restrictions would result in a readjustment of the ecological and economic anomaly.

The unrestricted freedom that continued for some fifteen years, 1791–1806, brought about some changes in the expected direction. Some Jews left their former abodes and took up residence where they had formerly been forbidden to do so. Metz Jews, who used to do business with the inhabitants of the surrounding villages where residence had been denied them, now settled among their customers.[9] This was a move in the expected and desired direction of dispersal. But most of the other changes went in directions contrary to those anticipated. More Jews from the countryside moved into towns than the other way around. Strassbourg had jealously guarded its privilege of excluding Jews and up to the Revolution the rich family Cerf Berr alone succeeded in securing permission to live there. Within less than a generation the town saw the establishment of a whole community. By 1807 the Jewish community counted 1,476 persons led by Rabbi David Sinzheim, who later acted as the President of the Sanhedrin in Paris.[10] Other towns, without Jews until the Revolution, also saw the establishment of populous Jewish communities.[11] Paris itself, which had only had a sprinkling of illegal Jewish inhabitants, became with nearly 3,000 souls a center for

Jews, for Sephardim and Ashkenazim alike.[12] Freedom to move and settle was indeed utilized but the result was less a dispersion than a greater concentration of Jews. Mobility was collective, for where one Jew moved, others tended to move as well.

The change in residence, in some cases at least, entailed a change in occupation as well. A few Jews in some localities took up agriculture, others turned artisan.[13] Isaac Cerf Berr could say in 1806, not without pride, that in spite of great obstacles they encountered "we have already among us tailors, carpenters, tinkers, goldsmiths and other artisans and artists." Cerf Berr also testified to an extension of the occupational map in another direction: "There are already those who have left the lycées and have been found worthy of occupying the chairs of mathematics and physics." Jews made a breakthrough, if not a spectacular one, then at least a beginning in the three new fields of agriculture, handicrafts, and the professions. The difficulties mentioned by Cerf Berr were of a social nature. "One of our children applies to a master artisan, a manufacturer, an artist, labourer etc., and he is rejected because he is a Jew." [14]

Jews still felt themselves to be discriminated against but circumstances changed in their favor. The Revolution was not restricted to the political domain; it had a powerful effect on economics as well. One of the most important effects was the confiscation of church property and estates belonging to the émigrés. This so-called national property was thrown on the market, probably enabling some Jews to take up agriculture in a country like Alsace where land was notoriously difficult to obtain. Still, the actual economic changes in the structure of the Jewish community were slight. The opportunities that arose were used by Jews, but more in varying and extending their traditional occupations than in taking up new ones. Jews also bought up national property — to what extent is contested and probably unverifiable — but not generally for the purpose of tilling the soil and not even as an investment of capital. They usually realized a profit on their investment by reselling either the whole or parcels of the acquired land.[15] The number of artisans was of course quite small — except possibly in Paris, where by 1804, of 840 Jews, 230 were artisans. Similarly, there were few professionals and clerks employed by the state.[16] Significant was not the alteration in occupational structure but what could be derived from it to evaluate the Jewish attitude. Even a small number of Jewish peasants and artisans gave the lie to the anti-Jewish charge that Jews would avoid occupations that involved physical labor as they had an innate propensity for easy gain. The small number of those who took to the new occupations could easily be accounted for by pointing to the short time that had elapsed since the opportunity arose and the difficulties that Jews still encountered. This was the tenor of Berr-Isaac Berr's argument when, in 1806, he summed up the results of one and a half decades of mobility, legally guaranteed for the Jews of Alsace.[17]

The experience of other Jewish communities that had been given an opportunity to move freely and change their occupations at will assumes a similar pattern. Where Jews had been confined to special quarters as in Frankfurt and Prague, many who could afford it moved now to other parts of the city, with the social consequences already observed.[18] Many left their former places of residence altogether. Most of these migrated to business centers, among them places where formerly no Jews had been permitted. Jews had been expelled from Cologne in the fifteenth century (1424). They returned only in 1794 after the French conquest of the town. By 1807 there were already 38 families with 138 souls.[19] Stuttgart, too, had been barred to Jews until the turn of the eighteenth century when some court Jews were admitted, but it was not until 1806 that the ban was lifted. In the space of two years, 14 families had settled, consisting of 109 persons.[20]

The two important commercial towns, Lübeck and Bremen, from which Jews had previously been excluded — though they had done business there by coming in for short periods from the neighboring towns — were now thrown open to them. During the short period of the French regime (between 1810 and 1814) a community of some importance made their home in Lübeck and some twenty families settled in Bremen — to the dismay of the local burghers who had to keep their reaction to themselves until the departure of the French.[21]

Unrestricted mobility produced here trends similar to those it had set in motion in France. The same can be said about the freedom of occupational choice. There are reports of Jews acquiring landed property in Germany where they were permitted to do so. Much of the property of the religious orders, dissolved by the French during their occupation — in the neighborhood of Halberstadt, Magdeburg, and Braunschweig — is known to have been bought up by Israel Jacobson. He resold most of the estates at a good profit, rented out some, but several he retained for his personal use. He was also in possession of estates in Mecklenburg, where he had large economic interests as well.[22] For a man like Jacobson the acquisition of estates was no doubt prompted by social aspirations. It was customary throughout Europe for businessmen of bourgeois origin and sufficient means to join the aristocracy by acquiring land. Now that the legal barriers had been removed, some Jews were attracted to this course. They did so, but only hesitatingly, for reasons that will be mentioned in a moment.

Theoretically the ground had been prepared for Jews to become peasants when they were granted citizenship. But reports of Jews using such economic opportunities are rare.[23] Jewish artisans appear here and there, as in the years following civil liberation. Siegmund Geisenheimer, the founder of the new Jewish school in Frankfurt, the Philantropin (and, as may be recalled, also of the Jewish lodge) tried in 1808 to convince his father in Bingen on the Rhine to have his younger son trained as an artisan. He himself, he explained in a letter, had already succeeded in collecting a substantial sum for the purpose of placing Jewish youngsters with Christian master craftsmen, and six boys had already been provided for in this way. To make his point, he wrote also that even wealthy Jewish children were being sent to train as artisans in Frankfurt. It was a shame that in the Rhine countries, where Jews had had this opportunity for twelve years, not a single Jew had availed himself of it.[24] In fact, Jewish artisans and would-be artisans were rare. The change, if at all, was a marginal one that left the core intact.

The real reason for the inertia, despite legal possibilities, is not difficult to explain. Legal permission may theoretically create new economic opportunities but these must be both economically and socially attractive if motivation is to be initiated that will encourage exploitation. These, however, were lacking for the individual Jew. On the contrary, any wish he may have had to make use of the new opportunities was probably frustrated by difficulties he encountered socially. The reluctance of Christian masters to take on Jewish apprentices in Alsace is but one example. Such behavior was the order of the day among artisans everywhere. Jewish societies founded for the purpose of helping Jews to become artisans — and of this later — had to pay exorbitant fees to Gentile masters for accepting Jews as apprentices.[25] Motivation was lacking for a spontaneous reversion to the occupation of peasant. The would-be peasant had to have the means for acquiring land. Why should he invest in an occupation followed in the main by those who had been born to it? Then, the acquisition of land was not all. The peasant had to be a member of a tightly-knit community to which peasants belonged by tradition and to which newcomers had no easy access. For a Jew this difficulty must have seemed insurmountable. Social isolation had, in addition, its economic repercussions as a peasant had to rely on his neighbors for help.[26]

Not unsimilar was the fate of the rich Jew who intended to retain an acquired estate under his own management. Public opinion was opposed to the Jew gaining an estate that had belonged for generations to the same old families even if the families had been forced to sell because of financial straits. The landed aristocracy was even more exclusive than most groups and the Jew, once settled, felt himself isolated from his neighbors, who were his only possible social contacts. The story of Israel Jacobson and his sons, who wanted to live on the estates they had bought but were ignored by their neighbors, illustrates this.[27] The observer who later, in the 1830's, said that such proprietors became an easy prey to conversion because of their social isolation may be believed.[28] As long as a Jew wished to retain his Jewishness — even when reduced to a minimum — he was handicapped in the choice of occupation. He could not afford to penetrate into non-

Jewish circles without endangering his attachment to his original religious and ethnic group.

Contemporaries cannot be expected to have insight into the factors commanding a social situation that a historian achieves in retrospect. Nevertheless, there were some who sensed that the desired occupational readjustment of the Jews would not automatically come about in the natural course of events and would not be accomplished unless measures were taken to direct Jewish youth toward occupations hitherto outside the traditional range. Berr-Isaac Berr was one of them. Immediately after the granting of citizenship in 1791, he suggested that an organized attempt be made to establish workshops where Jewish children could be trained as artisans. He thought that the wealthy, relieved of their special taxes by the new law of citizenship, were the natural sponsors of such a scheme and suggested that they should voluntarily contribute what they would have had to pay in the course of ten years, had not civil liberation made them a gift of this.[29] Clearly Berr-Isaac Berr, as a representative of the upper layer of Jewish society, felt a responsibility for indigent Jews. Jewish solidarity did not disappear with the abolition of the coercive community organization and although Berr's plan for organized action failed to be realized, it was taken up again at a later date. Voluntary associations of enlightened and rich Jews were to play a notable part in diverting young Jews to what was then regarded as productive occupations.[30]

Where the authorities sought to integrate Jews by means of reform, they took steps to channel Jews in the direction of the proper economic fields. These governments were far from granting Jews free choice of residence; in Austria, as has been shown, whole districts remained out of bounds for Jews unless they had made themselves worthy by choosing a desirable occupation such as establishing factories or — this was the case in Bohemia — were prepared to till the soil with their own hands. In such a case the restriction on marriage was also lifted as it was in the case of artisans who followed their professions in accordance with the rules of the guilds.[31] Thus the coveted mobility ought to have motivated Jews to enter new fields of occupation. Similar means were later employed by Napoleon, the Edict of 1808 restricting Alsatian Jews to their district unless they were prepared to become peasants.[32] Whether these regulations had any effect is doubtful. Jews did indeed develop some branches of industry in Austria,[33] as they did in other countries, as soon as these fields promised a good return on investment. Whether permission to live where they chose was an additional inducement is hard to say. Agriculture, where the economic rewards were small, did not attract Jews even when the prize, free choice of residence, was added as an inducement. Some Jews, in order to be permitted to establish a family, did become farmers or craftsmen and then later returned to the more traditional Jewish occupations. As such cases kept recurring, the authorities took steps to prevent the circumvention of their purpose.[34] Yet whatever they did to encourage the Jews through legal means to change their occupations did not meet with much success. On the other hand, wherever there were business prospects of a kind that suited the Jew, the restrictions failed to deter him. In spite of police control over Jews who had not the right of residence in Vienna, hundreds of them nevertheless managed to live there, many of them permanently.[35] As the metropolis, Vienna, became the center of the Empire's expanding economy that owed much to Jewish money and enterprise, it was only natural that Jews should gravitate there.

Legal restrictions in collision with economic interests were bound to give way as the following example will show. The Edict of Tolerance in Austria did not allow Jews to acquire landed property but did permit them to accept this as guarantee for loans. This was a typical half-measure, for if a debtor failed in honoring his obligations, his property automatically fell into the hands of the Jewish creditor. Small wonder that the law was circumvented; a fictitious third party could easily be invented and other subterfuges were not hard to find.[36] By the end of the period under consideration here, it was no secret that Jews were the owners of houses and property in spite of the official ban.[37]

Other countries besides Austria made similar attempts to direct the steps of the Jew in the desired direction. This was the case wherever integration was to be achieved through reform. The most elaborate system was in Baden. The Edict of 1809, which determined the status of the Jews in the country, made the granting of communal and civil rights dependent on the individual Jew's proving that he was engaged "in an accepted occupation." For instance, the sedentary merchants, those who purchased agricultural produce, could acquire the right of residence; but the hawker, the cattle dealer, the moneylender or pawnshop owner was refused this privilege. The same Edict of 1809 established the *Oberrat,* the organization that conducted the communal affairs of Baden Jewry. This body shouldered the responsibility of directing young Jews into the new occupations. At a meeting of representatives of Jewish communities it was decided that every Jewish child that left school at fourteen would be trained for a profession. The sum of 10,000 guilders required for training artisans and future peasants was obtained from the community. A child trained for agriculture was also provided with the means to acquire land but had to undertake to work it himself and not rent or sublet it.[38] In this way the *Oberrat* could keep a watchful eye on the careers of all Jewish children in the community and help them acquire useful occupations.

The result of these undertakings could only be assessed later. True, within a generation — by 1833 to be exact — there were 93 peasants and 403 artisans in Baden. Another estimate puts the number somewhat higher.[39] Since the Jewish population of Baden numbered approximately 19,000, artisans and peasants comprised not more than 3 percent. Not even the organized effort of the community and the genuine support of the government could overcome the natural resistance of the Jews to breaking with tradition, nor overcome the difficulties the Jewish peasants and artisans ran into. The results did prove the willingness and ability of some Jews to take up unorthodox occupations but not the sociological feasibility of transforming whole communities.

In spite of the more or less radical change in the political status of Jews in various countries during the thirty-odd years between 1780 and 1814, the occupational structure of the Jewish community changed only on the periphery. On the margin of Jewish society there appeared the artisan, occasionally the peasant, and the professional who had acquired a European education at the university or elsewhere and utilized it, sometimes even obtaining a position with the state. These were, to be sure, exceptional cases only. In Prague, a Jew who was admitted to the study of jurisprudence had in 1790 to struggle for permission to practice as an advocate — a privilege granted him finally by the liberal successor of Joseph II, but with the proviso that he would not be able to handle ecclesiastical issues.[40] In France a few Jewish civil servants appeared after the Revolution.[41] In Frankfurt, Ludwig Börne, at that time Juda Löb Baruch and unbaptized, was accepted as a clerk in the service of the police.[42] Karl Marx's father — although still unbaptized — was employed as Advocate at the High Court of Appeal in Trier.[43] These examples could be multiplied but would still be negligible numerically. The bulk of the Jewish population remained true to the old economic functions they had filled in the period preceding political emancipation, namely, the investment of money in trade and related undertakings. In general, Jews still held to the traditional Jewish fields where they had a comparative advantage, or entered new branches of economic activity that offered promising opportunities. That is the reason for the conspicuous part played by Jews in developing budding industry in Bohemia, Prussia, and elsewhere.[44] But this pertained to the upper layer of Jewish capitalists and did not affect the lower ranks. Peddling and hawking were designated pejoratively by the Baden and Bavarian authorities as *Nothandel* or *Schacherhandel,* and those engaged in these activities were precluded from obtaining the right of residence in any locality. In Austria and Bohemia such petty trade was severely restricted and in Hungary at times entirely forbidden.[45] But in spite of discouragement from moralists and economists alike, peddling remained in vogue and no amount of suppression could prevail over the obvious economic need that it came to satisfy.[46]

The education-minded legislator expected the Jewish trader to conform to the pattern of non-Jewish establishments. Some Jews emulated the non-Jewish businessman and, while in the previous period Jews had traded indiscriminately in all commodities, now Jewish firms specializing in a particular product appeared on the scene. Jews began to take an interest in branches of business which, until their acceptance as citizens, had been beyond their reach — inciting the protest of Christian traders who feared the competition.[47]

On the higher level of economic activity things changed once again, not because of ideological doctrine, but because of circumstances. The court Jew, who had served his master in multifarious ways — as agent, banker, purveyor, and so on — was slowly disappearing, or rather assuming new functions. The connection between the authorities of state and Jewish capitalists was certainly not severed, but it assumed a more specific character. The Jewish capitalist provided capital and handled state loans. The capitalist, now a citizen and protected by law from arbitrary dismissal or exploitation, dealt with the state as an independent contractor, using his bargaining power to his economic advantage.[48] This was the main difference between the court Jew of the eighteenth century and the great bankers of the nineteenth. Outstanding examples of the latter were the Rothschilds, who started their meteoric careers during the period under consideration here.[49] The unheard-of dimensions reached by the Rothschild fortunes can be ascribed to the greater opportunities that the expanding economy made available. But it was no less a result of the better legal standing of the Jew. The arbitrary treatment meted out to many a court Jew could not be wielded against the Rothschilds. When in cavalier times a new royal employer took over control of the state or when the old one wished to get rid of his obligations to the court Jew, he dismissed the latter or brought him to court, where any charge against him was in the hands of all-too-willing judges — certain to effect his ruin.[50] The Rothschilds, and even their less opulent colleagues, were not simply protégés of the mighty; they were citizens of their respective countries, and even though this citizenship did not as yet spell full political equality, they were no longer at the mercy of any capricious ruler. Under the new circumstances the Jewish firms could grow undisturbed by state intervention. On the contrary, they grew to be quite independent, their own interests governing whatever contracts they undertook.

No matter what layer of society is considered, there is no doubt that it changed considerably so far as its economic role or occupational distribution is concerned, and this change began with the first generation that had experienced legal acceptance if not complete emancipation. Reality, however, fell short of the expectation. Jewish and non-Jewish enlightened had harbored in their image of the future the realization of a complete transformation of the Jewish occupational structure. When this failed to materialize, the adversaries of Jewish integration were not slow to use this to prove that the whole idea was ill-conceived. Did not the Revolution give Alsatian Jews the opportunity of choosing any occupation they liked — asked their accusers, of Napoleon in 1806 — and what use did they make of it? [51] Moreover, even before that, during the Revolution, argued the burghers of Strassbourg, the Lettre Patente of 1784 gave the Jews of Alsace an opportunity to make themselves useful, and they even maintained — on doubtful grounds it is true — that no occupational restrictions had since 1753 deterred the Jews from the neighboring Lorraine.[52] Despite this, did not the Jews of Alsace and Lorraine cling to their old loves of trade, peddling, and usury? The Jewish answer to such recurring questions was that only a short period had elapsed, and hence these new opportunities had not yet been given a chance to take effect. "If it is true to say that evil works promptly and repairs itself only with extreme slowness, how can one demand that fifteen years . . . should suffice for affecting the disastrous and profound effects of many centuries of oppression and humiliation that pressed on the Jews," said Berr-Isaac Berr.[53] The main point in view was that Jews had shown themselves able to follow occupations which had, until that time, been regarded as beyond their capacities and ambition. The slowness of the process of economic transition did not destroy the belief in an eventual utopia where there would be an even distribution of Jews in all the occupational fields on which society is dependent.

Only later, and even then it only dawned on the most discerning observers, was it clear that the concentration of Jews in certain occupational fields was no ephemeral phenomenon but inherent in their status as a minority group with a special history and of a particular social and religious position.[54] As latecomers they were unable to enter en masse the fields of agriculture, handicrafts, civil services, or the standing army, for these areas were already occupied by other strata. On the other hand, Jews had their traditional occupations that gave them an advantage over others, and they had no reason to change these without particular motivation. Moreover, the very existence of the group as a religious and ethnic minority depended on their social cohesion which, in turn, drew them into common fields of economic activity. True, religion no longer represented too great a handicap in taking up any profession, since observance had dwindled and the neglect of it had the sanction of the Enlightenment and later the Reform movement. Nonetheless, being Jewish led toward certain occupations while discouraging others. Family ties bound the Jew closely to his own community and separated him from the bulk of the population. It was only natural that this social cohesion should influence the Jew in his choice of occupation; it would have been a risk to strike out for himself among strangers. When this happened and a Jew became an artisan, a proprietor, an army officer, he was probably isolated, and imagined, rightly or wrongly, that this was hampering his career. A Jewish father would have difficulty in apprenticing his son in those trades that were the prerogative of non-Jews. It was far easier to follow the line of least resistance and place him with a Jew. All this served to keep Jews within the range of the traditional occupations.

Where new economic possibilities arose as a result of new social and economic development, they attracted not one but many Jews who were on the lookout for new opportunities, thus once again concentrating them in the same profession. However much the range of Jewish occupation extended, Jews remained clustered together, whether in the old or in a new field of activity. Even where full emancipation had been achieved, most of the Jews were still engaged in occupations connected with the investment of capital, and around them hovered the newly hatched professionals and artists. In the eyes of observers, Jews appeared as a social group welded together by family, religious, social, and economic ties, a combination that very often led to their being designated, not too flatteringly, as "a caste." [55] Others called them — or at least the upper stratum of the rich — a new aristocracy that possessed a most important component of the economy, capital.[56] Such designations were not meant merely as sociological definitions but carried with them a critical and inimical undertone. Still, they were not fortuitous or whimsical inventions, for they owe their emergence to the fact that Jews were indeed a group, sui generis, among the other groups constituting European society in postrevolutionary times. Viewed in the light of two or three thousand years of Jewish history, this peculiarity of the Jewish group could be understood. Contemporaries, however, chose to ignore history and to judge the Jews of their time by the measure of the expectations that had emerged during the revolutionary era. Accordingly, it was assumed that entering European society would result in their shedding all Jewish peculiarities and possibly lead to complete absorption of the Jews by their environment. This was far from being the case. The tension that resulted from the tenacious Jewish peculiarities in conflict with the utopia of complete assimilation was a central feature in the history of the Jewish community in the postrevolutionary era.[57]

In perspective, the period of change and upheaval that swept through the Jewish communities in Western and Central European countries in the four to five decades that serve as background to this book may be viewed as an era of revolution. Transformations occurred in all walks of life and even the most conservative circles could not avoid being affected. This period in Jewish history has since then been recognized as a turning point, a period of transition that saw the dissolution of time-honored patterns and ushered in new trends and changes. Accordingly the period has been designated by a variety of names, depending on the different points of view. It was called "The Period of Enlightenment" or "Haskalah" when the intellectual climate of the time was considered, "Early Reform" when the issue of religion was in the foreground, and "Emancipation" when the period was evaluated from a political angle. There are no doubts about the propriety of the first two titles, naming the period one of Enlightenment or of incipient reform. That the period, in addition, deserves an appellation that reflects the change in the political status of the Jews is also clear. Still, the term Emancipation in this context is clearly a case of linguistic anachronism, for though it occasionally pops up in deliberations on the Jewish issue of that time, it was only from 1828 onward that the term became the magic formula for Jewish aspirations. Before that, other terms were in vogue such as "naturalization," the French term "régénération" and the German "Bürgerliche Verbesserung." [1]

This observation should not be dismissed as mere semantic quibble: for a disregard of the terminology applied by contemporaries may obscure the historical phenomena examined.

Naturalization, meaning the admittance of an alien to citizenship of a state, was admirably used, at the time the idea was first propounded, to indicate the change in the status of Jews in their respective countries. Where this Act of Naturalization was undertaken or performed by a state that did not uphold differences in estate or discriminate because of religious affiliation — and this was the case in France and Holland after the Revolution, and almost so in Prussia in 1812 — the Act of Naturalization implied full legal and political equality. In most countries under consideration, however, this was not the case. Austria and most of the other German states did somewhat reform the system of the Old Regime that was based on the different estates and the involvement of the state with Catholic or other Christian churches. As the estates lost ground and the influence of religion in public life diminished, it became possible to include the Jews in the body politic as members of a sort. Still, this certainly did not confer equality of rights and opportunities on them as the state hierarchy did not disappear overnight. The Jew became the subject of the state and occupied a very special place in the checkered pattern of its structure. True, the situation was not meant to be a final one; the whole state was on the move in the direction of reconstruction. Jews were on probation. Improvement in their situation was the bait dangled before their eyes — should they live up to expectations. The process of adaptation was adequately designated as civic betterment — a term introduced by Christian Wilhelm Dohm in his book *Über die bürgerliche Verbesserung der Juden* (1781), which hinted both at a reform of the Jews' habits, morals, and perhaps even religion, and a corresponding amelioration of their political status. The period depicted and analyzed in the previous chapters saw at least the initiation of this reform. The innovations in the different spheres of life were obvious and could scarcely be overlooked or contested. Still, their significance from the standpoint of the Jews' political status could be evaluated in several ways. Measured by the high expectations that accompanied the idea when it was first mooted — as summarized in the Image of the Future — the changes were rather slight, not affecting the layers of society too deeply, the reform being incomplete. The changes scratched only the surface; they certainly fell short of transforming Jewish society in accordance with what had been expected. Thus, when the period after the fall of Napoleon brought about a stagnation and even regression as far as Jewish rights were concerned, it could be justified by the inadequacy of the Jewish response in the preceding years when changes first occurred in the political status of the Jew.

The years 1814 to 1819 produced a new wave of anti-Jewish propaganda and animosity, ideologically nurtured by the awakening of nationalism and historical romanticism. The antagonists of Jews wished not only to stop any advances but even to reverse the trend. The Restoration period, following the Congress of Vienna, is characterized by tremendous efforts to reconstruct a political system resembling the Old Order and was thus most conducive to creating the climate of reaction also with regard to the status of the Jewish community.

But this was not to last. The ideas of 1789 were only slumbering and the political forces and social tendencies that led to the Revolution still had life in them. Increased industrialization and concomitant social mobility produced a comparatively independent middle class that felt rebuffed by the Restoration in France and entirely frustrated by the Reaction in Germany. Educated members of this class, and especially its intellectual elite, the intelligentsia, became the exponents of the Liberal movement that dreamt of and later fought for the reshuffling of the existing order supported by an enlightened social philosophy. An increasing number of Jews belonged to this striving and aspiring middle class — if it be defined by the economic function, social position, and intellectual equipment of its members. Thus, when the Liberal movement passed from social thinking to social action — and this started with the Revolution of 1830, Jews were abundantly represented among the rank and file and even the leaders of the movement.[2]

The Jewish community in the France of that day could already be regarded as an integrated part of state and society, although here, too, they faced some discrimination as evidenced in the retention of the special Jewish oath and the refusal of the state to defray the salaries of the rabbis when they were doing so in the case of clergymen.[3] Social acceptance and religious tolerance were certainly not yet complete facts. Thus Jews had very good reason to join the Liberals, who strove for a greater measure of social liberty and personal freedom. In Germany, Jews had more tangible complaints. In most German states they were still second-rate citizens — their inferiority marked by exclusion from state offices and teaching posts in universities as in Prussia, or as in Bavaria, where they were forced to submit to restrictions as regards rights of residence and permission to marry.[4] Still, it would not have done for Jews in Germany simply to support the Liberal movement and await the rectification of their grievances in the wake of its success. For the granting of Jewish rights unequivocally was not a settled issue with the Liberal movement. Many, otherwise liberal-minded, retained the traditional reservations against Jewish integration into state and society. If Jews wished to be heeded, they had to raise their voices separately, and this they did by initiating a campaign that was to influence public opinion as well as the organs and institutions of the state — the cabinets and parliaments where practical decisions would have to be taken.

The central figure of this campaign was Gabriel Riesser, an advocate from Hamburg, the grandson of Rabbi Raphael Cohen, who it will be recalled was one of the opponents of Mendelssohn's attempts at reform.[5] The grandson had come a long way from this conservatism. His religion, if any, was that of a deist who believed in God as the source of all goodness and morality, a creed he considered to be in harmony with original Jewish teaching. (Riesser's father, the son-in-law of Raphael Cohen, was an observant Jew with a leaning toward moderate reform). Indifferent toward religious observances, teachings, or ceremonies, Riesser kept aloof, preserving a superior distance from the internal struggle between Orthodox and Reform Jews. In his youth he was tempted by the possibility of conversion to Christianity, which would have opened the doors to a coveted academic career. Having rejected a private solution that, he thought, would impair his intellectual integrity, he could proudly evolve a loyalty, if not to any special Jewish doctrine, then to the political cause of the Jews. Committed to the idea of civic and

OUT OF THE GHETTO

personal freedom, he took up the cudgels on behalf of his Jewish brethren.[6]

At this juncture the fight for Jewish rights adopted the slogan Emancipation. The original word is from the Latin *emancipacio,* meaning the enfranchisement of a slave. The term entered the field of politics when the Irish Catholics at the end of the eighteenth century fought for political and religious freedom and "Catholic Emancipation" was the term that stuck to Catholic aspirations in Britain. The Catholics obtained their objectives in 1828; the Oath of Allegiance could now be taken on the Christian faith and no longer specifically on the Anglican. In the wake of this change the Jewish issue, which had lain dormant since the repeal of the Jew Bill in 1753, was brought up in Parliament. As long as non-Anglican Christians were excluded from office, Jews had no reason to feel discriminated against. Now that all restrictions were removed, Jews alone were left in the unenviable position of not being able to assume public office because they could not take the Oath of Allegiance. It may be recalled that Jews born in England were automatically British citizens, but the circumstances described here turned them into citizens with a politically exceptional and lower status. Against this status a struggle set in which, in its turn and following the Catholic example, was dubbed "Jewish Emancipation." From England the term traveled to Germany. Notwithstanding the differences between the two countries, they had one feature in common — that Jews at this time were acknowledged as citizens but did not enjoy equal rights with others. Thus the term Emancipation was appropriate here as in England.[7] It turned out to be a most efficient weapon: "A short but strong and impressive word" [8] as observed by the contemporary historian Isaac Marcus Jost. The struggle was fought in England, as in Germany and other countries, in protest against unjustified discrimination based on religious differences. The peculiarity of the Jewish group, formerly a national and ethnic unit of foreign origin, was well remembered. The opponents of emancipation saw to it that this should not be forgotten.[9] That, despite this, the Jews ultimately achieved full emancipation may be ascribed to two factors. First, the spirit of liberalism, which swept Europe in the middle of the nineteenth century, established the idea of the formal character of the state which, in return for certain obligations, safeguarded the security and legal rights of all its citizens. The state could disregard the qualities of citizens once their obligations had been rendered, and could include subjects of different religious and philosophical creeds and attitudes. True, there was an assumption that citizens would evolve a sentiment of loyalty for the state, stemming from their commitment to the national and cultural objectives it stood for. Jews, more and more, came to be regarded as being capable of similar sentiments. As the process of cultural assimilation continued they wore down immemorial barriers of estrangement so that amalgamation could be imagined in the foreseeable future. This was the second factor that assisted the progress of emancipation. Gabriel Riesser, in his argument, clearly anticipated the cultural adaptation of the whole Jewish community and, with this assumption, he vindicated the rights of the Jews to full emancipation.[10]

The actual progress of emancipation differed from country to country depending on what resistance it encountered as well as on the prevailing political structure and social system. In England, as mentioned, Jews took up the fight in the wake of Catholic emancipation. Thus the public debate on possible Jewish integration into a Christian commonwealth that had commenced in England some seventy-five years previously was reopened but, with liberalism in the ascendancy, the issue was fought in a more lenient spirit than either in eighteenth century England or in the countries on the Continent, where Jewish-Gentile relations were historically more burdened and actually a great deal more entangled. The number of Jews living in England in 1830 did not exceed 30,000, out of a population of about 15,000,000, and they were usually regarded as being foreign and strange but not especially obnoxious or objectionable. Yet there was some resistance to their occupying public offices that could only be worn down slowly and in the face of fierce resistance. The City of London elected Baron Lionel de Rothschild to Parliament as early as

1847 and he duly appeared to take his oath, believing that he would be allowed to take it in a way that would not conflict with his Jewish faith. As Parliament, however, insisted on retaining the Christian formula, Rothschild had to leave the House. Similar scenes were repeated in ensuing years when another Jew, Sir David Salomon, was elected to Parliament. Parliament was finally inclined to change the formula but the change depended on the consent of the House of Lords. This being the stronghold of the conservative element, it vetoed Parliament's decision until 1858 when it compromised, allowing a change in formula for the Commons but retaining the old formula for the House of Lords. This was the year when the first Jew, Lionel Rothschild, entered Parliament. In 1866 the impediment was also removed in the House of Lords.[11]

In Germany the struggle for emancipation was focused first on the legislative bodies of the respective states — the landtags and senates of the independent towns. Important improvement in their legal status was achieved by the Jews of Frankfurt and the country of Württemberg in 1824 and 1828 respectively. Free choice of occupation and rights of residence were obtained.[12] But these were piecemeal amendments that fell short of the coveted equality of rights. The principle of equality was accepted by the all-German assembly of Frankfurt in 1848–49 where Gabriel Riesser acted as vice-president and other Jews took part as members. But the Frankfurt assembly was a revolutionary body, unsuccessful in obtaining any of its aims. Jewish claims gained tremendous momentum in the revolutionary years 1848–49 without, however, managing to obtain full practical realization.[13] Jews, although undoubtedly citizens, labored under discriminatory restrictions. The fight against these went on during this whole period with alternating success, depending on circumstances and local conditions. A radical and universal remedy was secured only in 1866 and 1871 when, through the unification of the northern countries of Germany and then of the whole Reich by Bismarck, a new constitution, promulgated for the North German Federation in 1869, accepted the principle of citizenship independent of religious confession. As far back as 1847 Bismarck, as a member of the Landtag of Prussia, expressed his view that the access of Jews to all public offices including that of judge, would be incompatible with the Christian character of the state. Events, however, steered him to a more secular conception of the great state under his rule, and he accepted the consequences also with regard to the Jews.[14] Emancipation, in Germany as elsewhere, can be said to have been achieved more by the general trend of public sentiment in these countries than by the victory of its champions or the weight of their arguments in favor of the Jews.

Events in Austria-Hungary followed a similar course. The revolution of 1848–49 impelled the government here to grant its people a liberal constitution that included freedom of worship and equal rights, irrespective of religious affiliation. In Hungary the revolutionary government of Kossuth decided in favor of Jewish emancipation. As the Hungarian revolt was suppressed and the revolution in other parts of Austria abated, full emancipation failed to materialize; still, the old order of restriction — as regards residence, occupational choice, and permission to marry, especially in Moravia and Bohemia — was gone. The reshuffling of the Austrian Empire in the wake of its conflict with Prussia in 1866 brought about political equality in all parts of the empire, including Hungary, where the semi-independent government granted full emancipation in 1867.[15]

With the possible exception of France and Holland where emancipation was achieved at one stroke (though in France it still suffered a setback in the time of Napoleon), the emancipation of the Jews was the result of a struggle that merged with the process of social and political changes leading these countries to a greater measure of modernization and constitutionalism. It was possible to link the case of the Jews with the general trend toward modernization only because in the preceding period — that of reform and civic betterment — the Jew was tacitly or explicitly acknowledged as a citizen of the state. Once this was accepted, the aspiration toward full citizenship and equality followed immediately and a claim for citizenship could be made on good ideological grounds. The realization of this hope depended on general development in the country; where, as in Western countries, the transformation from a semifeudal to a constitutional state was achieved, there Jewish emancipation, too, became a legally secured fact.

The realization of civic equality for Jews should not be interpreted, however, as meaning that the reservations about their integration into state and society had disappeared or even substantially receded. The arguments against integration continued to be heard; they varied in accordance with the changing situation and the new trends in social philosophy that appeared on the scene. The late Napoleonic period saw the ascendancy of nationalism based on historical romanticism and Christian symbolism. The rejection of the past and its traditions by rationalists was now superseded by a revival of the values and concepts of former times by the romanticists. German nationalism and Christianity — conceived of in terms of a weltanschauung and a spiritual force rather than as a system of beliefs — were identified or at least strongly associated with each other. Jews found themselves excluded by definition from any social unit — whether the state or any voluntary association — based upon such criteria. Indeed, this philosophy of historical romanticism produced some of the strongest negations of Jewish integration and even Jewish existence, voiced especially by the Berlin historian Friedrich Rühs and the philosopher Jacob Friedrich Fries of Heidelberg. These two appeared on the scene after the Congress of Vienna when Jewish aspirations to civic rights suffered a setback, helped along by anti-Jewish theories and ideologies that sprouted into being.[16] When the Liberal movement gained support in the 1830's, the prospects of the Jewish cause seemed brighter; still, among liberals, too, there arose opponents of the Jewish cause, as exemplified by Heinrich E. G. Paulus, who found Jews to be morbidly attached to their particularistic laws and customs, which precluded their belonging to a society based upon laws of universal validity. In virtue of this argument, Paulus rejected the claims Gabriel Riesser put forward in favor of Jewish emancipation and became his most virulent antagonist.[17] Ten years later the Jewish issue became entangled with the emerging radicalism of Hegelian origin. This revolutionary school, rejecting religion as well as all social tradition, wished to remodel society in accordance with preconceived principles. In the light of such a philosophy it would have seemed likely that the differences between Jews and non-Jews would disappear. Yet one of the great radical exponents of the school, Bruno Bauer, found that Jews represent the incarnation of petrified tradition and therefore had no place in the new society conceived by the radical philosophers.[18]

These novel doctrines about Jewish incompatibility were evolved in German countries, where they served as ideological crutches for the resistance to full emancipation for Jews. But anti-Jewish theories were alive also in France, where the legal equality of Jews was a long established fact. In Alsace the old charges against the Jewish usurer who effected the ruin of the unprotected peasant were still alive, and were being hauled forth to substantiate the claim that a remedy lay in the revocation of complete emancipation.[19] But the anti-Jewish theories did not always have an immediate political target. They were sometimes combined with general social criticism as, for instance, in the case of Pierre J. Proudhon, who sought to replace the regime based on capitalism by a social system consisting of free associations of a cooperative nature. The society of that day came in for severe criticism, no section more so than the Jews who, in Proudhon's view, represented the characteristic features of capitalism such as avidity and greed.[20] This combination of anticapitalism and anti-Jewishness found its concise expression in the title of a book *Les Juifs, rois de l'époque. Histoire de la féodalité financière* by Alphonse Toussenel, a follower of Proudhon.[21] Jews were identified with those in possession of capital and the old prejudice against Jews merges with the socialist rejection of developing capitalism.[22]

The anti-Jewish theories and ideologies could not undo the results of emancipation where it had been achieved, nor prevent its accomplishment where it had not yet been fully implemented. The theories, firstly, were not held by everyone, and for every anti-Jewish pamphlet there were other publications favoring Jews. Then, as observed, the political fate of the Jews did not depend on whether or not their cause was espoused. Rather, it was the result of the general way in which the modern state was developing. This was, however, different when social acceptance or cultural integration was in question.

The social amalgamation of the Jews with their neighbors was one of the main features conceived by the promoters of Jewish emancipation. Yet even at the height of ideological rapprochement they were unable to create more than a semineutral society where the inferior status of the Jews was ignored by conscious effort rather than eliminated by actual equality. The number of Jews who became regular members of non-Jewish social groups remained small — and not because of a lack of self-appointed candidates. The more traditional Jewish society disintegrated, the greater became the number of enlightened Jews who looked around for new social ties and commitments. In most cases, however, they had to find their own circles in order to satisfy their social needs and only in exceptional cases did they succeed in making an entry into non-Jewish societies. Even where on the plane of ideological reasoning the anti-Jewish attitude was rejected as obsolete prejudice, reservations against associating with Jews persisted. This is well borne out by the history of Freemasonry, a society that owed its conception to the idea of religious tolerance. Although the admissibility of Jews was implied in the wording of the consitution, resistance to actual acceptance or even evasion by a reinterpretation of the letter of the constitution became the order of the day wherever substantial numbers of Jewish candidates for Freemasonry appeared on the scene. In such cases Jews had to put up their own Jewish lodges conforming to others in principle, but consisting exclusively of Jews. In spite of some conspicuous social rapprochement between Jews and non-Jews, such as the Berlin salons that made a great stir in the public eye, the bulk of the Jewish population and even the enlightened section of it remained aloof.[23]

When ideologies and politics took a turn toward Christian romanticism and nationalism, the social gap between Jew and Christian was bound to widen. Even while the process of legal equalization went on in the latter phase of the Napoleonic rule in

Europe, the reaction against mixing with Jews in society was already setting in. When the Berlin and Frankfurt burghers had to put up with the granting of civil rights in their states (1811 in Frankfurt, 1812 in Prussia), the Freemason lodges introduced new paragraphs in their constitution excluding Jews from membership.[24] Then, during the era of Restoration and Reaction, Christian exclusiveness became the order of the day in all Christian circles. That was a time of great frustration for the well-educated Jew who thought himself qualified for the surrounding society but was nevertheless rejected by it. When Liberalism gained the upper hand in the thirties, the balance was once again somewhat corrected. Voluntary societies, among them many of the Freemason lodges — even in Germany — were open to Jews and in artistic, intellectual, and other less conventional groups Jews did mix with non-Jews.[25]

But these achievements in the social sphere remained a far cry from the vision that had sustained Jews when they first started to leave behind the boundaries of their traditional society. This vision embraced the idea of free contact between Jew and non-Jew that would lead to cooperation and friendship resting on personal association, unhampered by the prejudices which clung to the image of the Jews. This utopian view of the future was never to become reality. Jews, even in countries where they had obtained political freedom, were economically advanced, and assimilated culturally, remained separate, even conspicuously so.

The phenomenon of social disassociation even when Jews enjoyed political equality received conflicting interpretations. The apologetic approach attributed it to persistent Christian exclusiveness, maintaining that Jews never had a real chance to integrate socially. The inimical explanation or interpretation maintained that it was the Jewish inclination to particularism that prevented them from crossing the boundaries of their own society — in anti-Semitic version adding a vicious intention to this adhesion. Thus the controversy on Jewish sociability followed in the wake of the polemic on Jewish emancipation. It loomed large not only among the Freemasons, to whom the question of the social adaptability of Jews was a central issue,[26] but it played a part also among those whose main concern was with the Jews' political status. Opponents of complete emancipation such as Heinrich E. G. Paulus (1830)[27] and, some years later, Karl Streckfuss,[28] used the argument that Jews would not associate themselves with others and therefore were not worthy of full citizenship, which presupposes cultural adaptation and social amalgamation. The protagonists of Jewish rights retorted that Jews would be only too glad to associate with non-Jews but were hindered in this by Christian exclusiveness.

Viewed historically or sociologically, the share of Jews or Christians respectively in producing the phenomenon of social cleavage between them cannot be neatly apportioned. Both groups simply retained some of their reservations toward each other that had in the not-too-distant past kept them divided, to all intents and purposes, as two separate entities. At that time, Jews and Christians did not intermarry, in fact, did not even mix socially, their contact being restricted to the economic field or other circumscribed situations of a businesslike nature. The mutual avoidance was buttressed by religious ideas and prescriptions and reinforced by legal discrimination. When this discrimination disappeared, the breakdown of social and religious barriers became a theoretical possibility at times, and in some places some of the barriers did disappear. Many Jews, and perhaps most Christians, ignored prohibitions with regard to eating one another's food or in each other's company. This made convivial meetings a possibility. But the removal of ritual restrictions, though it made social contact between Jews and non-Jews possible, did not necessarily encourage or promote it. Meetings between Jews and non-Jews continued to be regarded as encounters between members of separate societies that differed in both status and quality. Special motivation was needed for such meetings and when they took place they were accompanied by self-conscious evaluation of the event. All things being equal, the Jew was the one who gained when a Gentile of similar cultural and economic standing deigned to meet him just for the meeting's sake. The non-Jew was at once suspect, an ulterior motive was immediately ascribed to him and the meeting robbed of whatever ease or innocence it might have had. Accordingly, such meetings became events that could not pass unobserved. When the diplomats of the Congress of Vienna feasted in the rich house of the Arnheims[29] or the emissaries of the German state, meeting at Frankfurt, dined at the generous table of the Rothschilds,[30] this was carefully noted by contemporaries and so were similar occurrences in Berlin and Paris fifty years later when the Paris Rothschilds were honored by the presence of high society[31] or the Bleichröders gave a great ball — excluding their own kith and kin.[32] Jews were noted for their exaggerated hospitality and show on these occasions and Gentiles laid themselves open to criticism for taking advantage of this opulent hospitality and returning it only by a gracious bestowal of their presence. Probably meetings on a lower social level called forth similar comments.

The lower status of the Jews was not the main cause for their comparative social seclusion. Even when granted freedom to choose their occupations where they would, Jews adhered to certain economic fields. This alone would have facilitated contact between Jew and Jew. Religious institutions, too, fostered social relations; synagogues, Orthodox or Reform, and voluntary societies established for charitable or other purposes, which will be described in a moment, assisted a lively social intermingling. The chance for a Jew to know a fellow Jew really intimately was statistically greater than his chance to know a non-Jew. His social separation from non-Jewish society was thus influenced by his professional preference and his religious affiliation; conversely, it would also be true to say that his social exclusiveness reinforced his inclination for certain professions and adherence to the religious community into which he had been born.

But there is a third factor that markedly reinforced the Jewish tendency to remain a society apart, namely, an inclination for endogamy, that is, the wish among Jews to marry among themselves which corresponded to a similar inclination among Christians. In pre-emancipation times the ban on intermarriage between Jews and non-Jews was ensured by the strengh of ecclesiastical and Halakic — respectively for Christians and Jews — laws, supported by the state. When and where civil marriage was introduced, as for instance in France after the Revolution and in most modern countries in the course of time, intermarriage became legally possible. Still, the number of intermarriages remained small;[33] Jews resisted it socially and ideologically as strongly as they did conversion. If it did happen, it was tantamount to defection from the Jewish family and society, for marrying out of the faith led, in most cases, to a conversion to Christianity. The practical result of intermarriage was a loss to the Jewish community. The character of community as such remained untouched by the intermarriages of individuals, for they did not create family or social ties. On the contrary they created, by way of rejection and reaction, a greater measure of reservation.

Critics of Jewish society, friendly and unfriendly alike, often took it to task for its stubborn resistance to intermarriage. They interpreted this as a sign of arrogance and indicative of the Jews' contempt for their neighbors or even for all their fellow men. As long as the division between Jews and Christians was socially complete and both legally and religiously sanctioned, there was little room for such reproach. Mutual exclusiveness was only natural. With the crumbling of the social structure that supported separation, the ideological justification for intermarriage was impaired. Of course, among those over whom religion still retained its authority and control, the ban on intermarriage could be represented as simply part of a larger system. But, in fact, resistance to intermarriage persisted even where Jews had already become casual as to faith and indifferent to religious observance. This type of resistance to intermarriage could be dubbed atavistic in that it represented an adherence to a pattern of behavior after the reason for it had disappeared.

Historically the Jewish aversion to create family connections with external groups is of course one of the central factors that ensured their survival in the Diaspora. As a minority group living in the midst of other nations they faced the possibility of absorption by the majority — unless some force of resistance would manifest itself in what the sociologist would call a defense mechanism. The whole system of Jewish religious practice, dietary laws as well as the observance of special days of feast and fast, backed by faith in the divine significance of Jewish separateness, can be seen as such a mechanism of defense. This definition can be accepted without conceding an underlying vitalistic assumption, an innate drive for self-preservation that lay at the root of Jewish survival. Whatever the explanation of the origin of Jewish perseverance, whether historical, philosophical, or theological, it is a fact that at the end of the traditional period it became a force in itself, independent of the continued existence of the factors that had brought it forth. In spite of the crumbling of tradition and the weakening of religious commitments, Jewish cohesion persisted.

Many of those who strove for the legal acceptance of the Jews maintained the hope that as a result of their new status the Jewish community would dissolve and its members merge with the surrounding society. This expectation, however, failed to materialize even where full emancipation became a fact. Although suffering some erosion numerically, Jewry continued to exist. It survived the dissolution of the organizational framework that had kept the Jews separated from their neighbors and the passing of those ideas and ideologies that had sustained that apartness. The attachment of most of the members of the Jewish community to one another, although difficult to account for, remained a source of strength and the mainspring of the community's survival.

It will be remembered that the critics of Jewish integration defined the Jews, even after emancipation, as a caste.[34] The basic argument for this charge was Jewish inbreeding and social apartness. Political equality, economic advance, or cultural adaptation did not dispel the charge. The alterations that had occurred in the status, position, and attitude of the Jews seemed to its adversaries insignificant in view of the fact that socially — especially as far as family ties were concerned — they remained aloof from the wider society around them. The Jewish response and adaptation to the new conditions seemed to have been fictitious or superficial only.

Protagonists of Jewish emancipation and integration dismissed the charge as malevolent, maintaining that such inimical evaluation of Jewish attitudes was itself the reason for Jewish apartness that under more favorable conditions would disappear. Radical assimilationists accepted the thesis that in the long run Jews would have to amalgamate with the society in whose midst they lived. They demanded that Jewish religion give up its emphatic reservations about intermarriage and some even fancied that legal or social pressure could be exercised to facilitate family ties between Jews and Gentiles.[35] Most supporters of integration, however, preferred to minimize the problem rather than to seek practical solutions. As the choice of mate is a personal matter, it could obviously not be the concern of political institutions; the state has only to legalize whatever the choice proves to be. Indeed, liberal-minded Jews often advocated civil marriages in those states where it had not yet been introduced, even when from the Jewish standpoint they would have disapproved of intermarriage with Christians. They wished to assure the legal possibility of intermarriage but hoped, nevertheless, that Jews would not avail themselves of it.[36] This hope could be rationalized on religious grounds. The recommendation that Jew should marry Jew could be based upon the observable fact that the Jewish religion could hardly be preserved — not to speak of bringing up children as Jews — in a mixed family.[37] Jewish apartness could then be presented as a result of the religious commitment of Jews.

In theory Jewish religion could be defined as resting on personal faith and conviction. As early as 1816, Michael Hess, a teacher in the Philantropin School in Frankfurt, defined Judaism (in his polemic with Friedrich Rühs) as a mere confession of faith, on the same plane as other religious denominations.[38] In the following decades, this conception gained much currency and was held by politicians like Gabriel Riesser[39] and expounded by theologians like Abraham Geiger.[40]

From the politicians' standpoint the definition of Jewish religion as the individual's confession of faith was an appropriate and convenient one. The theory provided justification for the claim that Jews could be regarded as just one more religious group among others. The Jewish theologian, who had to vindicate this definition in the light of Jewish tradition, was hard put to do so, for the literary sources of the Bible and Talmud and the facts of Jewish history did not tally with this concept; rather, they revealed the Jews as a people, or at least a community, constituted by common descent and attachment to a cultural heritage. Jewish law and teachings conceived of the Jewish community as not only a religious congregation but as a people with a distinct ancestry, a documented history, and a well-defined destiny. The process of dissolving the community into separate and unrelated parts living in different countries was a revolutionary trend, and the hope that they would amalgamate with the surrounding nations was one that defied three thousand years of history and tradition. Many of those who sought to bring about this change, particularly the non-Jews, saw in it a liquidation of Jewish history and a termination of the existence of the Jewish community. Most Jewish theologians and lay leaders, however, wished the community to go on existing and even to find its ideological moorings in tradition. They had then to make an effort to reconcile their notions of Jewish religion with the traditional elements. This was no easy task. All the mental energy of the first two or three generations of the emancipation period went into this undertaking.[41] The first attempts have already been analyzed. The reform movement had a double purpose. It sought a legitimate way to ease the yoke of the law for the modern Jew so that he could pursue his career, achieve his economic aims, and make his way into non-Jewish society. This was, so to speak, the practical aspect of reform. Not less important was its theoretical objective: to evolve a comprehensive philosophy of Judaism that would be in harmony with the status of the modern Jew as a citizen of the non-Jewish state and a member of a non-Jewish society. This could only be effected by a thorough sifting of traditional tenets, omitting parts that seemed irreconcilable with the new position of the Jews, and introducing, or at least reemphasizing, tenets that seemed to be appropriate to the new situation.

Biblical and even Talmudic Judaism, although it focused for the most part on the Jewish people, and was in this sense particularistic, nevertheless also had universalistic elements, containing laws that were obligatory for all men and envisaging a time when all mankind would be united in the worship of the one true God. Reform Judaism chose to accentuate these elements or to omit or neglect the conflicting notions that were no less a part of that same tradition. The turning point when the conception of Judaism as revealed law — as it was still maintained by Mendelssohn — was discarded in favor of its acceptance as a body of dogma and moral teachings has already been observed. This view was first propounded by Saul Ascher and pursued subsequently by most theologians and philosophers who expounded Judaism in the liberal era. Seen in this light, Judaism appeared as a confession of faith like other confessions and the Jewish community as a group united by its adherence to an abstract body of teachings.

This was the theory. In the realm of fact and actual attitude, the adherence to Judaism scarcely depended upon a conviction of the truth of any particular set of doctrines. Actually the Jew faced a dilemma: should he succumb to the temptation of society-at-large if it involved accepting Christianity or remain a member of the socially inferior minority. The deciding factor in his choice was not so much his conviction of the truth of Judaism as a reluctance to impair his intellectual integrity, unconvinced as he was of the validity of the Christian dogmas. The unconverted remained Jews and were regarded as such whatever their attitude was toward Judaism. During the nineteenth century this meant, in most countries of Europe, that they had to belong to a Jewish community that was organized under the protection of the state. Of course, although membership in the Jewish community was compulsory, it could remain a formality and be limited to the payment of dues and taxes. Whether the member participated in the organizational and spiritual activities of the community was up to him. Reform communities, one supposes, attracted some congregants by adapting to contemporary taste and by omitting what seemed to contradict accepted convictions. Still, this does not mean that Judaism became a mere profession of faith. A Jew was considered as such not so much because of his religious attitude but because he had been born of Jewish parents. Being Jewish had its social implications, which could not be evaded, quite apart from the individual's disposition toward Jewish teachings or religious obligations. As a somewhat cynical observation of Heinrich Heine had it, "Jewishness was an incurable malady." Paradoxically, the status that had its basis in a biological fact could only be escaped through baptism, an act that was by definition a purely spiritual one. In reality, baptism carried with it a social transition, the transference of the baptized from his original minority group to the majority, where, in the course of time, traces of his origin tended to disappear. In contrast, to remain a Jew meant belonging to a social group whose nature, primarily, had been historically determined and owed less to the personal and spiritual characteristics of its members.

The tendency to fashion a Judaism that was simply a confession of faith was not shared by all. Orthodoxy, whether old-fashioned or modernized, could not but adhere to the traditional conception, by whose lights a Jew is one who is born of a Jewish mother — irrespective of his actions or convictions. True, Orthodoxy condemned any deviation from Jewish tradition in point of dogma or observances, and, in some countries — Hungary in 1869 and Prussia in 1875 — this led to a formal schism with the Reform communities. Orthodoxy went so far as to declare itself a religion, apart from the Reform.[42] But this position was primarily a tactical one. They won thereby the right to set up under government auspices separate communal organizations, but they never sought to deny that anyone born of a Jewish mother, be he Orthodox or Reform, observant or atheist, belonged to the Jewish nation. As Orthodoxy adhered to Jewish tradition and especially to the Halakah (religious law), it could hardly dismiss one of the law's basic principles: that being Jewish was a question of descent rather than of conviction.

Concepts deriving from Jewish tradition were, however, no longer the only means of defining and understanding the phenomenon of Judaism. Enlightenment had provided the tools of rationalistic criticism. Under the harsh light of reason the integrity of Jewish tradition began to dissolve, and distinctions between essential and nonessential features of Judaism seemed to reveal themselves to the rationalistic observer. The Reform movement, especially in its early days, made much use of this differentiation, and by claiming to discard only the nonessential elements, dispensed with many of the traditional religious practices.

In the course of time, however, a third method of assessing Judaism arose, that of historical criticism. This was evolved, or rather adopted, from current European scholarship by the founders of the so-called Wissenschaft des Judentums.[43] This group, headed by Yomtov Lipman Zunz (1794–1886) attempted to understand Judaism by employing the generally accepted tools of historical research. Seen in historical perspective, Judaism appeared as a unique phenomenon, but still not beyond the reach of historical categories. The members of the historical school took different stands with regard to contemporary problems of Judaism, and, some of them, like Zunz himself, at first a radical reformer and later inclined to a conservative stand, tended to vacillate in their attitude to tradition. The first proponents of Judaic studies thought that historical research and understanding would also serve as a sure guide in establishing the new shape that Judaism was to take, or to be more precise, in recapturing the pristine one that had been lost in the course of centuries. In fact, however, instead of providing a sure guide to the future, historical research only encouraged every shade of Reform to strive for and assert its claim to history, on the basis of differing interpretations of the past. Everyone agreed that the essential parts of tradition should be salvaged for future generations and the accidental discarded. But they differed radically on where to draw the line. Zechariah Frankel (1801–1875) reached the conclusion that the bulk of ritual and Halakah had to be retained while Abraham Geiger wished in principle to discard almost the whole body of ritual precepts and ceremony in the hope that the spirit of Judaism — whatever this meant in abstracto — would re-create the proper continuation of Judaism both in content and in expression. Surely the historical approach did not settle the controversy between the different schools, but it did provide a term of reference. By focusing attention on history, it checked the tendency toward abstraction that had been instrumental in turning Judaism into a confession of faith.[44]

When speaking of the beginning of reform, it was noted that Saul Ascher hoped that Halakic experts — those who ensured the continuity of Judaism by constant reinterpretation of the law — would be superseded by the theologians, who would expound the obligatory tenets of the Jewish faith.[45] The Halakist disappeared or lost his hold on the community but the theologians were slow to assume the roles that had been allotted them in his scheme of things. They almost failed to put in an appearance. Instead, Judaism fell into the hands of historians who described the events of the past and reinterpreted them historically. Then along came the philosophers with their interpretation of Judaism as a system of beliefs, a weltanschauung. Historians and philosophers alike were however unable to offer a direct guide as to what was obligatory observance or essential beliefs. True, both offered new terms of reference. A knowledge of the past at least gave some meaning to the Judaism of the present and held out some hope for the future. Both philosophical and historical works on Judaism dwelt on the beneficial role it had assumed in the past and hinted at a possible destiny where it might furnish its adherents with a cause worth serving. Indeed, it is the much discussed and reviled idea of the Jewish mission that colored the ideas of many Jewish thinkers of the nineteenth century. Sometimes this was carefully and exactly spelled out, setting out what role Jewish teaching and example had to fill. In its less explicit form, the historical and philosophical analysis of Jewish teaching conveyed an idea of what Judaism may still stand for — at least assuring the contemporary Jew that his being a Jew is not an altogether deplorable fact.[46]

Theories that vindicated Judaism were of importance if only to keep the Jew within the fold. The continuation of Jewish organizations and public functions were no less in need of justification. Their maintenance ran counter to the expectation of assimilationists, who thought Jews would find their social and spiritual needs fulfilled — with the exception of the strictly religious —

OUT OF THE GHETTO

within the institutions of their Christian neighbors. Any organization catering for specifically Jewish needs seemed needlessly conspicuous. This view was held even by benevolent observers, such as the historian Theodor Mommsen, who looked aghast at the profusion of Jewish societies and organizations dedicated to some purpose that could theoretically have been just as well achieved by non-Jewish institutions already in existence.[47] These associations included the traditional charitable institutions: distribution of alms, education of the poor, supporting the sick, and so on. Some had been founded to sustain Jewish research and learning; others to further the interests of Jewish communities abroad that had not yet been emancipated; some of them were only created for social purposes. All these societies and their communal activities were publicized by the Jewish press, which, far from being dedicated to religious subjects, gave prominence to all community and political matters.

A look at Jews and the activities of Jews in the decades of the growing emancipation — between 1848 and 1880 — shows that the picture is not a process of assimilation pure and simple. Assimilation, it is true, makes progress insofar as some Jews are coming into more intimate contact with non-Jews and all Jews more and more adopt the cultural patterns of their surroundings. But, at the same time, Jews also create the instruments that continue to hold them together and help them to maintain a separate social identity. The conception of Jews as a congregation existing merely by virtue of a common confession of faith functioned only on the theoretical level. In reality they retained the characteristics of a subgroup in society, recognizable by its ethnic origin, its economic concentration, its comparative social isolation, and by its nonconformist minority religion. The social countenance of this group differs greatly of course from the face the Jewish community presented a hundred years previously when Jews were a tolerated group, ecologically concentrated, economically strictly limited, and socially and culturally thoroughly isolated. At that time the group was tightly organized and disciplined while religion served as a mighty force for unification. Now, in the second half of the nineteenth century, Jews were divided among themselves in point of religion — the common denominator may almost be said to have been the rejection of Christianity. Cultural isolation was almost completely gone, and the economic one-sidedness at least ameliorated. What remained unimpaired was Jewish inbreeding, the maintaining of exclusively Jewish family ties. This, and the residues of that religious nonconformity, comparative economic concentration and social isolation, and some cultural peculiarity still gave the Jewish group a special physiognomy. If the group was different from what it had been a century before, it certainly had not assumed the characteristics expected by those who propounded the idea of fusion with Christian society.

Yet another expectation that had been held by those who struggled for emancipation failed to be realized in the wake of their success. The promoters of the Jewish cause, together with many Jews, imagined that emancipation of the Jewish inhabitants of any particular country would mean their absorption by the rest of the population and concomitantly the connection between them and the Jewish communities of different countries would be weakened and perhaps even cease altogether. The governments that granted citizenship to Jews of their countries at the same time took legislative steps to prevent the influx of foreign Jews.[48] The idea behind these measures was, and sometimes it was stated in so many words, that as each country absorbed its portion of Jews the phenomenon of an interstate community would disappear.

In the first decade of Jewish integration there were actually some indications of a loosening of the ties that bound together the Jewish communities all over the world. The acquisition of citizenship by Jews in the lands of their residence created bonds of allegiance to political institutions. It bred a genuine patriotism, albeit not always free of the ardor of the newly converted. The new generation, reared in the modern educational institutions, was molded into the prevailing cultural pattern. Jews learned the language of their environment, losing at the same time the common Jewish language, Hebrew, and the lingua franca of the Ashkenazim, Yiddish, and of the Sephardim, Ladino. The linguistic diversification reflected also a difference in culture, mentality, and outlook. If until the era of emancipation, the Jews of Frankfort, Amsterdam, Prague, and Lemberg could understand one another's language, several generations later this was no longer true. At times it might have seemed to some observers that the Jewish nation was about to disintegrate and the pieces to merge into their surroundings.

This trend toward disintegration did not however run its full course. Jews adapted themselves to the customs of their countries but did not entirely divest themselves of the ties with Jews beyond their immediate borders. Economic as well as cultural and family connections between Jews living in different countries persisted. Businessmen continued to deal with each other; rabbis, teachers, and scholars accepted appointments in foreign countries;[49] and rich families sought suitable matches across the borders. Jewish interest in public affairs was not confined to what happened in one country; on the contrary, the very struggle for emancipation was conducted with an eye on what was happening throughout Western Europe, the achievement in one place serving as an incentive to another.

Similarly, attempts at educational and religious reform within Judaism became rapidly a Continental movement, and advocates in one country looked upon those in another as brothers in arms. The opponents of reform similarly joined forces, as can be seen in the Hamburg polemic of 1819 when rabbis from Germany, Italy, Holland, and Austria united in the common cause.[50] Jewish periodicals multiplied from the 1840's on, and these catered not only to the local population but also served to disseminate information on Jews and Judaism all over the world.[51]

Thus not only the persistence of old habits, but paradoxically, the very attempts at integration with the environing society, reinforced a sense of international community. The old solidarity between Jews remained. Although dissolution into particular communities in different countries was envisaged, sympathy and practical help went forth from Jew to Jew whenever the need arose. Though immigration was impeded by legislation, it could not be entirely suppressed. Polish Jews continued to emigrate to

Germany and Hungary; Bohemian and Moravian Jews flocked to Hungary; German Jews found their way to Paris, Amsterdam, and London. Poorer immigrants were assured the assistance of the local Jews even if the migration was viewed unfavorably by those Jews themselves. While the dissolution of Jewry into regional communities may have had the support of an ideology, the sentiment of solidarity was a living force.

The extent of this force was illustrated by the events of 1840 in Damascus. Jews were accused by local authorities of causing the death of a French monk and his servant. Jewish communities and notables all over Europe exerted themselves to extricate their fellow Jews, by political pressure and public protest. The rescue was finally effected by the visits of Sir Moses Montefiore from England and Adolphe Cremieux from France, who proceeded to Alexandria and intervened with Mehemet Ali.[52] This event marked a turning point for cooperation between already integrated Jewish communities. Significantly the trend emerged first in France in the community most advanced in political equality. French Jewry felt itself politically secure and could allow itself to assist other Jewish communities without incurring the accusation of dual loyalty. As an outcome of this struggle the idea was born of an organization of emancipated Jews bridging national barriers, for the purpose of furthering the emancipation of other Jews and stimulating their cultural advancement. This then became the program of the Alliance Israélite Universelle, which was finally established in 1860,[53] a step that demonstrated even on the level of formal organization that the integration of Jews into their respective countries does not mean the severing of their international ties. Indeed the trend as well as the activities of the Alliance — among them establishing the first agricultural school in Palestine (1870) and thereby initiating modern Jewish colonization there — foreshadowed the Jewish National Renaissance that was eventually to turn back the tide of disintegration.

Jews entered European society but did not merge with it. Rather, their community became a novel and singular social entity, and at the same time, a thoroughly changed but recognizable variation of the ancient Jewish community. This variation of the community both in internal structure and external appearance differed basically from what the promoters of Jewish integration had imagined. Instead of a new religious community belonging entirely to the surrounding society, there emerged a kind of subgroup differing from the general population in occupational distribution, in family attachment, and in its connections with, and commitments to, a community beyond the local units. It could, of course, be argued — and Jewish apologists did so emphatically — that similar features were to be found in other subgroups of society. Protestants in France were a socially recognizable group and Catholics everywhere were bound in allegiance to the ultramontane church and its head. Still, their adhesion locally and their interstate solidarity were more conspicuous in Jews than in other groups. Then, too, Jews scarcely stood a chance of being judged on a par with others.

The dissimilarity, indeed the uniqueness, of their past; the singularity of their contemporary social situation; plus the web of superstitions about them current for centuries rendered the Jewish position in society anomalous. Anomaly of this kind was not necessarily a reason for arousing opposition. In England, Holland, and in the Scandinavian countries, the Jewish influx was accepted as a special addition to the social spectrum. This was also the case with benevolent and tolerant elements in France, Germany, Austria, and Hungary. The bulk of the population, however, hardly ever overcame its reservations against the Jewish variant in their society; and intolerant, malcontent, and intransigent elements would single out Jews as targets for criticism and even as a source of evil to which all the burdens and shortcomings of modern society could be attributed. Such accusations accompanied the process of Jewish integration from the very beginning, though they did seem to disappear when in the 1860's and '70's the Jewish cause prospered and full emancipation was achieved; nevertheless, they were only to return later at the end of the 1870's and '80's with the onset of the new anti-Semitic movements. Even then no one could foretell to what excesses this would lead within two or three generations in the 1930's and '40's. Indeed, only a fatalistic conception of history would take for granted that the eventual catastrophe was predetermined by earlier events.

The expectations connected with the exodus from the ghetto might better have been realized had that exodus taken place simultaneously in the entire Jewish world; if the Jews had been granted emancipation in all countries at the same time. Exposed to the influence of its environment and undisturbed by external factors, each community could have adapted itself to the social and cultural patterns of its surroundings. Rapid and radical assimilation might have overcome the reservation and resistance of the absorbing society and a fusion of Jews and gentiles could indeed have resulted.

Although speculation on the possible results of a contingency that did not arise is not the métier of the historian, he may be permitted to indulge himself if his speculation puts real events in a sharper perspective. Of course, Jewish emancipation was not contemporaneous. As indicated in the introductory chapter, even in the Western countries there was a lag; two or three generations passed between the emancipation of French Jewry during the Revolution and that of the Jewish communities of such countries as Austria-Hungary and Germany toward the end of the liberal era. Only then with the ascent of Alexander II (1855–1881) did the great Russian Jewish community, still laboring under repressive laws and restrictive conditions, see the first glimmer of hope for emancipation. However, this was not to be realized until the revolution of 1917. Throughout this period, the Jews of the Balkans and those of the Near East and North Africa either engaged themselves in the struggle for equality or endured passively the status of a degraded minority, while seeking help from their more fortunate brethren in the West. In fact, the fate of the unemancipated communities held the attention of those who had already achieved citizenship or even equality. At the same time a slow but steady migration brought Jews from the less emancipated communities to the more emancipated ones. Both concern for their unemancipated brethren and their emigration to liberated communities slowed down the assimilation of those communities. The time gained permitted the incursion of forces that counteracted assimilation — anti-semitism from without and the national movement from within.

Since the diaspora extended throughout the Christian and Moslem world, the Jews found themselves in countries at varying stages of social and political development. Consequently, simultaneous emancipation could never have been expected. A retardation of the process of assimilation was historically conditioned and inevitable. The anticipation of an abruptly dissolving Jewish community in the wake of emancipation was no more than a dream; the wishful thinking of Jewish as well as gentile ideologues. It was inherent in the nature of Jewish existence that emancipation become a turning point in Jewish history, but by no means its termination.

NOTES   INDEX

NOTES

Abbreviations Used in the Notes

AZJ   *Allgemeine Zeitung des Judenthums*

BLBI   *Bulletin des Leo Baeck Instituts*

CCAR   *Central Conference of American Rabbis*

HUCA   *Hebrew Union College Annual*

JGJCR *Jahrbuch für Geschichte der Juden in der Čechoslovakischen Republik*

JJLG   *Jahrbuch der jüdisch-literarischen Gesellschaft in Frankfurt am Main*

JJS   *The Jewish Journal of Sociology*

JSS   *Jewish Social Studies*

LBIYB *Leo Baeck Institute Year Book*

MGWJ *Monatsschift für die Geschichte und Wissenschaft des Judenthums*

PAAJR *Proceedings of the American Academy for Jewish Research*

REJ   *Revue des Études Juives*

ZGJD   *Zeitschrift für die Geschichte der Juden in Deutschland*

I. SOCIAL REVOLUTION—WITH A DIFFERENCE

1. See Jacob Katz, "The Term 'Jewish Emancipation'; Its Origin and Historical Impact," *Studies in Nineteenth-Century Jewish Intellectual History*, ed. Alexander Altman (Cambridge, Mass., Harvard University Press, 1964), pp. 1–25.

2. See Jacob Katz, *Tradition and Crisis; Jewish Society at the End of the Middle Ages* (New York, Free Press of Glencoe, 1961).

3. Comparisons of the situation of the Jews with that of the Huguenots were often made. See Selma Stern, *Der preussische Staat und die Juden* (Tübingen, Mohr-Siebeck, 1962), I/1, 10, 14. Stern stresses the inferior position of the Jews in comparison with that of the Huguenots. The anti-Jewish writer Karl Wilhelm Friedrich Grattenauer (*Ueber die physische und moralische Verfassung der heutigen Juden* [Berlin], 1791, p. 119), made the comparison to show the disadvantage for the state of accepting Jews in contradistinction to the French immigrants. The Berlin Jewish leader David Friedländer referred to the French colony to show what immigrants can achieve under appropriate conditions. See David Friedländer, *Aktenstücke, die Reform der jüdischen Kolonien in den preussischen Staaten betreffend* (Berlin, 1793), pp. 110–111.

4. It was different in the United States, where, as Ben Halpern has pointed out, emancipation was never a problem. See Ben Halpern, *The American Jew* (New York, Theodor Herzl Foundation, 1956), pp. 13–14. Halpern expressed the view that the American Jews gained a great advantage from not having to struggle for their emancipation.

5. From the vast literature on the Jewish stereotype of the Middle Ages, I should like to mention only the following: Marcel Simon, *Verus Israel; étude sur la relation entre chrétiens et juifs dans l'Empire Romain (135–425)* (Paris, E. de Boccard, 1964); Joshua Trachtenberg, *The Devil and the Jews: The Medieval Conception of the Jew and its Relation to Modern Antisemitism* (Cleveland, World Publishing Co. and Philadelphia, Jewish Publication Society of America, 1943).

II. GHETTO TIMES

1. This chapter relies heavily on two of my earlier books: Katz, *Tradition and Crisis*; and Katz, *Exclusiveness and Tolerance; Studies in Jewish-Gentile Relations in Medieval and Modern Times* (London, Oxford University Press, 1961).

2. I follow Raphael Mahler, *History of the Jewish People in Modern Times* (In Hebrew, Merhavyah, Sifriat Hapoalim, 1952–1956), I, 93, 103, 211; II, 14, 183, 248, 333–336. Somewhat different figures are given in Arthur Ruppin, *Soziologie der Juden* (Berlin, Jüdischer Verlag, 1930–31), I, 7, 25.

3. Albert Montefiore Hyamson, *A History of the Jews in England* (London, Methuen, 1928), p. 221; Mahler, *History of the Jewish People*, I, 93.

4. Exact figures about the growth of the Jewish population of Amsterdam, half of Dutch Jewry, are to be found in Herbert Ivan Bloom, *The Economic Activities of the Jews of Amsterdam in the Seventeenth and Eighteenth Centuries* (Williamsport, Pa., The Bayard Press, 1937), pp. 31–32.

5. Alajos Kovács, *A zsidóság térfoglalása Magyarországon* (Budapest, Szerzö kiadása, 1922), p. 9, has 12,000, and this is regarded as being too low. See Nathaniel Katzburg, *Encyclopaedia Hebraica*, XIII (Jerusalem-Tel Aviv, Encyclopaedia Publ. Comp., 1961), 864.

6. The latest summary on the resettlement of the Jews in France is given by Arthur Hertzberg, *The French Enlightenment and the Jews* (New York, Columbia University Press, 1968), pp. 12–17, 22–28.

7. *Ibid.*, pp. 18–20.

8. Elie Scheid, *Histoire des Juifs d'Alsace* (Paris, 1887), pp. 167–198.

9. Eljakiem Menachem Bolle, "De Opheffing van de Autonomie der Kehilloth (Joodse Gemeenten) in Nederland 1796" (diss., Amsterdam, 1960), p. 197.

10. Joseph Melkman, *Encyclopaedia Hebraica*, XIII, 753.

11. Henry Straus Quixano Henriques, *The Jews and the English Law* (Oxford, Hart, 1908), pp. 162–164, 171, 177–178.

12. Hugo Barbeck, *Geschichte der Juden in Nürnberg und Fürth* (Nuremberg, 1878), pp. 55–73.

13. Stern, *Der preussische Staat und die Juden*, I/1, 6–8, 19–22, 65–66, 71–73.

14. Richard Wilhelm Markgraf, *Zur Geschichte der Juden auf den Messen in Leipzig von 1664–1839* (Bischofswerden, 1894), especially p. 92.

15. Alfred Francis Pribram, *Urkunden und Akten zur Geschichte der Juden in Wien*, I (Vienna, Braumüller, 1918), pp. XXXVIII, XLVI, CLXIV.

16. Sándor Büchler, *A zsidók története Budapesten, a legrégibb idöktöl 1867–ig* . . . (Budapest, IMIT, 1901), pp. 332–335.

17. Bernhard Wachstein, *Urkunden und Akten zur Geschichte der Juden in Eisenstadt und den Siebengemeinden* (Vienna, Braumüller, 1926), pp. XIII–XIX; M. Pollák, *A zsidók története Sopronba* (Budapest, 1896), pp. 197–198, 206–222.

In Bohemia, Jews were forbidden from entering its *Bergstädte*, towns where rare metals were coined. This prohibition remained intact even after the Edict of Tolerance of 1781. See Ludwig Singer, "Zur Geschichte der Toleranzpatente in den Sudetenländern," *JGJCR*, V (1933), 236, 261. In Moravia the Jews were forbidden residence in the royal towns, for instance in Brünn, *ibid.,* p. 276.

18. Joseph Bergl, *Geschichte der ungarischen Juden* (Leipzig, 1879), pp. 69–71.

19. Hertzberg, *The French Enlightenment and the Jews*, pp. 17–20.

20. See note 13 above.

21. Robert Anchel, "La tolérance au Moyen-Age," *Les Juifs en France* (Paris, J. B. Janin, 1946), pp. 93–124.

22. Hyamson, *A History of the Jews in England*, pp. 130–134. Cecil Roth, *A Life of Menasseh ben Israel; Rabbi, Printer, and Diplomat* (Philadelphia, Jewish Publication Society of America, 1934), pp. 206–208.

23. Luther's anti-Jewish tirades had a great impact on his contemporaries as well as the ensuing generations. Much of the effort of the great defender of Jewish interests, Josel von Rosheim, was directed against Luther's attacks. See Selma Stern, *Josel von Rosheim, Befehlshaber der Judenschaft im Heiligen Römischen Reich Deutscher Nation* (Stuttgart, Deutsche Verlags-Anstalt, 1959). Catholic zeal plays a part in the expulsion from Vienna in 1670.

24. The court Jew has been described by Selma Stern, *The Court Jew; Contribution to the History of the Period of Absolutism in Central Europe* (Philadelphia, Jewish Publication Society of America, 1950). Extensive research on that subject is to be found in Heinrich Schnee, *Die Hoffinanz und der moderne Staat; Geschichte und System der Hoffaktoren an deutschen Fürstenhöfen im Zeitalter des Absolutismus nach archivalischen Quellen*, I–VI (Berlin: Duncker and Humblot, 1952–1967).

25. Johann Ulrich von Cramer, *Wetzlarische Nebenstunden* (Ulm, 1756), III, 95.

26. Endeavors to prevent the expulsion from Prague are described in Barouh Mevorah, "Jewish Diplomatic Activities to Prevent the Expulsion of Jews from Bohemia and Moravia in 1744–1745" (In Hebrew), *Zion*, XXVIII (1963), 125–164. There are no allusions to legitimate rights of the Jews to residence.

27. Moses Mendelssohn, *Gesammelte Schriften*, V (Leipzig, 1844), 545. See Meier Kayserling, *Moses Mendelssohn: sein Leben und seine Werke* (Leipzig, 1862), pp. 272–274; Kaim Isidor Sidori, *Geschichte der Juden in Sachsen* (Leipzig, 1840), pp. 91–96.

28. Rudolf Glanz, "Die unterste Schicht von deutschem Judentum im 18. Jahrhundert," *YIVO Bletter*, XI (1937), 356–368. *Idem, Geschichte des niederen jüdischen Volkes in Deutschland* (New York, 1968), 82–171.

29. Katz, *Tradition and Crisis*, chaps. 6 and 7.

30. *Ibid.,* chaps. 9 and 10.

31. Jizchak Fritz Baer, *Das Protokollbuch der Landjudenschaft des Herzogtums Kleve*, I (Berlin, Schwetschke, 1922). Berthold Altmann, "The Autonomous Federation of Jewish Communities in Paderborn," *JSS,* III (1941), 159–188. Daniel J. Cohen, "The Organisation of the 'Landjudenschaften' Jewish Corpo-

rations in Germany during the XVII and XVIII Centuries" (diss., in Hebrew, Jerusalem, 1967). A general summary is given by Salo Wittmayer Baron, *The Jewish Community; Its History and Structure*, (Philadelphia, Jewish Publication Society of America, 1942), I, 79–80.

32. Tobias Jakobovits, "Das Prager und böhmische Landesrabbinat Ende des siebzehnten und Anfang des achtzehnten Jahrhunderts," *JGJCR*, V (1933), 79–80; Baron, *The Jewish Community*, I, 339–340.

33. The statutes of the organization were published first in German translation by Gerson Wolf, *Die alten Statuten der jüdischen Gemeinden in Mähren* (Vienna, 1880). In 1952 the original Hebrew version was published by Israel Halpern, *Constitutiones Congressus generalis Judaeorum Moraviensium* (Jerusalem, Mekize Nirdamim, 1952).

34. Katz, *Tradition and Crisis*, chaps. 5, 16, and 17.

35. *Ibid.*, chaps. 9 and 10.

36. *Ibid.*, chaps. 16 and 18; Tobias Jakobovits, "Die jüdischen Zünfte in Prag," *JGJCR*, VII (1936), 57–141.

37. Katz, *Tradition and Crisis*, chap. 19.

38. *Ibid.*, chap. 12.

39. *Ibid.*

40. *Ibid.*, chaps. 3 and 18; Katz, *Exclusiveness and Tolerance*, pp. 138–146.

41. Gershom Scholem, *Major Trends in Jewish Mysticism* (New York, Schocken Books, 1954), pp. 287–324.

42. Heinrich Graetz, *Geschichte der Juden von den ältesten Zeiten bis auf die Gegenwart* (Leipzig, 1878–1897), X (1887), 347–377; Mortimer Joseph Cohen, *Jacob Emden; A Man of Controversy* (Philadelphia, Dropsie College, 1937), pp. 118–242.

43. Simon Ginzburg, *The Life and Work of Moses Hayyim Luzzatto, Founder of Modern Hebrew Literature* (Philadelphia, Dropsie College, 1931), pp. 64–65.

44. Simon Ginzburg, *R' Moshe Hayyim Luzzatto u-vne doro* (Tel Aviv, Dvir, 1937), p. 360. This formulation is of Moses Hagiz, the chief persecutor of the Sabbatian heresy.

45. Katz, *Exclusiveness and Tolerance*, pp. 148–150.

46. Johann F. A. de Le Roi, *Die evangelische Christenheit und die Juden unter dem Gesichtspunkt der Mission geschichtlich betrachtet* (Karlsruhe, 1884–1891), I, 246–269.

47. Azriel Shohet, *Beginnings of the Haskalah among German Jewry in the First Half of the Eighteenth Century* (In Hebrew, Jerusalem, Bialik Institute, 1960), pp. 174–197.

48. Katz, *Exclusiveness and Tolerance*, pp. 156–162.

49. *Ibid.*, pp. 162–168.

III. THE PORTENTS OF CHANGE

1. The history of the court Jews has been dealt with mainly by two historians: Stern, *The Court Jew*; and Schnee, *Die Hoffinanz und der moderne Staat*. An excellent summary of the main results of the research of the two above-mentioned historians is given by Francis Ludwig Carsten, "The Court Jews; a Prelude to Emancipation," *LBIYB*, III (1958), 140–156.

2. Schnee, *Die Hoffinanz und der moderne Staat*, III, 205–207, 209–211, 214, 222–227.

3. On Muslim Spain and other Muslim countries, see Salo Wittmayer Baron, *A Social and Religious History of the Jews* (New York, Columbia University Press, 1957), III, 150–161. On Christian Spain, see Abraham Aaron Neuman, *The Jews in Spain; Their Social, Political and Cultural Life During the Middle Ages* (Philadelphia, Jewish Publication Society of America, 1942), II, 221–274; Jizchak Fritz Baer, *A History of the Jews in Christian Spain* (Philadelphia, Jewish Publication Society of America, 1961–1966), according to the Index under Court officials, Fiscal administrators, Tax farming.

4. Schnee, *Die Hoffinanz und der moderne Staat*, III, 215.

5. Schnee has been criticized by Carsten ("The Court Jews," *LBIYB*, III [1958], 155–156) for his anti-Semitic bias, which manifests itself in a general overtone and in uncalled-for derogatory remarks. But Schnee is due for criticism even more for his lack of perspective and perceptiveness. His historical conclusions, assembled especially at the end of Book III, are uncritical inferences from details rather than a product of an analysis of the vast material collected by him. His attributing the emancipation to the activity of the court Jews is a case in point.

6. On Austria, see Pribram, *Urkunden und Akten*, I, pp. LXVI–LXXVI. On France, see Hertzberg, *The French Enlightenment and the Jews*, pp. 338–368.

7. See Herbert Ivan Bloom, "Felix Libertate and the Emancipation of Dutch Jewry," *Essays on Jewish Life and Thought Presented in Honor of Salo Wittmayer Baron*, ed. Joseph Leon Blau (New York, Columbia University Press, 1959), pp. 105–122.

8. Ismar Freund, *Die Emanzipation der Juden in Preussen unter besonderer Berücksichtigung des Gesetzes vom 11. März 1812; Ein Beitrag zur Rechtsgeschichte der Juden in preussen* (Berlin, Poppelauer, 1912), especially I, 208–226. Freund stresses the active role of the Jewish leaders (p. 208), but agrees that as far as the results are concerned it mattered little or not at all. Friedländer's role has recently been analyzed by Michael A. Meyer, *The Origins of the Modern Jew; Jewish Identity and European Culture in Germany, 1749–1824* (Detroit, Wayne State University Press, 1967), pp. 64–70, 78–81.

9. Salo Wittmayer Baron, *Die Judenfrage auf dem Wiener Kongress* (Vienna-Berlin, K. Löwit, 1920), pp. 131–145.

10. Egon Caesar, Conte Conti, *The Rise of the House of Rothschild* (London, Gollancz, 1928), pp. 183, 209–212, 223–240, 244–245, 288–294, 323–324; *idem, The Reign of the House of Rothschild* (London, Golancz, 1928), pp. 174–175, 295–298, 328–336; Cecil Roth, *The Magnificent Rothschilds* (London, Halle, 1939), pp. 42–54.

11. Mevorah, "Jewish Diplomatic Activities," *Zion*, XXVIII (1963), 125–164.

12. See note 2 above.

13. Felix Priebatsch, "Die Judenpolitik des fürstlichen Absolutismus im 17.und 18.Jahrhundert," *Festschrift zum 70.Geburtstag von Dietrich Schäfer* (Jena, 1915), pp. 564–651. Shohet, *Beginnings of the Haskalah among German Jewry*, pp. 58, 284.

14. Stern, *Der preussische Staat und die Juden*, II/1, 123–149.

15. A. Weber, *Die Entwicklung der Judenemanzipation in Würtenberg bis zum Judengesetz von 1828* (Stuttgart, 1940).

16. Cohen, "The Organisation of the 'Landjudenschaften' Jewish Corporations in Germany," pp. 86–106.

17. Stern, *Der preussische Staat und die Juden*, II/1, 148–149.

18. The possibility of the Jews' expulsion was publicly discussed in Vienna and Prague, when rumors of the impending Edict of Tolerance reached the public. See *Ueber die Juden und deren Duldung* (Prague, 1781), pp. 42–47; *Die Juden so wie sie sind, und wie sie seyn sollen* (Vienna, 1781), p. 29. During the discussion of the Jews' case in the National Assembly in Paris none other than Clermont-Tonnerre, their most ardent advocate, mentioned the possible banishment of the Jews from France as the only alternative to their acceptance as full citizens (Achille Edmond Halphen, *Recueil des lois, decrets, ordonnances . . . concernant les Israélites depuis la Révolution de 1789* (Paris, 1851), p. 185. Similarly, two most important participants in the consultations preceding the Edict of 1812 in Prussia, namely Franz Ferdinand von Schrötter and Wilhelm von Humboldt, told the king that unless full amalgamation of the Jews into the body politic could be achieved, their expulsion from the land would be the logical answer to the problem (Freund, *Die Emanzipation der Juden in Preussen*, II pp. 227, 273). The idea of establishing special Jewish colonies was discussed by Dohm and others (Christian Wilhelm von Dohm, *Ueber die bürgerliche Verbesserung der Juden*, I–II (Berlin, 1883), I, 124–125; II, 118–123). The idea of a kind of semicitizenship for German Jews was maintained by the opponents of the full citizenship in the era of Restoration and forcefully propagated by Heinrich Eberhard Gottlob Paulus, *Die jüdische Nationalabsonderung nach Ursprung, Folgen und Besserungsmitteln, oder über Pflichten, Rechte und Verordnungen zur Verbesserung der jüdischen Schutzbürgerschaft in Teutschland. Allen Teutschen Staatsregierungen und Landständischen Versammlungen zur Erwägung gewidmet* (Heidelberg, 1831).

19. Hertzberg, *The French Enlightenment and the Jews*, pp. 74–76, 142–153.

20. Shohet, *Beginnings of the Haskalah among German Jewry*.

21. Shohet's book has been critically reviewed by Barouh Mevorah in *Kirjath Sepher*, XXXVII (1961–62), 150–155. See also Jacob Toury, "Neue Veröffentlichungen zur Geschichte der Juden im deutschen Lebenskreise," *BLBI*, IV (1961), 55–73.

22. On the extensive charitable activities of the court Jews, see Stern, *The Court Jew*, pp. 219–226, and Schnee, *Die Hoffinanz und der moderne Staat*, III, 191–192, 222–224.

23. See Jacob Katz, "Marriage and Sexual Life among the Jews at the Close of the Middle Ages," (In Hebrew) *Zion*, X (1945), 46–47; Katz, *Tradition and Crisis*, end of chap. xiv, 147–148.

24. Shohet, *Beginnings of the Haskalah among German Jewry*, pp. 198–235, 259–260.

25. Trevor-Roper came to a similar conclusion in his inquiry into the persistence of the belief in witchcraft in spite of widely spread skepticism concerning the matter. Acquaintance with new ideas contradicting details of the tradition did not affect the general attitude. Only the replacement of the whole system of thought changed the general outlook. Hugh Redwald Trevor-Roper, "The European Witchcraft of the Sixteenth and Seventeenth Centuries," in *Religion, The Reformation and Social Change* (London-Melbourne-Toronto, Macmillan 1967), pp. 175–182.

26. Some data on this has been collected by Barouh Mevorah, "The Problem of the Messiah in the Emancipation and Reform Controversies, 1781–1819" diss., Jerusalem, 1966), pp. 18–25. As late as 1710, there appears in Amsterdam a tractate — (Isak Cantarini, *Et Kez*) — predicting the date of the messianic year. See Zalman Shazar, *Ha-Tiqva Li-Shnat Hataq; The Messianic Hope for the Year 1740* (Jerusalem, Magnes Press, 1970).

27. Jizchak Fritz Baer was the first to pay attention to the sources indicating this deviation. See Jizchak Fritz Baer, *Galuth* (Berlin, Schocken, 1936), pp. 96–98 (English translation, New York, Schocken Books, 1947, pp. 112–114); Mevorah, "The Problem of the Messiah," pp. 19–21.

28. See Shmuel Ettinger, "The Beginnings of the Change in the Attitude of European Society towards the Jews," *Scripta Hierosolymitana*, VII (1961), 193–219; Katz, "The Term 'Jewish Emancipation'."

29. The quotation is from the edition of J. W. Gough, *The Second Treatise of Civil Government and a Letter Concerning Toleration* (Oxford, Blackwell, 1945), p. 160.

30. In the following I draw on my article quoted in note 28 above.

31. Toland's views are presented in his anonymous pamphlet, *Reasons for Naturalising the Jews in Great Britain and Ireland* (London, 1714).

32. Thomas Whipple Perry, *Public Opinion, Propaganda, and Politics in Eighteenth-Century England; a Study of the Jew Bill of 1753* (Cambridge, Mass., Harvard University Press, 1962).

33. On this point I do differ from Perry's presentation (see note 32 above). See Katz, "The Term 'Jewish Emancipation'," p. 9, n. 39.

34. Voltaire, *Essai sur les Moeurs et l'Esprit des Nations*. The best edition is by René Pomeau (Paris, Garnier Frères, 1963). See Vol. II, 63; Emmerich, *Das Judentum bei Voltaire*, p. 47.

35. The original pamphlet, published in Berlin in 1753, is unavailable, but it had been republished in Hamburg in 1759 anonymously. *Schreiben eines Juden an einem Philosphen nebst der Antwort. Mit Anmerkungen.* (Hamburg, 1759). Even this is a rarity. Eichstädt No. 71A found it only in the university library at Hamburg, but this was destroyed during the Second World War. The library of the Hebrew Union College in Cincinnati has one copy, and a photocopy of it reached me. The original pamphlet by Levi Israel had been written in the form of a correspondence between him and a Gentile philosopher, but there is no doubt this was only a literary device; in fact the entire pamphlet was written by him, as the Hamburg publisher noted in his introduction.

IV. THE SEMINEUTRAL SOCIETY

1. See chap. x below.

2. Stern, *The Court Jew*, pp. 234–235, and Schnee, *Die Hoffinanz und der moderne Staat*, III, 224–231, cited many instances of the highest dignitaries honoring Jews by their presence at Jewish celebrations and the like.

3. See Shohet, *Beginnings of the Haskalah among German Jewry*, pp. 38–39.

4. Graetz, *Geschichte der Juden*[3], X, 266–274. See note 6 below.

5. Louis Lewin, "Die jüdischen Studenten an der Universität Frankfurt an der Oder," *JJLG*, XIV (1921), 217–238; Guido Kisch, "Der erste in Deutschland promovierte Jude," *MGWJ*, XL (1934), 350–363.

6. Gerson Wolf, "Der Prozess Eisenmenger," *MGWJ*, XVIII (1869), 379–380; Meier Wiener, "Des Hof- und Kammeragenten Leffmann Berens Intervention bei dem Erscheinen judenfeindlicher Schriften," *Magazin für die Wissenschaft des Judenthums*, VI (1879), 52.

7. Jacob Katz, *Jews and Freemasons in Europe 1723–1939* (Cambridge, Mass., Harvard University Press, 1970). I have summarized some of the main points of my book in Jacob Katz, "Freemasons and Jews," *JJS*, IX (1967), 137–148. Here I follow this summary in part.

8. James Anderson (comp.), *The Constitutions of the Freemasons* (London, 1723), p. 50.

9. Lawrence Dermott, *Ahiman Rezon* (London, 1756).

10. The standard biography of Mendelssohn is still that of Meier Kayserling, *Moses Mendelssohn: sein Leben und seine Werke* (Leipzig, 1862), see pp. 8–14. A full bibliography has recently been published by Herrmann Meyer, *Moses Mendelssohn Bibliographie, mit einigen Ergänzungen zur Geistesgeschichte des ausgehenden 18.Jahrhunderts* (Berlin, W. de Gruyter, 1965). On Moses Mendelssohn's childhood see the recent study by Alexander Altmann, "Moses Mendelssohns Kindheit in Dessau," *BLBI*, X (1967), 237–275.

11. That is the much-debated Koheleth Mussar. See the recent article of Jacob Toury, "On the Authorship of 'Koheleth Mussar' " (In Hebrew), *Kirjath Sepher*, XLIII (1968), 279–284. *Idem*, "Die Anfaenge des juedischen Zeitungswesens in Deutschland," *BLBI*, X (1967), 93–110. Herrmann M. Z. Meyer, "Kohelet Mussar, Berichtigungen, Ergaenzungen, Meinungen," *BLBI*, XI (1968), 48–60.

12. Moses Mendelssohn, *Gesammelte Schriften, Jubiläumsausgabe* (Berlin, Akademie-Verlag, 1929–1932), XVI, 119. See the observations of the editor (Leo Strauss), III, pp. XVIII, XL. Mendelssohn ultimately preferred to base his thesis on rational arguments disregarding Revelation. But this does not change the fact that this entailed writing for an entirely different audience.

13. Kayserling, *Moses Mendelssohn*, p. 70.

14. David Kaufman and Max Freudenthal, *Die Familie Gomperz* (Frankfurt a.M., J. Kauffmann, 1917), pp. 167–189.

15. Julius Fürst, ed., *Henriette Herz, ihr Leben und ihre Erinnerungen* (Berlin, 1858), pp. 93–101.

16. Salomon Maimon, *Salomon Maimons Lebensgeschichte. Von ihm selbst geschrieben und hrsg.von K.P. Moritz in zwei Theilen* (Berlin, 1792–93. Republished by Jacob Fromer, Munich, 1911).

17. See Katz, *Jews and Freemasons*, pp. 24–25.

18. Mendelssohn, *Gesammelte Schriften, Jubiläumsausgabe*, XI, 338, 494.

19. Kayserling, *Moses Mendelssohn*, pp. 229–233.

20. *Ibid.*, pp. 184–190. Simon Rawidowitz, "Zum Lavater-Mendelssohn-Streit," Mendelssohn, *Gesammelte Schriften, Jubiläumsausgabe*, VII, pp. XI–LV.

21. Kayserling, *Moses Mendelssohn*, pp. 190–198. Rawidowitz, "Zum Lavater-Mendelssohn-Streit."

22. See Katz, *Exclusiveness and Tolerance*, pp. 170–177.

23. See Mendelssohn, *Gesammelte Schriften, Jubiläumsausgabe*, XVI, 148–149; Kayserling, *Moses Mendelssohn*, pp. 192, 493.

24. Kayserling, *Moses Mendelssohn*, pp. 201–216; Rawidowitz, "Zum Lavater-

Mendelssohn-Streit," Mendelssohn, *Gesammelte Schriften, Jubiläumsausgabe*, VII, pp. LXXIII–LXXVII; [Friedrich Wilhelm von Schütz,] *Leben und Meinungen Moses Mendelssohn, nebst dem Geiste seiner Schriften in einer kurzen Abrisse dargestellt* (Hamburg, 1787), p. 175.

25. *Das Forschen nach Licht und Recht in einem Schreiben an Herrn Moses Mendelssohn auf Veranlassung seiner merkwürdigen Vorrede zu Manasseh ben Israel* (Berlin, 1782. See Jacob Katz, "To Whom Was Mendelssohn Replying in 'Jerusalem'?" (In Hebrew), *Zion*, XXIX (1964), 112–132 and in the forthcoming issue of *Zion*, XXXVII. English translation to appear in a forthcoming issue of *Scripta Hierosolymitana*, and see especially the Appendix there.

26. Meier Kayserling, *Der Dichter Ephraim Kuh: Ein Beitrag zur Geschichte der deutschen Literatur* (Berlin, 1864), especially pp. 15–19.

27. In my doctoral thesis (Jacob Katz, *Die Entstehung der Judenassimilation in Deutschland und deren Ideologie* [Frankfort a.M. D. Droller, 1935]), I used the expression "die neutralisierte Gesellschaftsform." Now it seems to me that semi-neutral is a more appropriate term.

28. Details on this in Katz, *Jews and Freemasons*, chap. iii, especially pp. 26–37.

29. *Ibid.*, pp. 37–53.

30. Much has been written on these salons. See Meyer, *The Origins of the Modern Jew*, pp. 102–114; Baron, *Die Judenfrage auf dem Wiener Kongress*, pp. 117–145; Hilde Spiel, *Fanny von Arnstein oder Die Emanzipation: Ein Frauenleben an der Zeitenwende 1758–1818* (Frankfurt a.M., S. Fischer, 1962).

31. Julius Fürst, *Henriette Herz, ihr Leben und ihre Erinnerungen* (Berlin, 1858), p. 130.

V. THE IMAGE OF THE FUTURE

1. Christian Wilhelm von Dohm, *Über die bürgerliche Verbesserung der Juden, I–II* (Berlin, 1781–1783). The first volume of Dohm's writings has been enlarged and republished with the second. On Dohm, see W. Gronau, *Christian Wilhelm von Dohm nach seinem Wollen und Handeln: Ein biographischer Versuch* (Lemgo, 1824), and Ilsegret Dambacher, "Christian Wilhelm von Dohm: Ein Beitrag zur Geschichte des preussischen aufgeklärten Beamtentums und seinen Reformbestrebungen am Ausgang des 18.Jahrhunderts" (diss., Munich, 1957).

2. Mendelssohn's contribution to the program for the Jewish future is contained in his introduction to Menasseh ben Israel's *Vindiciae Judaeorum*, which was translated on his initiative or possibly by himself (see Alexander Altmann, "A New Evaluation of Moses Mendelssohn's *Jerusalem* in the Light of Bibliographical Data" (In Hebrew), *Zion*, XXXIII (1968), 49, n. 15) and published in 1782. The introduction is included in Moses Mendelssohn, *Gesammelte Schriften*, III, 179–202. Similarly his major work *Jerusalem* published in 1783, in his *Gesammelte Schriften*, III, 257–362. English translation of *Jerusalem* by Alfred Jospe, *"Jerusalem" and other Jewish Writings by Moses Mendelssohn* (New York, Schocken Books, 1969).

3. Wessely wrote a Hebrew pamplhet *Divre Shalom ve-Emeth* (Berlin, 1782). German translation: *Worte der Wahrheit und des Friedens an die gesammte jüdische Nation* (Berlin, 1782).

4. See Katz, "The Term 'Jewish Emancipation,' " pp. 10–11, and above, chap. iii, n. 35.

5. See *An die jüdische Nation, Brief 1, 2* (Frankfurt and Leipzig, 1776–77); Wilhelm Ludwig Wekhrlin, "Über das Project, die Juden in Deutschland zu naturalisieren," *Chronologen* (1779), I, 76–87. One year later, the anonymous pamphlet *Versuch über die Frage: ob die Juden zu einer reichsschlussmässigen Toleranz unter gewissen Bedingungen gelangen könnten* (Regensburg, 1780) deals with the issue of admission only. See Katz, "The Term 'Jewish Emancipation'," pp. 10–12.

6. Dohm, *Über die bürgerliche Verbesserung der Juden*, I, 126–128; II, 168–171.

7. See Katz, "The Term 'Jewish Emancipation'," pp. 12–13; Dambacher, "Christian Wilhelm von Dohm," pp. 72–84.

8. During the Lavater controversy in 1769, Mendelssohn said unequivocally that the Jews "are content if they are tolerated and protected," *Gesammelte Schriften*, III, 47, Jospe, *"Jerusalem,"* pp. 119–120. Signs of resignation have been observed, even as late as 1777 (see chap. iii above). It was only the simultaneous promulgation of the Edict of Tolerance and the publication of Dohm's book, as well as the appearance of Lessing's play *Nathan der Weise* on the German stage, that convinced him that times were changing *Gesammelte Schriften*, III, 179–180. See Katz, *Die Entstehung der Judenassimilation in Deutschland*, pp. 72–73.

9. Expounded at length in his *Jerusalem*, part 1, *Gesammelte Schriften*, III, 297–298, Jospe, *"Jerusalem,"* pp. 47–49. Ernst Cassirer, "Die Philosophie Moses Mendelssohns," *Moses Mendelssohn, zur 200jährigen Wiederkehr seines Geburtstages* (Berlin, Schneider, 1929), pp. 62–66. Altmann, "A New Evaluation," *Zion*, XXXIII, 56–57, stressed that Mendelssohn retained the idea of cooperation between state and religion, ensuring the welfare of man. But this cooperation is to be achieved in spite of the separation of the respective institutions of state and church.

10. Mendelssohn, *Gesammelte Schriften*, III, 194–202, 264–269, 285–289, 296–298, Jospe, *"Jerusalem,"* pp. 18–23, 35–40, 46–49, 143–144.

11. Dohm, *Über die bürgerliche Verbesserung der Juden*, I, 117–122; II, 270–290.

12. Mendelssohn, *Gesammelte Schriften*, III, 183, 187–193; see also his letter to Herz Homberg on the limited choice of occupations open to his son, *Gesammelte Schriften*, V, 673–674, also 679–680.

13. These questions were anticipated by Dohm and asked by his critics. The learned Michaelis and the preacher Schwager were among his critics. Dohm included their comments in his second volume: Dohm, *Über die bürgerliche Verbesserung der Juden*, I, 143–155; II, 46–51, 100–103. Others who wrote such arguments in order to reject the possible integration of Jews altogether will be seen in the next chapter.

14. Dohm, *Über die bürgerliche Verbesserung der Juden*, I, 134–137.

15. Moses Mendelssohn, *Ritualgesetze der Juden, betreffend Erbschaften, Vormundschaften, Testamente und Ehesachen* . . . (Berlin, 1778). The book was authorized by the Berlin Rabbi Hirschel Lewin.

16. Mendelssohn, *Gesammelte Schriften*, III, 193–202, Jospe, *"Jerusalem,"* pp. 143–144.

17. Kayserling, *Moses Mendelssohn*, pp. 289–297; Perez Sandler, *Mendelssohn's Edition of the Pentateuch* (In Hebrew) (Jerusalem, Rubin Mass, 1940), pp. 194–208. Moshe Samet proved that no actual ban was ever pronounced against the

Pentateuch or its author (M. S. Samet, "Mendelssohn, Weisel and the Rabbis of their Time," in A. Gilboa, ed., *Studies in the History of Jewish People and the Land of Israel* (In Hebrew) (Haifa, The University of Haifa, 1970), pp. 233–297). But rumors of it reached Mendelssohn before he published his statement on the issue of the rabbis' right to use the ban.

18. This consideration was raised first by Michaelis; see his observations in Dohm, *Über die bürgerliche Verbesserung der Juden*, II, 42–43.

19. Mendelssohn's answer is printed in *ibid.*, II, 74–75.

20. "And even today, no better advice than this can be given to the House of Jacob: Adopt the mores and constitution of the country in which you find yourself, but be steadfast in upholding the religion of your fathers, too. Bear both burdens as well as you can. True, on the one hand, people make it difficult for you to bear the burden of civil life because of the religion to which you remain faithful; and, on the other hand, the climate of our time makes the observance of your religious laws in some respects more burdensome than it need be. Persevere nevertheless; stand fast in the place which Providence has assigned to you; and submit to everything which may happen, as you were told to do by your Lawgiver long ago." Jospe, *"Jerusalem,"* p. 104. Mendelssohn, *Gesammelte Schriften* III, 355.

21. Dohm, *Über die bürgerliche Verbesserung der Juden*, I, 145–155; II, 171–187, 214–215, 222–224, 236–246, 259–262, 290–294, 358–360.

22. See the passages quoted in the previous note, especially II, 178–179.

23. Mendelssohn's theory of Judaism has been repeatedly analyzed. See Max Wiener, *Jüdische Religion im Zeitalter der Emanzipation* (Berlin, Philo Verlag, 1933), pp. 36–40; Julius Guttmann, *Die Philosophie des Judentums* (Munich, E. Reinhardt, 1933), pp. 303–317; English translation: *Philosophies of Judaism* (New York, Holt, Rinehart and Winston, 1964), pp. 291–303.

24. Dohm, *Über die bürgerliche Verbesserung der Juden*, II, 171–179.

25. Volume XVI of the *Jubiläumsausgabe* contains besides the Hebrew the jüdisch-deutsch letters.

26. See the sources listed by Shohet, *Beginnings of the Haskalah among German Jewry*, p. 58, n. 84. The Edict of Tolerance annulled the validity of any document written in Hebrew or using Hebrew letters. Pribram, *Urkunden und Akten*, I, 498. In other countries, similar proscriptions were introduced.

27. On the changing evaluation of Jüdisch-Deutsch, see Leopold Zunz, *Die gottesdienstlichen Vorträge der Juden, historisch entwickelt; Ein Beitrag zur Alterthumskunde und biblischen Kritik, zur Literatur-und Religionsgeschichte* (Frankfurt a.M., 1892), pp. 466–468.

28. Isaac Eisenstein-Barzilay, "The Ideology of the Berlin Haskalah," *PAAJR*, XXV (1956), 25–26. The changing pattern of education at this time has been exhaustively described by Mordehai Eliav, *Jewish Education in Germany in the Period of Enlightenment and Emancipation* (In Hebrew) (Jerusalem, The Jewish Agency, 1960).

29. *Ibid.*, pp. 8–9, 22, 71.

30. On Wessely, see Joseph Klausner, *Historiya shel ha-Sifruth ha-Hadasha* (The History of Modern Hebrew Literature), (Jerusalem, Achiasaf Publ. House Ltd., 1952), pp. 103–120.

31. *Ibid.*, pp. 112–113.

32. See note 3 above.

33. Eliav, *Jewish Education in Germany*, pp. 39–49.

34. Katz, *Die Entstehung der Judenassimilation in Deutschland*, pp. 55–57.

35. Katz, "The Term 'Jewish Emancipation'," pp. 13–14.

36. In his early years Mendelssohn protested against the generalization of Michaelis, who denied the possibility of a virtuous Jew as was portrayed by Lessing in his *Der Jude* (*Gesammelte Schriften*, III, 476–480). During the Dohm controversy he spoke of "misuse rampant among traders" (*ibid.*, pp. 190–193). He recommended free competition as the only sure remedy. On other occasions he spoke of the "Unsittlichkeit des gemeinen Mannes" and attributed it partly at least to the use of the "jüdisch-deutsche Mundart" (*ibid.*, V, 605). He probably regarded this as the indication of the social gulf that created the moral indifference of the Jews toward the Gentile. See also the sources listed in my article quoted in the previous note. See Eliav, *Jewish Education in Germany*, pp. 32–33.

37. On the whole problem see Katz, *Exclusiveness and Tolerance*, pp. 143–155.

38. [Toland], *Reasons for Naturalizing the Jews in Great Britain and Ireland*, pp. 17–21.

39. The novel is called *Das Leben der schwedischen Gräfin*. It appeared in 1746 and was reprinted in Christian Fürchtegott Gellert's *Sammlung der sämmtlichen Schriften*, I, 1765.

40. See Gotthold Ephraim Lessing, *Sämmtliche Schriften* (Stuttgart, G. J. Göschen, 1886–1924), VI (1890), 159–166; see Katz, "The Term 'Jewish Emancipation'," p. 10.

41. Pinto's reply to Voltaire is quoted in Antoine Guenée, *Lettres de quelques Juifs Portugais, Allemands et Polonais à M. de Voltaire Avec un petit commentaire extrait d'un plus grand* (Paris, 1765), pp. 10–44. The relevant passage is on pp. 25–26.

42. Hertzberg, *The French Enlightenment and the Jews*, pp. 158–159.

43. There is a whole literature on the Berlin Haskalah; see Klausner, *Historiya*, pp. 151–190; Eisenstein-Barzilay, "The Ideology of the Berlin Haskalah," *PAAJR*, XXV, 1–37.

44. See the *Nachschrift* to Dohm's *Über die bürgerliche Verbesserung der Juden*, I, 161–164.

45. The Alsace Jews formulated their wishes in a *Mémoire sur l'état des Juifs en Alsace*, printed by Dohm on pp. 165–210. These are not too far reaching but still are based on the concept of natural rights and humanity; see especially pp. 176–178. On the chain of events, see Gronau, *Christian Wilhelm von Dohm*, pp. 84–85; Graetz, *Geschichte der Juden*, XI, 58–61; Zosa Szajkowski, *The Economic Status of the Jews in Alsace, Metz and Lorraine 1648–1789* (New York: Editions historiques franco-juives, 1954), pp. 123–140.

46. See Katz, "The Term 'Jewish Emancipation'," pp. 12–16.

47. The whole matter is exhaustively treated by Abraham Cahen, "L'emancipation des Juifs devant la Société royale des Sciences et Arts de Metz en 1787 et M. Roederer," *REJ*, I (1880), 83–104.

48. Abbé Henri-Baptiste Grégoire, *Essai sur la régénération physique, morale et politique des Juifs* (Metz: Devilly, 1789), p. 108.

49. Thiéry, *Dissertation sur cette question: Est-il des moyens de rendre les Juifs plus heureux et plus utiles en France?* (Paris, 1788), pp. 46–50, 152–153.

50. Grégoire, *Essai sur la régénération des Juifs*, pp. 130–133. Paul Grunebaum-Ballin, "Grégoire convertisseur? ou la croyance au 'Retour d'Israel'," *REJ*, CXXI (1962), 383–407.

51. Hertzberg, *The French Enlightenment and the Jews*, pp. 264–265.

52. Zalkind Hourwitz, *Apologie des Juifs* (Paris, 1789), pp. 64–68, 72.

53. *Ibid.*, pp. 56–57; Grégoire, *Essai sur la régénération des Juifs*, pp. 44, 99, 107, 109, 111. Michaelis's criticism of Dohm's first volume was included in the second (Dohm, *Über die bürgerliche Verbesserung der Juden*, II, 31–71). This was Grégoire's source. In addition, Dohm's and Mendelssohn's ideas became known in France by Mirabeau's *Sur Moses Mendelssohn, sur la réforme politique des Juifs, et en particulier sur la révolution tentée en leur faveur en 1753 dans la Grande Bretagne* (London, 1787). This pamphlet is also quoted by Grégoire, p. 214.

54. See Hertzberg, *The French Enlightenment and the Jews*, pp. 178–179.

55. M. Liben, "Les Juifs et la convocation des États Généraux," *REJ*, LXIII, (1912), 185–210; LXIV (1912), 89–108, 244–277; LXV (1913), 89–133; LXVI (1913), 161–212.

56. Liben, *REJ*, LXV (1913), 117–128; Hertzberg, *The French Enlightenment and the Jews*, p. 344.

57. The proceedings of the National Assembly concerning Jews are printed in Achille Edmond Halphen, *Recueil des lois, décrets, ordonnances, avis du Conseil d'Etat, arrêtés et règlements concernant les Israélites depuis la Révolution de 1789* (Paris, 1851). On Grégoire's role see pp. 178–179, 181, 196.

58. On the political aspect of the emancipation in France and the other countries, see chap. x below.

59. Halphen, *Recueil des lois*, p. 210.

60. *Actenstücke zur Geschichte der Erhebung der Juden zu Bürgern in der Republik Batavien* (Neusterlitz, bei dem Hofbuchhändler Michaelis, 1797), pp. 9–10.

61. On Jacobson's activity see Schnee, *Die Hoffinanz und der moderne Staat*, II, 109–154. Schnee's treatment is not too sympathetic, nor is Jacobson's role objectively evaluated by many Jewish historians. An exception is the exhaustive biography by Jacob Rader Marcus, "Reform Judaism and the Laity: Israel Jacobson," *Central Conference of American Rabbis*, XXXVIII (1928), pp. 386–498.

62. See Immanuel Heinrich Ritter, *David Friedländer: Sein Leben und sein Wirken* (Berlin, 1861); Freund, *Die Emanzipation der Juden in Preussen*. Meyer, *The Origins of the Modern Jew*, pp. 57–84, added substantially to a detached evaluation of Friedländer's not too attractive figure.

63. Prussia at the time of the Edict of 1812 had shrunk by the loss of territory after the defeat in 1806; therefore the number of Jews who immediately became citizens was comparatively small. See Mahler, *History of the Jewish People in Modern Times*, II, 333–335.

64. See Freund, *Die Emanzipation der Juden in Preussen*, II, 192, 227, 251–253.

65. See chap. iv above.

66. Freund, *Die Emanzipation der Juden in Preussen*, II, 269.

67. He speaks of "nie ganz zu entzifferndem Nationalcharakter," *ibid.*

68. *Ibid.*, p. 271.

69. *Ibid.*, pp. 274–276.

70. The main points of Humboldt's view were well summed up by Freund (*ibid.*, I, 149–152) but he ignored Humboldt's expectation of the ultimate conversion of Jews. It has been stressed by Franz Rosenzweig in one of his letters, (Franz Rosenzweig, *Briefe* (Berlin, Schocken, 1935), pp. 278–279.) Franz Rosenzweig was aware of Humboldt's expectations and accepted it as the natural attitude of the Christian partner to emancipation.

VI. GENTILE OBJECTIONS

1. Sabattja Joseph Wolff, *Maimoniana. Oder Rhapsodien zur Charakteristik Salomon Maimon's. Aus seinem Privatleben gasammelt* (Berlin, 1813), pp. 210–211.

2. August Friedrich Cranz, *Heuss und die Juden, oder Nachtrag zu den sämtlichen fariseirenden Abgeordneten in Rostadt insinuirten Schrift, die Stimme der Menschheit, von einem Weltbürger betrachtet* (Altona, 1798); The Gesellschaft der Freunde founded in Berlin in 1798 was said to have had the function of harboring Jewish young men who were not admitted to any Ressource (club) attended by Christians. Ludwig Lesser, *Chronik der Gesellschaft der Freunde in Berlin* . . . (Berlin, 1842), p. 29.

3. See chap. v above about the negative attitude of the Jewish enlightened toward Yiddish or Jüdisch-Deutsch.

4. On Knigge, see Karl Gödeke, *Adolf Freiherr Knigge* (Hannover, 1844).

5. Adolf Franz Friedrich Ludwig, Freiherr von Knigge, *Über den Umgang mit Menschen* (Hannover, 1804; first edition appeared in 1788), p. XII; on the sociological background and significance of the book, see Barbara Zaehle, *Knigge's Umgang mit Menschen und seine Vorläufer; ein Beitrag zur Geschichte der Gesellschaftsethik* ("Beiträge zur neueren Literaturgeschichte, N.F., Heft 22," Heidelberg, 1933), pp. 163–206.

6. Knigge, *Über den Umgang mit Menschen*, pp. 151–152.

7. *Ibid.*, pp. 152–157.

8. *Ibid.*, pp. 154, 157. In 1796, Knigge published his *Über Eigennutz und Undank* (Leipzig, Jacobäer, 1796), a sequel to his *Umgang mit Menschen*, as the subtitle has it: *Ein Gegenstück zu dem Buche: Über den Umgang mit Menschen*. The Jew is here (pp. 169–173) depicted as the prototype of Eigennutz, that is, selfishness.

9. Guenée, *Lettres de quelques Juifs portugais, allemands et polonais à M.de Voltaire*, pp. 16–19.

10. Katz, *Jews and Freemasons*, pp. 11–25.

11. The greater skill of the Jewish woman in acquiring the social graces was often observed, *Schattenrisse von Berlin* (Amsterdam, 1788), pp. 30–31. Wolf Davidsohn wrote in 1792 "Die Erziehung ist die Ursache, dass das weibliche Geschlecht bei den Juden schöner und wohlgebildeter ist, als das männliche, und neben den hässlichen, schmutzigsten Jungen steht das niedlichste, schönste Mädchen . . . Nächst dem Gelde hat auch das schöne Geschlecht unsere Aufklärung sehr befördert. N.O.S.D.J.V.A.D.W. (to be read in reverse W. Davidso(h)n, *Ein Wörtchen über Juden. Veranlasst durch die von Herrn Friedländer herausgegebenen Aktenstücke* (Berlin, 1792). (This booklet is most rare: Volkmar Eichstädt, *Bibliographie zur Geschichte der Judenfrage* [Hamburg, Hanseatische Verlagsanstalt, 1938], p. 42), has no indication of where it can be found, nor did he decipher the initials of its author. I found a copy of the pamphlet in the library of Jews College, London (Montefiore) that contains the books of Leopold Zunz. The name of the author is here inserted in Zunz's handwriting). See the observation of Ignaz Aurelius Fessler, *Rückblicke auf seine siebzigjährige Pilgerschaft. Ein Nachlass an seine Freunde und an seine Feinde* (Breslau, 1824), pp. 245–246. Fessler was a guest of the family Ephraim in Berlin and frequented the houses of other rich Jews. The Jewess he found to be highly cultured and excelling in the social graces while the men were still grappling with first elements of secular education. See also Fürst, *Henriette Herz*, pp. 121–122.

12. On the history of the order see chap. iv above and for more detailed comments, Katz, *Jews and Freemasons*, chap. 3.

13. (Carl Ferdinand von Boscamp, genannt Laspolski) [Hans Carl von Ecker und Eckhoffen], *Werden und können Israeliten zu Freymaurern aufgenommen werden?* (Hamburg, 1788), pp. 46–49.

14. Karl Wilhelm Friedrich Grattenauer, *Über die physische und moralische Verfassung der heutigen Juden* (Berlin, 1791), pp. 111–132; ". . . aber diese kann man auch nicht mehr zu den Juden rechnen, sie sind Deisten und Naturalisten dem Glauben nach," *ibid.*, pp. 113–114.

15. *Ibid.*, p. 114.

16. The most famous play of this sort was *Unser Verkehr* by Karl B.A. Sessa. According to Graetz (*Geschichte der Juden*, XI (1902), 308), the piece was first played in Breslau in 1812. The bibliographies mention only the later editions from 1815 on. On the contents and intention of the play, see Herbert Carrington, *Die Figur des Juden in der dramatischen Litteratur des XVIII. Jahrhunderts* (Heidelberg, 1897), pp. 60–76. See the *Schattenrisse von Berlin* quoted in note 11 above.

17. Julius von Voss, "Über des Schauspielers Herrn Wurm jüdische Deklaration," *Jüdische Romantik und Wahrheit, von einem getauften Israeliten* (Berlin, 1817), pp. 291–300.

18. Grattenauer, *Über die physische und moralische Verfassung der heutigen Juden*, p. 3 of the unpaged "Vorwort."

19. On Schulz, see Martin von Geismar (pseud.), *Bibliothek der deutschen Aufklärer des achtzehnten Jahrhunderts* (Leipzig, 1846–47), III, 139–144.

20. Mendelssohn expressed this view in his *Jerusalem, Gesammelte Schriften*, III, 287 (Jospe, *"Jerusalem,"* p. 37).

21. Johann Heinrich Schulz, *Philosphische Betrachtung über Theologie und Religion überhaupt und über die jüdische insonderheit* (Frankfurt and Leipzig, 1784), see especially pp. 65–89, 229–241.

22. See chap. iv above.

23. Dohm, *Über die bürgerliche Verbesserung der Juden*, II, 30, 103.

24. Cahen, "L'Emancipation des Juifs," *REJ*, I (1880), 88.

25. Dohm, *Über die bürgerliche Verbesserung der Juden*, II, 103.

26. The main exponent of the theory of the Christian state was the Jewish convert Julius Stahl, the spiritual father of the conservative party in Prussia. See Julius Stahl, *Der christliche Staat und sein Verhältnis zu Deismus und Judenthum; eine durch die Verhandlungen des vereinigten Landtags hervorgerufene Abhandlung* (Berlin, 1847).

27. Friedrich Traugott Hartmann, *Untersuchung, ob die bürgerliche Freiheit den Juden zu gestatten sei* (Berlin, 1783), p. 3.

28. *Allgemeine Deutsche Biographie* (Leipzig, Duncker and Humblot, 1875–1912), XXI, 685–692.

29. Dohm, *Die bürgerliche Verbesserung der Juden*, II, 37, 41–51; reprinted from the *Orientalische und exegetische Bibliothek*, 19 (1782).

30. Dohm, *Die bürgerliche Verbesserung der Juden*, II, 42–43.

31. See chap. ii, note 22 above.

32. Hartmann, *Untersuchung*, pp. 142–146 followed Michaelis and so did some of the participants of the Metz discussion. From there on, the Messiah motive became a recurring one in the Jewish issue. See details in Mevorah, "The Prob-

lem of the Messiah in the Emancipation and Reform Controversies 1781–1819."

33. Dohm, *Über die bürgerliche Verbesserung der Juden*, II, 34–36, 38–39, 54–56.

34. Hartmann, *Untersuchung* pp. 17, 44–65, 115–117, 157–175, 183–186.

35. *Ibid.*, pp. 109–111. On Eisenmenger, see note 41 below.

36. *Ibid.*, pp. 8, 40, 124–134, 145.

37. Schulz, *Philosophische Betrachtungen*, pp. 216, 219.

38. Jews tried to prevent the publication of the book but succeeded only in postponing it by some ten years. See Graetz, *Geschichte der Juden* (1897), X, 275–280.

39. Dohm, *Die Bürgerliche Verbesserung der Juden*, II, 38–39.

40. See note 35 above.

41. The title of the last chapter of Eisenmenger's work is "Warumb die Juden sich so standhafft in ihrer Religion erweisen und so wenig den Christlichen glauben annehmen; und wie mit denselben zu verfahren seye, damit sie sich in mehrer anzahl alss bisshero geschehen ist, bekehren mögen."

42. The literature on Voltaire's attitude toward Jews is immense. The standard work is still Hanna Emmrich, *Das Judentum bei Voltaire* (Breslau, Priebatsch's Buchhandlung, 1930). The latest treatment of the subject is that of Hertzberg, *The French Enlightenment and the Jews*, pp. 280–313.

43. Emmrich, *Das Judentum bei Voltaire*, pp. 256–259.

44. The anti-Jewish trend of rationalistic deism has been stressed by Shmuel Ettinger, "Jews and Judaism as seen by the English Deists of the 18th Century" (In Hebrew), *Zion*, XXIX (1964), 182–207.

45. Max Wiener, "John Toland and Judaism," *HUCA*, XVI (1941), 215–242; Ettinger, "Jews and Judaism as seen by the English Deists," *Zion*, XXIX, 188–190. Similarly Jean Bodin is a philo-semitic; see Jakob Guttmann, *Jean Bodin in seinen Beziehungen zum Judentum* (Breslau, M. & H. Marcus, 1906). Georg Roellenblech, *Offenbarung, Natur und jüdische Überlieferung bei Jean Bodin; eine Interpretation des Heptaplomeres* (Gütersloh, G. Mohn, 1964).

46. From the vast literature on anti-Semitism in the ancient world, I will mention only Isaac Heineman, "Antisemitismus," Pauly-Wissowa, *Real-Encyclopedie der classischen Altertumswissenschaft*, Supplement V (1931), 3–43; and Johanan Hans Lewy, *Studies in Jewish Hellenism* (In Hebrew) (Jerusalem, Bialik Institute, 1969), pp. 79–196.

47. Schulz does not quote Voltaire and it may well be that Voltaire reached him indirectly. Voltaire styled himself a deist, while Schulz confessed to atheism. Still the arguments of both are on similar lines and Voltaire's influence was at the time of Schulz already generally absorbed.

48. On the following see Jacob Katz, "A State within a State — the History of an anti-Semitic Slogan," *The Israel Academy of Sciences and Humanities Proceedings*, IV (1971), 32–58.

49. [Johann Gottlieb Fichte], *Beitrag zur Berichtigung der Urteile des Publikums über die Französische Revolution* ([Berlin] 1793), p. 188.

50. Halphen, *Recueil des lois*, pp. 186–187.

51. See my article quoted in note 48 above.

52. Details in Freund, *Die Emanzipation der Juden in Preussen*, I, 89–100.

53. Christian Ludwig Paalzow, *Über das Bürgerrecht der Juden übersetzt von einem*

Juden (Berlin, 1803), pp. 98–99 (Original title *Tractatus historico-politicus de civitate Judaeorum* [Berolini, 1803].)

54. Karl Wilhelm Friedrich Grattenauer, *Wider die Juden. Ein Wort der Warnung an alle unsere christlichen Mitbürger*. 2nd ed. (Berlin, 1803), p. 5. On his indebtedness to Eisenmenger, pp. 28–31.

55. Freund, *Die Emanzipation der Juden in Preussen*, II, 177.

56. See the end of chap. v.

57. Freund, *Die Emanzipation der Juden in Preussen*, II, 208–209. On the reason for the change of mind of Schroetter, see *ibid.*, I, 109–118.

58. See the end of chap. V.

VII. THE DEFECTING FRINGE

1. See chap. x below.

2. This was the case for instance in Prussia; see Freund, *Die Emancipation*, I, 28–30.

3. Katz, *Exclusiveness and Tolerance*, pp. 148–150.

4. See chap. ii, n. 46 above.

5. *Merkwürdige Bekehrungsgeschichte aus dem Judenthum von 8, 10, und 12 Jahren getauft* (Berlin, 1798).

6. On Berlin see Ludwig Geiger, "Vor hundert Jahren," *ZGJD*, III (1889), 223–233; on Vienna see Pribram, *Urkunden und Akten zur Geschichte der Juden in Wien*, I, 384–388, 414–417; II, 18, 77.

7. See Eichstädt, *Bibliographie*, pp. 175–178.

8. A striking example for the first type can be taken from Gottfried Selig, and for the second, Johann Friedrich Heinrich Selig. Both told their respective life stories. Gottfried Selig, *Geschichte des Lebens und der Bekehrung Gottfried Seligs, lect. publ., seiner drey Schwestern und einiger nahen Anverwandten, welche sämmtlich das Judenthum verlassen und treue Bekenner Jesu geworden sind. Von ihm selbst beschrieben*. I–III (Leipzig, 1775–1779). Johann Friedrich Heinrich Selig, *Johann Friedrich Heinrich Seligs, eines Bekehrten aus dem Judenthume eigene Lebensbeschreibung*. I–II (Leipzig, 1783). The story of the first, though embellished in retrospect, reflects a genuine estrangement from Judaism and genuine acceptance of the Christian dogmas. The second is a clear case of pretended conversion.

9. See chaps. v and vi above.

10. See Barouh Mevorah, "The Background of Lavater's Appeal to Mendelssohn," (In Hebrew), *Zion*, XXX (1965), pp. 158–170.

11. See Mevorah's article quoted in the previous note.

12. See chap. iv above.

13. *Das Forschen nach Licht und Recht*, pp. 10–11.

14. *Ibid.*, p. 25. See Katz, "To Whom Was Mendelssohn Replying in 'Jerusalem'," *Zion*, XXIX, 120–125, XXXVI, 116–117.

15. On Hezel, see *Allgemeine Deutsche Biographie*, XII, 381–382.

16. Wilhelm Friedrich Hezel, *Die Allgemeine Judenbekehrung, oder die Möglichkeit, die Juden, mit Vernunft und Billigkeit, zu Christen und zu nützlichern und glücklichern Staatsbürgern zu machen* (Giessen, 1792), I, 3–11, 17–21, 28–33.

17. The letter is printed by Spiel, *Fanny von Arnstein*, pp. 86–89. The letter is undated and signed Michael Joseph Edler v.Arnsteiner. He is the fifth son of

Adam Isak Arnstein. See Bernhard Wachstein, *Die Inschriften des alten Juden-friedhofes in Wien*, I–II (Vienna and Leipzig, Braunmüller, 1912–1917), II, 463–464.

18. [Grattenauer], *Über die physische und moralische Verfassung der heutigen Juden*, pp. 20–21.

19. Geiger, "Vor hundert Jahren," *ZGJD*, III (1889), 205–211. See also notes 20 and 21.

20. *Olof Gerhard Tychsen's Nachtrag zu des Herrn Oberconsistorialraths Teller Beytrag zur neuesten jüdischen Geschichte über die Streitfrage: Ob der Ausdruck: nicht bey der jü-dischen Religion bleiben, nach jüdischen Sprachgebrauch heisse die christliche Religion an-nehmen?* (Rostock, 1788). On the tenet of Jewish religious law concerning the convert, see Katz, *Exclusiveness and Tolerance*, pp. 68–73. In some respects the convert was to be regarded as a Jew and Tychsen was able to quote sources which prima facie supported his view. Still, with regard to the case in point, his arguments were rather arbitrary and they were energetically rejected by the liberal-minded theologian Teller. See Wilhelm Abraham Teller, *Beytrag zur neusten jü-dischen Geschichte für Christen und Juden gleich wichtig und veranlasst durch die vor dem Königl. Cammergerichte zu Berlin erhobene Streitfrage: Bleibt der Jude, der zum Christen-thum übergeht, bey der jüdischen Religion?* (Berlin, 1788).

21. Heinrich Friedrich von Diez, *Kann die von jüdischen Vätern verbotene Glau-bensänderung ihren Kindern den angedrohten Verlust des Erbtheils nach sich ziehen?* (Dessau and Leipzig, 1783), pp. 14–20.

22. Katz, *Jews and Freemasons*, pp. 28–37.

23. On the Gesellschaft, see Ludwig Lesser, *Chronik der Gesellschaft der Freunde zu Berlin, zur Feier ihres fünfzigjährigen Jubiläums* (Berlin, 1842), pp. 8–16. I have lost the reference of the decision of the Gesellschaft mentioned in the text, but that this was the accepted attitude is clear from the facts. Many of the founders converted, but some of them remained members nonetheless, as for instance Abraham Mendelssohn-Bartholdy and Gerhard Friedrich Eschwe, alias Jere-mias Baruch. See Jacob Jacobson, ed., *Die Judenbürgerbücher der Stadt Berlin, 1809–1851* (Berlin, W. de Gruyter, 1962), pp. 16–17, 77; and Lesser, *Chronik*, pp. 19–20. On Saul Ascher's Attitude, see Clause Günther Reissner, *Eduard Gans, ein Leben im Vormärz* (Tübingen, Mohr [Siebeck], 1965), p. 54. On Gan's activity after his conversion see *ibid.*, p. 154.

24. Quoted by Meyer, *The Origins of the Modern Jew*, p. 98.

25. Øgvind Andreasen, *Aus den Tagebüchern Friedrich Münters* (Copenhagen-Leipzig, 1937), p. 41. See Katz, "To Whom Was Mendelssohn Replying in 'Je-rusalem'," *Zion*, XXIX, 116–118.

26. See Katz, *Jews and Freemasons*, p. 54 and the sources cited there.

27. Maimon told his life story in his famous autobiography first published in 1792–93. Solomon Maimon, *Lebensgeschichte* (My references are to the Schocken edition [Berlin, 1935].) On Maimon's philosophical contribution see Schmuel Hugo Bergmann, *The Philosophy of Solomon Maimon* (Jerusalem, Magnes Press; Hebrew University, 1967).

28. Maimon, *Lebensgeschichte*, pp. 173–176.

29. On Friedländer see Immanuel Heinrich Ritter, *Geschichte der jüdischen Re-formation*, I–III (1858–1865), vol. II, "David Friedländer. Sein Leben und sein Wirken im Zusammenhange mit den gleichzeitigen Culturverhältnissen und

Reformbestrebungen im Judenthum dargestellt (1861)." Substantial additions to understanding Friedländer's personality have been given by Meyer, *The Origins of the Modern Jew*, pp. 57–84.

30. [David Friedländer], *Sendschreiben an seine Hochwürden, Herrn Oberconsistorialrath und Probst Teller zu Berlin, von einigen Hausvätern jüdischer Religion* (Berlin, 1799), pp. 21–25.

31. At the same time Friedländer was prepared to accept the ceremonies of the Protestant church as a matter of formality. See *ibid.*, pp. 85–86.

32. Meyer, *The Origins of the Modern Jew*, p. 63.

33. The ideas of Friedländer are included in his *Akten-Stücke, die Reform der jüdischen Kolonien in den Preussischen Staaten betreffend* (Berlin, 1793). See Meyer, *The Origins of the Modern Jew*, pp. 62–64.

34. These hopes are hinted at in the public utterences of Friedländer (*Akten-Stücke*, pp. 23–24) and clearly expressed in his private correspondence with an Orthodox friend from Glogau. See Josef Meisl, "Letters of David Friedländer," *Yivo Studies in History* (In Yiddish), II (1937), 390–412.

35. This is the purpose of the appeals contained in the *Akten-Stücke*.

36. The views of those who participated in the Friedländer-Teller affair are well summed up by Ellen Littmann, "David Friedländers Sendschreiben an Probst Teller und sein Echo," *ZGJD*, VI (1935), 92–112.

37. Wilhelm Abraham Teller, *Beantwortung des Sendschreibens einiger Hausväter jüdischer Religion an mich, den Probst Teller* (Berlin, 1799), pp. 32–33.

38. See Littmann, "David Friedländers Sendschreiben an Probst Teller," p. 108. Meyer, *The Origins of the Modern Jew*, pp. 76–78.

39. On Schleiermacher and especially on his attitude during the controversy, see Wilhelm Dilthey, *Leben Schleiermachers* (Berlin, W. de Gruyter, 1922), pp. 467–471.

40. Friedrich Schleiermacher, *Briefe bei Gelegenheit der politisch theologischen Aufgabe und des Sendschreibens jüdischer Hausväter. Von einem Prediger ausserhalb Berlin* (Berlin, 1799), pp. 9–10.

41. *Ibid.*, pp. 45–48, 55–59.

42. Teller, *Beantwortung des Sendschreibens*, pp. 19–21, 48–49.

43. Andreasen, *Aus den Tagebüchern Friedrich Münters*, p. 42. See Katz, "To Whom Was Mendelssohn Replying in 'Jerusalem'," *Zion*, XXIX, 118.

44. Schleiermacher, *Briefe*, pp. 30–38.

45. Hilde Hüttmann, "August Neander [David Mendel] in seiner Entwicklung (diss., Hamburg, 1936), pp. 18, 20–26, 33–36. See also Karl Axenfeld, "Ueber Dr. August Neander's Stellung zum christlichen Glauben bei seinem Uebertritt zur christlichen Kirche." Appendix to *Moses Mendelssohn im Verhältnis zum Christentum. Nebst Anhang* (Erlangen, 1866), pp. 31–32; Justus Ludwig Jacobi, *Erinnerungen an D. A. Neander* (Halle, 1882), pp. 1–6.

46. Dilthey, *Leben Schleiermachers*, pp. 462–471.

47. See Julius Guttmann, "Kant und das Judentum," *Schriften herausgegeben von der Gesellschaft zur Förderung der Wissenschaft des Judentums* (Leipzig, 1908), pp. 41–61. Nathan Rotenstreich, "Hegel's Image of Judaism," *JSS*, XV (1953), pp. 36–37. *Idem*, "Kant's Interpretation of Judaism," (In Hebrew), *Tarbiz*, XXVII (1958), pp. 404–405. Guttmann and Rotenstreich point out the consequences of Mendelssohn's theory in denying the ethical character of Judaism. The conse-

quences were even more severe when it came to the evaluation of Judaism from the standpoint of emotion and devotion.

48. The devastating influences of the salons from the standpoint of Jewish self-preservation has often been described. See the latest treatment of the subject by Meyer, *The Origins of the Modern Jew*, pp. 85–114.

49. Hans Landsberg, *Henriette Herz; ihr Leben und ihre Zeit* (Weimar, Kiepenheuer, 1913), pp. 113, 135. See Meyer, *The Origins of the Modern Jew*, pp. 105–106.

50. *Ibid.*, pp. 20–101.

51. Friedländer, *Akten-Stücke*, p. 140.

52. Friedländer, *Sendschreiben*, pp. 78–80. See note 54 below.

53. See note 44 above.

54. Freund, *Die Emanzipation der Juden in Preussen*, pp. 421–422. See Geiger, "Vor hundert Jahren," *ZGJD*, III (1889), 232–233. Geiger was in possession of the list but did not see fit to publish it. See his note on p. 233.

55. Schnee, *Die Hoffinanz und der moderne Staat*, III, 216–220. Here Schnee summarizes his findings.

56. See Graetz, *Geschichte der Juden*, XI, 155–156. The editor of the second edition (Leipzig, 1900), Markus Brann, took exception to Graetz's statement; see appendix by S. Neumann, pp. 579–580. Similarly Nathan Samter, *Judentaufen im neunzehnten Jahrhundert* (Berlin, Poppelauer, 1906), p. 5. Correct evaluation by Mahler, *History of the Jewish People in Modern Times*, ii, 160.

57. Schleiermacher, *Briefe*, pp. 31–32.

58. E. G. Adolf Böckel, "Noch einige Worte ueber die Frage: Ob Israeliten als Freimaurer aufgenommen oder als Besuchende zugelassen werden können," *Archiv für Freimaurerei*, Bd. 3, H.2, 1845, pp. 57–58.

59. Grattenauer, *Ueber die physische und moralische Verfassung der heutigen Juden*, pp. 19–21.

60. "Politisch-theologische Aufgabe über die Behandlung der jüdischen Täuflinge," *Berlinisches Archiv der Zeit*, I (1799), 228–239.

61. "Ja, ein judaisierendes Christenthum das wäre die rechte Krankheit, die wir uns inokulieren sollten!", Schleiermacher, *Briefe*, pp. 36–37.

62. *Die Kinder Israels in den Wüsten; ein Beytrag zur Geschichte der Fehden unseres Jahrhunderts* (Boston-Sorau, 1804), p. 57.

VIII. A BLOW FOR REFORM

1. John Seiler Brubacher, *A History of the Problems of Education* (New York, McGraw-Hill, 1947), pp. 117–119; Robert Freeman Butts, *A Cultural History of Education; Reassessing Our Educational Traditions* (New York, McGraw-Hill, 1947), pp. 316–326.

2. See chap. v above.

3. On the educational ideologies of the Jewish Enlightenment, see Eliav, *Jewish Education in Germany*, pp. 52–70; Ernst Akiba Simon, "Philanthropism and Jewish Education," *Mordecai M. Kaplan Jubilee Volume on the occasion of his seventieth birthday* (New York, Jewish Theological Seminary of America, 1953), Hebrew section, pp. 149–187.

4. Joseph Klausner, *Historia shel ha-Sifruth ha-Ivrith ha-Hadasha*, I, 151–164.

5. Siegfried Stein, "Die Zeitschrift 'Sulamith'," *ZGJD*, VII (1937), 193–226.

6. Boaz Shahewitch, "Arba Leshonoth, iyunim shel Sifruth be-Lashon ha-Maskilim al pi 'Hameasef' " (Four Versions; literary observations concerning the language of the Maskilim of 'Hameasef'), *Molad*, XXIV (1967), 236–242.

7. Israel Zinberg, *The History of the Jewish Literature* (In Yiddish) (New York, Morris S. Sklarsky, 1943), VII, 113–132. (Hebrew translation, Tel Aviv, Merhavia, 1959, V, 63–72).

8. Hayyim Yosef David Azulai, *Ma'agal-Tob Hashalem* (Jerusalem, Mekize Nirdamim, 1934), p. 114; see Hertzberg, *The French Enlightenment and the Jews*, p. 159.

9. Eliav, *Jewish Education in Germany*, pp. 22–24.

10. Mordecai Levin, "The Problem of Productivization in the 'Haskalah' Period" (In Hebrew, diss., Jerusalem, 1964), pp. 43–50, 65–73.

11. Eliav, *Jewish Education in Germany*, pp. 71–118.

12. Zvi Scharfstein, *History of Jewish Education in Modern Times* (In Hebrew, Jerusalem, Rubin Mass, 1960), pp. 145–188, 226–228.

13. See notes 11 and 12 above.

14. Eliav, *Jewish Education in Germany*, pp. 52–70; Simon, "Philanthropism and Jewish Education," pp. 167–169.

15. Eliav, *Jewish Education in Germany*, pp. 72–73.

16. The history of the Mendelssohn translation has been repeatedly told, most exhaustively by Sandler, *Mendelssohn's Edition of the Pentateuch*.

17. Wessely, *Divre Shalom ve-Emeth*, chap. 5.

18. Eliav, *Jewish Education in Germany*, pp. 162–165.

19. *Ibid.*, pp. 165–167.

20. *Ibid.*, pp. 99, 117–118.

21. *Freimüthige Gedanken über die vorgeschlagene Verbesserung der Juden in den preussischen Staaten, von einem Juden, mit Zusätzen eines Christen* (Halle, 1792), pp. 25, 30. Eichstädt, *Bibliographie*, Nr. 540, attributes this book to Sabbattja Joseph Wolff. In the copy of the Universitätsbibliothek from Halle, Weil is indicated as the author.

22. See chap. v above.

23. Eliav, *Jewish Education in Germany*, pp. 57–60, 67–68, 76–79, 85–87.

24. Lazarus Bendavid, *Etwas zur Charakteristick der Juden* (Leipzig, 1793), pp. 45–52; Aaron Wolfssohn, *Jeschurun, oder unpartheiische Beleuchtung der dem Judenthume neuerdings gemachten Vorwürfe* (Breslau, 1804), pp. 111–116. Bendavid had four categories, Wolfssohn five.

25. Wolfssohn, *Jeschurun*, p. 114.

26. Mendelssohn, *Gesammelte Schriften*, III, 355–357; V, 669; Jospe, *"Jerusalem,"* pp. 104–107, 148; see Guttmann, *Die Philosophie des Judentums*, pp. 312–316; English translation, p. 115. See Wolfssohn, *Jeschurun*, pp. 114–115.

27. According to Henriette Herz this was the accepted view among contemporaries of Mendelssohn, though she herself disagreed with it. Landsberg, *Henriette Herz*, p. 147.

28. Saul Ascher, *Leviathan, oder, Über Religion in Rücksicht des Judenthums* (Berlin, 1792).

29. Fritz Pinkuss, "Saul Ascher, ein Theoretiker der Judenemanzipation aus der Generation nach Mendelssohn," *ZGJD*, VI (1935), 28–32; Ellen Littmann,

"Saul Ascher, First Theorist of Progressive Judaism," *LBIYB*, V (1960), 107–113.

30. Ascher's theory, ignored until a generation ago, has lately been repeatedly but not quite adequately analyzed; see Wiener, *Jüdische Religion im Zeitalter der Emanzipation*, pp. 40–41, 46–47; Hans Joachim Schoeps, *Geschichte der jüdischen Religionsphilosophie in der Neuzeit* (Berlin, Vortrupp Verlag, 1935), pp. 49–60. Littmann, "Saul Ascher," *LBIYB*, V, 113–119; Meyer, *The Origins of the Modern Jew*, pp. 122–125. See also the article by Pinkuss quoted in note 29 above.

31. Ascher, *Leviathan*, pp. 19–25, 212–213.

32. *Ibid.*, pp. 14–15, 220, 227. See Pinkuss, "Saul Ascher," p. 30; Wiener, *Jüdische Religion*, p. 41.

33. Ascher, *Leviathan*, pp. 172, 229. It is therefore irrelevant whether the tenets Ascher suggests are rational or not. He is prepared to accept dogmas on the basis of faith alone. Schoeps's critical observations have the Christian conception of dogma in mind, but irrationality is not necessarily one of the basic characteristics of dogma.

34. *Ibid.*, p. 237.

35. See Schoeps, *Geschichte der jüdischen Religionsphilosophie*, p. 53, n. 4.

36. Ascher, *Leviathan*, pp. 229, 237–239.

37. The news was printed in *Staats- und Gelehrte Zeitung des Hamburgischen unpartheyischen Correspondenten*, 1796, Nr.57, Freytag den 8.April. There it is quoted from *Gazette des Deux-Ponts*. The German translation of the dementi from Florence (see note 39) mentions the *Altonaischer Gelehrter Merkurius* (*ibid.* 4) and see there p. 8; see also note 38 below.

38. *Hameasef*, VII, 271–273. Ruth Kestenberg-Gladstein, *Neuere Geschichte der Juden in den böhmischen Ländern*; I: Das Zeitalter der Aufklärung (Tübingen, Mohr [Siebeck], 1969), pp. 145–146.

39. *Mihteve ha-Rabbanim* (Livorno, 1796). That the protest was launched at the request of Raphael Cohen is stated by Hayyim Joseph David Azulai, *Yosef Omez* (Livorno, 1798), no. 7. The Hamburg edition with a German translation appeared in the same year.

40. Azulai, *Yosef Omez*.

41. Schleiermacher interpreted Friedländer's intention, voiced in the *Akten-Stücke* (1792), that the state should exercise pressure upon Jews who might object to the planned reform because of religious apprehensions; Schleiermacher, *Briefe*, pp. 57–58. Elkan Henle wished to regard Jews who were not willing to accept citizenship because of the possible encroachment on religious observance as sick persons: "Der kluge und menschenfreundliche Arzt versucht in solchen Fällen gewiss alles, dem Kranken einige Hülfe, durch Ueberredung, auch im Nothfalle durch Anwendung einiger Gewalt zu verschaffen." [Elkan Henle], *Ueber die Verbesserung des Judenthums* (Frankfurt a.M., 1803), pp. 22–23. An anonymous writer propagated in 1804 expressis verbis compulsion in order to fuse Jews with Christians: *Ein freundliches Wort an die Christen, zur gänzlichen Beylegung ihres Streites mit den Juden. Von einem Juden* (Königsberg, 1804), pp. 45–51. From the non-Jewish side, the *Judenreformator* (*Der Judenreformator oder wie können die Juden vertilgt werden, ohne einem einzigen den Kopf abzuschneiden?* [Hamburg, 1805]) recommended the dissolution of the Jewish community and the suppressing of Jewish education by force; see especially pp. 132–138. See below on the activity of the Westphalian Consistoire.

42. Graetz, *Geschichte*, XI, 150–152. See the recent article of Moshe Samet, "Rabbi Saul Berlin and his Works," *Kiryath Sepher*, XLIII (1968), 427–441.

43. *Besamim Rosh* (Berlin, 1793), Nr. 18–20, 36, 64. See Mahler, *History of the Jewish People*, II, Appendix, 336–342. Mahler sees in Berlin a radical reformer altogether.

44. Jacob R. Marcus, "Reform Judaism and Laity, Israel Jacobson," *Central Conference of American Rabbis*, XXXVIII (1928), 452–456.

45. *Sulamith*, III, 1 (1810), 15–20; Marcus, "Reform Judaism and Laity," pp. 453, 490, n. 72.

46. Menahem Mendel Steinhardt, *Divre Igereth* (Rödelheim, 1812), pp. 1–9.

47. Ascher, *Leviathan*, p. 212.

48. (Rabbi Assa) [Abraham Asch], *Der Messias, oder Reform der Juden in religiöser und moralischer Hinsicht, philosophisch und theologisch erläutert* (Berlin, 1805), pp. 74–95. The author is identified in Zunz's copy in the Jews College Library, London.

49. Similar to Asch's argument are those of the pamphlet *Licht und Wahrheit, die Umbildung des Israelitischen Kultus betreffend. In zwei Briefen gewechselt zwischen zwei Freunden der Wahrheit* (Leipzig, 1813).

50. The letter is not extant but its contents were reproduced in *Les Premiers pas de la nation juive vers son bonheur sous les auspices du grand monarque Napoléon* (Paris, [1806]), pp. 7–14. See note 51 below.

51. Marcus, "Reform Judaism," pp. 413–418, and especially n. 30 on p. 485. Marcus did not see *Les premiers pas* (quoted in the previous note), but knew its contents from a quotation by Alexander Bran, *Gesammelte Actenstücke und öffentliche Verhandlungen über die Verbesserung der Juden in Frankreich* (Hamburg, 1806–07). His reconstruction is in all probability correct.

52. On Napoleon's policy toward Jews, see Robert Anchel, *Napoléon et les Juifs* (Paris, 1928), pp. 128–225, and Barouh Mevorah, *Napoleon u-Tekufato* (Napoleon and his Era), (Jerusalem, Bialik Institute, 1968).

53. The following rests on my analysis in Katz, *Exclusiveness and Tolerance*, pp. 182–193.

54. Rabbi Moses Sopher paid tribute to the way in which Sinzheim availed himself of his task as the president of the Sanhedrin. See chap. ix below.

IX. CONSERVATIVES IN A QUANDARY

1. On the significance of messianism in Jewish society see Gershom Scholem, "Zum Verständnis der messianischen Idee im Judentum," *Eranos-Jahrbuch*, 28 (1959), 193–239.

2. See chap. iii.

3. The letter is printed in Mendelssohn, *Gesammelte Schriften, Jubiläumsausgabe*, XVI, 2–3.

4. *Ibid.*, pp. 178–179. This letter is of a later date but it indicates an earlier inquiry of Mendelssohn on the same matter.

5. See Katz, *Exclusiveness and Tolerance*, pp. 174–177.

6. Kayserling, *Moses Mendelssohn*, pp. 276–280. The problem has been dealt with exhaustively by Moshe Samet in his unpublished doctoral thesis "Halaha ve-Reforma" (In Hebrew; Jerusalem, 1967), pp. 76–172.

7. The relevant correspondence on the subject is pointed out in Mendelssohn, *Gesammelte Schriften, Jubiläumsausgabe*, XVI, 154–159, 161–168.

8. *Ibid.*, pp. 172, 178–183.

9. Eliav, *Jewish Education in Germany*, pp. 41–42.

10. Naphtali Herz Wessely, *Yen Levanon* (Berlin, 1775). The approbation of Landau is printed on pp. 1a–b.

11. The content of this poem has been discussed by Bolle, *De Opheffing van de Autonomie der Kehilloth*, pp. 66–67, 200.

12. This has been done especially by Shohet, *Beginning of the Haskalah among German Jewry*. See chap. iii above, where the significance of Shohet's findings are discussed.

13. Zerah Eidlits, *Or la-Jesharim* (Prague, 1785), pp. 96b–97a.

14. Yehezkel Landau said in so many words that the Sabbatians are worse than the deists who deny Revelation and Divine Providence; *Drushe ha-Zelah* (Warsaw, 1897), p. 79. See also p. 106. Eleazar Fleckeles had a clash with this group as late as 1799, and wrote his condemning pamphlet, *Ahavat David* (Prague, 1800), against them.

15. Landau, *Drushe ha-Zelah*, p. 76. The date of the sermon is indicated on pp. 77 and 80.

16. Jaroslaus Schaller, *Kurzgefasste Geschichte der kais. kön. Bücherzensur und Revision im Königreich Böhmen* (Prague, 1796), p. 9.

17. Salomon Hugo Lieben, "Rabbi Eleazar Fleckeles," *JJLG*, X (1913), pp. 4–7.

18. Eleazar Fleckeles, *Olath Hodesh Hasheni, Olath Zibur* (Prague, 1796), pp. 54b–56a, 86b–87b, 97a. In the same vein are some of the later sermons of Yehezkel Landau, *Drushe ha-Zelah*, pp. 47–48, 103–104. The date of the last one is clearly after the eighties; of the first there is no evidence, but judged by the content, it seems to be of late date.

19. [August Friedrich Cranz], *Über den Missbrauch der geistlichen Macht oder der weltlichen Herrschaft in Glaubenssachen, durch Beyspiele aus dem jetzigen Jahrhundert ins Licht gesetzt* (Berlin, 1781–82). Mendelssohn referred to the Altona (Hamburg) rabbi's intolerance in his letter of July 13, 1779 (Kayserling, *Moses Mendelssohn*, p. 524); and his public protest a year later against the rabbis' right to use the ban was clearly directed at this and similar cases. Mendelssohn, *Gesammelte Schriften*, III, 198–208. See also Friedländer, *Akten–Stücke*, pp. 19–20.

20. Abraham Meir Habermann, *Encyclopaedia Hebraica*, XIV, 882–884.

21. See the condemnation of David Tewele, rabbi in Lissa, published by Louis Lewin in *JJLG*, XII (1918), 182–183. Partly reprinted in Simha Assaf, *Mekoroth le-Toldoth ha-Hinuh be-Yisrael* (Tel Aviv, Dvir, 1925), I, 1, pp. 236–238. Similar is the tone of the letter sent by Rabbi Yehezkel Landau to community wardens of Berlin in the same matter: *Ibid.*, pp. 239–240.

22. See Mendelssohn's letter to Avigdor Levi in *Gesammelte Schriften, Jubiläumsausgabe*, XVI, 251–253. See Eliav, *Jewish Education in Germany*, pp. 33–34. There is no indication that Mendelssohn later appealed for an authorization, as Eliav assumes. The words of Yehezkel Landau that Eliav quotes refer to Salomon Dubno and not to Mendelssohn.

23. See the source quoted by Sandler, *Mendelssohn's Edition of the Pentateuch*, pp. 196–197.

24. Fleckeles, *Olath Hodesh Hasheni*, pp. 12b–13a.

25. In the introduction to the Pentateuch edition of Sussmann Glogau in 1785 reprinted in Assaf, *Mekoroth le-Toldoth ha-Hinuh be-Yisrael*, pp. 240–241. I see no reason to doubt Landau's authorship of this introduction.

26. Fleckeles, *Olath Hodesh Hasheni*, p. 13b.

27. This controversy has been dealt with very often. See Graetz, *Geschichte*, XI, 86–90; Eliav, *Jewish Education in Germany*, pp. 36–51.

28. Moshe S. Samet, "Mendelssohn, Weisel, and the Rabbis of their Time," *Studies in the History of the Jewish People and the Land of Israel in Memory of Zvi Avneri*, pp. 233–257, has clearly shown this to be the case.

29. However, see note 9 above.

30. Marcus Herz, *An die Herausgeber des hebräischen Sammlers über die frühe Beerdigung der Juden* (Berlin, 1787). A year later an enlarged edition appeared.

31. See Klausner, *Historiya*, I, 254–260. On Pappenheim's philosophical contribution, see Harry Austin Wolfson, "Solomon Pappenheim on time and space and his relation to Locke and Kant," *Israel Abraham's Memorial Volume* (New York, Press of the Jewish Institute of Religion, 1927), pp. 426–440; Pappenheim expressed his apprehension of a possible reform tendency that would emerge out of the Sanhedrin convoked by Napoleon. Solomon Seligmann Pappenheim, *Nachruf an den Rabbiner Levi Schauelsohn Fränkel in Angelegenheit seiner unternommenen Reise nach Paris* (Breslau, 1807).

32. Solomon Pappenheimer (sic), *An die Barmherzigen aus En-dor; oder, über die zu früh scheinende Beerdigung der Juden* (Breslau, 1794); *Idem, Deduction seiner bereits herausgegebenen Apologie für die frühe Beerdigung der Juden* (n.p., 1798).

33. Kestenberg-Gladstein, *Neuere Geschichte der Juden in den böhmischen Ländern*, I, 124–146.

34. Louis Lewin, "Materialien zu einer Biographie Wolf Heidenheims," *MGWJ*, XLIV (1900), 134–138; XLV (1901), 422–432; *Idem*, "Heidenheimiana," *Jeschurun*, (Berlin), X (1923), 212–214.

35. Lesser, *Chronik der Gesellschaft der Freunde in Berlin*, pp. 10, 25–27.

36. Eliav, *Jewish Education in Germany*, pp. 80–87.

37. Benjamin Hirsch Auerbach, *Geschichte der Israelitischen Gemeinde Halberstadt. Nebst einem Anhange ungedruckter, die Literatur wie die religiösen und politischen Verhältnisse der Juden in Deutschland in den letzten 2 Jahrhunderten betreffender Briefe und Urkunden* (Halberstadt, 1866), p. 146. Jost as an eye-witness testifies to the resistance of the communities against the Consistoire's prescription: Israel Marcus Jost, *Geschichte des Judenthums und seiner Sekten* (Leipzig, 1857–1859), III, 327.

38. Saul Berlin, Isaac Eichel, and Aaron Wolfsohn were productive in this field; see Zinberg, *The History of the Jewish Literature*, VII, 1, pp. 171–184, 232–234 (Hebrew edition, V, 91–97, 122–125).

39. Zvi Hirsch Horowitz, *Lahme Toda* (Offenbach, 1816), pp. 18a, 33b.

40. Isidor Krakauer, *Geschichte der Juden in Frankfurt a.M. [1150–1824]* (Frankfurt a.M., Kauffmann, 1925–1927), II, 355–431.

41. See Katz, *Jews and Freemasons*, pp. 56–59.

42. See Horowitz, *Lahme Toda*, pp. 36a–b, 44a–47a. Every one of the sermons ends with the drawing of conclusions which lead him to rebuke the community.

43. Shlomo Sofer (ed.), *Igroth Sofrim* (Vienna-Budapest, Schlesinger, 1929, reprinted New York, Ziegelheim, 1946), section 2, pp. 1–2.

44. Nahman Berlin, *Et ledaber* (Breslau, 1819), pp. 66b–67a.

45. Yekutiel Arieh Kammelhaar, *Mofet Hador* (Munkacs, Kahn and Fried, 1903), p. 76.

46. Landau, *Drushe Ha-Zelah*, p. 53.

47. Herbert Juan Bloom, "Felix Libertate and the Emancipation of Dutch Jewry," *Essays on Jewish Life and Thought, presented in honor of Salo Wittmayer Baron* (New York, Columbia University Press, 1959), p. 114.

48. Eleazar Fleckeles, *Tshuva me-Ahava* (Prague, 1804–1820), III, 71a; see Samet, "Halaha ve-Reforma," pp. 141–143.

49. See chap. viii above.

50. *Organisation civile et réligieuse des Israélites de France et du Royaume d'Italie* (Paris, 1808), p. 144.

51. Jacob Katz, "Contribution towards a biography of R. Moses Sofer," *Studies in Mysticism and Religion presented to Gershom G. Scholem* (Jerusalem, Magnes Press, 1967), Hebrew section, pp. 142–143.

52. *Ibid.*, pp. 141–142.

53. The conscious conservative attitude assumed by Moses Sofer has been stressed by Josef Bendavid, "Beginning of Modern Jewish Society in Hungary during the First Half of the Nineteenth Century" (In Hebrew), *Zion*, XVII (1952), pp. 122–128.

54. *Ibid.*; Katz, "Contribution towards a Biography of R. Moses Sofer," pp. 133–136.

55. See note 54 above.

56. Katz, "Contribution towards a Biography of R. Moses Sofer," pp. 138–141.

57. *Ibid.*, pp. 143–144.

X. LEGAL STEPPINGSTONES

1. Dohm, *Ueber die bürgerliche Verbesserung der Juden*, I, 152–153.

2. Pribram, *Urkunden und Akten*, I, pp. LXXIX–LXXX; Yehezkel Landau, *Drushe ha-Zelah*, p. 105; on Mendelssohn's attitude toward the Edict, see Katz, "To whom was Mendelssohn replying in 'Jerusalem'," *Zion*, XXIX (1964), 127–129; on Wessely see chap. v, note 3 above.

3. Friedrich Gottlieb Kloppstock, *Sämmtliche Werke* (Leipzig, 1854), pp. 262–263. The poem was first published in 1782.

4. Pribram, *Urkunden und Akten*, I, pp. 494–500. Ludwig Singer, "Zur Geschichte der Toleranzpatente in den Sudetenländern," *JGJCR*, V (1933), 231–311. Joseph Bergl, *Geschichte der ungarischen Juden* (Leipzig, 1879; Kaposvar, 1879), pp. 74–79.

5. Pribram, *Urkunden und Akten*, I, p. 494. Singer, "Zur Geschichte der Toleranzpatente," p. 293.

6. Eduard Winter, *Der Josefinismus; die Geschichte des Reformkatholizismus, 1741–1848* (Berlin, Rütten and Löning, 1962), pp. 172–176.

7. Pribram, *Urkunden und Akten*, I, pp. 440–494. Singer, "Zur Geschichte der Toleranzpatente," pp. 248–258, 278–287.

8. Singer, "Zur Geschichte der Toleranzpatente," pp. 260, 295.

9. Pribram, *Urkunden und Akten*, I, pp. CII–CXXVI.

10. Simon Adler, "Das Judenpatent von 1797," *JGJCR*, V (1933), 199–229, especially p. 205.

11. Pribram, *Urkunden und Akten*, I, pp. CXVI–CXVIII.

12. Rabbi Landau is known to have addressed the first Jewish recruits with tears in his eyes: Ruth Kestenberg-Gladstein, *Neuere Geschichte der Juden in den böhmischen Ländern*, pp. 70–72. Against the right of the emperor to draft Jews, wrote Saul Ascher his *Bemerkungen über bürgerliche Verbesserung der Juden veranlasst bei der Frage: Soll der Jude Soldat werden?* ([Frankfurt a.0], 1788).

13. Adler, "Das Judenpatent von 1797," p. 224.

14. The preamble of the Judenpatent of 1797 spoke of "christliche und jüdische Unterthanen," *ibid.*, p. 205.

15. Paul Tänzer, *Die Rechtsgeschichte der Juden in Würtenberg 1806–1828* (Berlin, Kohlhammer, 1922), pp. 22–27, 97.

16. *Sammlung der im Grossherzogtum Baden in bezug auf die Israeliten erschienenen Gesetze und Verordnungen* (Karlsruhe, 1837), p. 3. Selma Täubler-Stern, *Die Emanzipation der Juden in Baden* (Frankfurt a.M., Kauffmann, 1934), pp. 30–33.

17. Stefan Schwarz, *Die Juden in Bayern im Wandel der Zeiten* (Munich, Olzog, 1963), pp. 77–180.

18. The regulations of 1808 stated "Die Einwohner der jüdischen Nation . . . sind als erbfreie Staatsbürger zu behandeln," *Sammlung*, p. 3.

19. Täubler-Stern, *Die Emanzipation der Juden in Baden*, pp. 51–52.

20. On the history of the Leibzoll see Ulrich Friedrich Kopp, "Vom Juden-Leibzoll," *Bruchstücke zur Erläuterung der Teutschen Geschichte und Rechte* (Cassel, 1799), pp. 97–154; for details on the abolition of the Leibzoll, see: Michael Silberstein, "Wolf Breidenbach und die Aufhebung des Leibzolles in Deutschland," *ZGJD*, V (1892), 126–145.

21. In Würtemberg Jews could exempt themselves from military service for payment. Friedrich Fr. Mayer, *Sammlung der würtembergischen Gesetze in Betreff der Israeliten* (Tübingen, 1847), p. 6, but other groups had similar privileges. J. M. Jost, *Neuere Geschichte der Israeliten* (Berlin, 1846), I, 167.

22. Carl August Buchholz, *Actenstücke, die Verbesserung des bürgerlichen Zustandes der Israeliten betreffend* (Stuttgart, 1815), p. 99.

23. Halphen, *Recueil des lois*, p. 15. Problems of halakic nature that arose from the state of affairs reached Moses Sofer, at that time rabbi in Mattersdorf, West Hungary, from Trieste, as early as 1804. See Jacob Katz, "Contribution towards a biography of R. Moses Sofer," *Studies in Mysticism and Religion Presented to Gershom G. Scholem* (Jerusalem, Magnes Press, 1967, Hebrew section), p. 138, n. 159.

24. Buchholz, *Actenstücke*, p. 100. The Mecklenburg-Schwerin regulations follows in the main the Prussian ones, but the end of this paragraph is a novelty compared to the Prussian ones. Compare Buchholz, *Actenstücke*, p. 90.

25. Mayer, *Sammlung*, pp. 6, 11. The Baden authorities seem to have imagined that rabbis, like Catholic priests, are capable of giving dispensation of religious prescriptions when a conflict arises between these and the demands of other duties; see Täubler-Stern, *Die Emanzipation der Juden in Baden*, p. 55.

26. Robert Anchel, "Les lettres-patentes du 10 juillet 1784 pour les Juifs d'Alsace," *Les Juifs en France* (Paris, Janin, 1946), pp. 213–233.

27. Whether Jews of pre-Revolutionary France were to be regarded as

Frenchmen has been discussed by scholars. See M. Maignial, *La question juive en France en 1789* (Paris, 1903). Maignial concluded that Jews were regarded as foreigners. Morice Liber's objections to this conclusion ("Les Juifs et la convocation des Etâts généraux," *REJ*, LXIV [1912], p. 245), are unconvincing apologetics.

28. This phase in the history of the Jews' emancipation has been repeatedly described. The latest treatment is that of Herzberg, *The French Enlightenment and the Jews*, pp. 338–368.

29. Ludwig Horwitz, *Die Israeliten unter dem Königreich Westfalen: Ein aktenmässiger Beitrag zur Geschichte der Regierung König Jérôme's* (Berlin, Kommissionsverlag von S. Calvary, 1900), p. 6.

30. See Bolle, *De Opheffing van de Autonomie der Kehilloth*, pp. 123–177 (English summary, pp. 196–207).

31. Isidor Kracauer, *Geschichte der Juden in Frankfurt a.M.* (Frankfurt a.M., I. Kauffmann, 1927), II, 402–419.

32. Anchel, *Napoléon et les Juifs*, pp. 260–352, 412–426.

33. Ludwig von Rönnes and Heinrich Simon, *Die früheren und gegenwärtigen Verhältnisse der Juden in den sämmtlichen Landestheilen des Preussischen Staates* (Berlin, 1843), p. 373.

34. Freund, *Die Emanzipation der Juden in Preussen*, II, 49, 76–88, 206–207.

35. *Ibid.*, I, 451–452; II, 226; Ludwig Geiger, *Geschichte der Juden in Berlin* (Berlin, 1871), I, 142–145; Ludwig Geiger, "Aus den Gemeindeakten," *Gemeindeblatt der jüdischen Gemeinde zu Berlin*, II (1912), pp. 34–36; *Sulamith*, IV (1812), vol. 1, 45–46. On Friedländer's hopes in connection with the Edict, see Meyer, *The Origins of the Modern Jew*, pp. 79–81; [Gotthold Solomon], *Licht und Wahrheit, die Umbildung des Israelitischen Kultus betreffend* (Leipzig, 1813), pp. V–XI; Abraham Asch, *Der heilige Verein oder die wahre Vaterlandsliebe* (Berlin, 1813), pp. 30–32. This booklet is, as far as I can see, nowhere listed in the bibliographies. A copy of it is to be found in the Jews College Library, London, Montefiore Collection.

36. Freund, *Die Emanzipation der Juden in Preussen*, II, 457 (paragraphs 18–19); 458–459 (paragraphs 31, 32, 34, 36). On Mecklenburg-Schwerin, Bavaria, and Denmark, see Buchholz, *Actenstücke*, pp. 95–96 (paragraph 3); 132 (paragraph 2); 152 (paragraph 19); Mayer, *Sammlung*, pp. 17–18 ("Verordnung gegen das Eindringen fremder Juden in das Königreich"). This ordinance is from 1814 but it refers to earlier issues of similar content.

37. Leopold Löwenstein, "Die Juden im Elsass vor und während der Schreckensscherrschaft," *Blätter für jüdische Geschichte und Literatur*, I (1900), 17–18, 33–34, 49–50, 65–69; II (1901), pp. 1–3. Moïse et Ernest Ginsburger, "Contributions à l'histoire des Juifs d'Alsace pendant la terreur," *REJ*, XLVII (1903), 283–299.

38. Halphen, *Recueil des lois*, p. 15.

39. [Nathan] Netter, *Die Schuldennot der Metzer Gemeinde* (Metz, n.p., 1913), pp. 48–56; Nathan Netter, *Vingt siècles d'histoire d'une communauté juive; Metz et son grand passé* (Paris, Libschutz, 1938), pp. 207–211, 229–233.

40. *The Cambridge Modern History*, IX (1907), pp. 203–204.

41. Diogène Tama, *Collection des actes de l'Assemblée des Israélites de France et du Royaume d'Italie* (Paris, 1807), pp. 274–303. The preamble to the Constitution of the Consistoire presents the work as the decision of the Assembly. Halphen, *Recueil des lois*, p. 38.

42. *Ibid.*, pp. 38–42.
43. See chap. ii above.
44. Halphen, *Recueil des lois*, pp. 41 (paragraph 23), 39–40 (paragraph 12).
45. *Sulamith*, II (1808), vol. 1., 3–9.
46. Täubler-Stern, *Die Emanzipation der Juden in Baden*, pp. 30–32.
47. Pribram, *Urkunden und Akten*, I, pp. 494–495.
48. Adler, "Das Judenpatent von 1797," pp. 199–200.
49. Alfred Willmann, "Die mährischen Landesrabbiner," in Hugo Gold, ed., *Die Juden und Judengemeinden Mährens in Vergangenheit und Gegenwart* (Brünn, Jüdischer Buch-und Kunstverlag, 1929), pp. 45–49.
50. Freund, *Die Emanzipation der Juden in Preussen*, II, 459.
51. Leopold Auerbach, *Das Judenthum und seine Bekenner in Preussen und in den anderen deutschen Bundesstaaten* (Berlin, 1890), pp. 281–283, 288–301.

XI. THE FUTILE FLIGHT FROM JEWISH PROFESSIONS

1. See above, especially chap. v.
2. Halphen, *Recueil des lois*, pp. 185, 211. In Holland, too, a more variated distribution and a better moral standard on the part of the Jews were expected. See *Actenstücke zur Geschichte der Erhebung der Juden zu Bürgern in der Republik Batavien* (Neustrelitz, 1797), pp. 12–13, 25–26, 56–63; Bolle, *Die Opheffing von de autonomie der Kehilloth*, pp. 128–129, 202.
3. See the sources quoted in chap. x above.
4. The Edict of Tolerance permitted Jews to take residence in any part of Vienna; Pribram, *Urkunden und Akten*, I, 498 (paragraph 18). In Prague the permission was limited to the merchant. Singer, "Zur Geschichte der Toleranzpatente in den Sudetenländern," *JGJCR*, V, 270. The other regulations implicitly permitted the taking of residence in any part of the city where Jews were admitted. In Bavaria, there is an exception for Munich, the capital. There a special permission was necessary for a Jew to buy a house for his residence. Buchholz, *Actenstücke*, p. 135.
5. Zosa Szajkowski, *The Economic Status of the Jews in Alsace, Metz, and Lorraine (1648–1789)* (New York, Editions historiques Franco juives, 1954), pp. 50–67, 73–76, 91–99.
6. The criticism of the Jews by the Alsatian because of their demeanor is well summed up in the memorandum of the Strasbourg citizens to the National Assembly in Paris in 1790 expressing the objection against possible admittance of Jews to their town. The Jews are accused of "watching for the needs or even perhaps making them arise by presenting deceptive enticements" especially of young people and domestics, offering them their wares etc. *Très-humble et très respectueuse Adresse que présente à l'Assemblée Nationale la Commune toute entière de la Ville de Strasbourg*, p. 11. On the background of this, see Paul Hildenfinger, "L'Adresse de la commune de Strasbourg à l'Assemblée Nationale contre les Juifs," *REJ*, LVIII (1909), 112–120.
7. This is a much debated point; see Szajkowski, *The Economic Status of the Jews*, pp. 50–54.
8. This is the recurring motive in the pleas of the Jews and their defendants. See "Mémoire sur l'état des Juifs en Alsace," Dohm, *Ueber die bürgerliche Verbes-*

serung der Juden, pp. 174–175; Henry Grégoire, Essai sur la régénération physique, morale et politique des Juifs (Metz, 1789), pp. 84–85.

9. Solomon V. Posener, "The Immediate Economic and Social Effects of the Emancipation of the Jews in France," JSS, I (1939), 281–293.

10. Alfred Glaser, Geschichte der Juden in Strassburg (Strassburg, 1891), pp. 31–44; Erwin Schnurmann, La statistique de la population juive de Strasbourg (Strasbourg, n.p., 1933), p. 3.

11. Posener, "The Immediate Economic and Social Effects," pp. 281–293.

12. S. Posener, "Les Juifs sous le premier Empire," REJ, XCIII (1932), p. 202; Léon Kahn, Les Juifs à Paris depuis le VIe siècle (Paris, 1889), pp. 99–105.

13. Posener, "The Immediate Economic and Social Effects," pp. 297–304.

14. Berr Isaac Berr, Lettre du Sieur Berr-Isaac-Berr, Manufacturier, membre du conseil municipal de Nancy, à M. Grégoire, sénateur, à Paris (Nancy, 1806), p. 15.

15. Zosa Szajkowski, "Jewish Participation in the Sale of National Property during the French Revolution," JSS, XIV (1952), 291–316.

16. Posener, "The Immediate Economic and Social Effects," pp. 293–307; Léon Kahn, Les professions manuelles et les institutions de patronage (Paris, 1885), pp. 11–15, 65–74.

17. The letter referred to in note 14 above.

18. [D. Ring], Vierzig Jahre von Frankfurt am Main, oder Frankfurt im Jahr 1792, im Jahr 1832 und im Jahr 1872 (Frankfurt am Main, 1834), p. 62. Ring describes the places outside the Judengasse where it was forbidden for Jews to enter or where they were permitted only during certain hours. These restrictions were finally removed after much controversy in the time of the French hegemony in 1811. See Kracauer, Geschichte der Juden in Frankfurt am Main, pp. 395–417. On Prague, see Singer, "Zur Geschichte der Toleranzpatente," pp. 270–271. The same tendency in Hamburg during the short period of equality under French rule; Helga Krohn, Die Juden in Hamburg, 1800–1850 (Frankfurt am Main, Europäische Verlagsanstalt, 1967), p. 17. On the social and religious consequences, see chap. ix above.

19. Ernst Weyden, Geschichte der Juden in Köln am Rhein (Cologne, 1867), pp. 273–277.

20. Maria Zelzer, ed., Weg und Schicksal der Stuttgarter Juden; ein Gedenkbuch (Stuttgart, Klett, 1964), pp. 23, 508.

21. The repeal of the Jews' rights in Bremen and Lübeck was one of the main causes for bringing the Jewish issue before the Congress of Vienna; see Baron, Die Judenfrage auf dem Wiener Kongress, pp. 39–45, 47–49, 86–100.

22. Schnee, Die Hoffinanz und der moderne Staat, II, 137–139, 144–145.

23. From Bohemia direct evidence is available that Jews failed to be attracted to agriculture: Josef Johann Schiffner, Gallerie der interessantesten und merkwürdigsten Personen Böhmens (Prague, 1804), p. 344. On the continuation of political and other motivation, see notes 24 and 25 below.

24. Hermann Baerwald, "Zur Geschichte der Schule: Das Philanthropin 1804–1813," Einladungsschrift zu der am 15. März 1869 stattfindenden Prüfung der Real und Volksschule der israel. Gemeinde (Frankfurt a.M., 1869), p. 16. See also Krohn, Die Juden in Hamburg, p. 17.

25. Die Kinder Israels in den Wüsten (Boston) [Sorau, 1804], p. 65; Sulamith, VI, 2 (1824), 195; VII, 1 (1825), pp. 17, 132–133, 365, 373 (an optimistic report). In

the forties, Ludwig Philippson (*wie sich der Statistiker Staatsrath etc. Dr. J. G. Hoffmann verrechnet!* (Leipzig, 1842), pp. 37–39), described the difficulties a would-be Jewish artisan encountered.

26. Instances for the difficulties were given by an anonymous writer in *Gespräch zwischen dem Schuhmacher Ehrlich und einem hausierendem Juden Israel in einer Dorfschenke ohnweit Breslau* (Berlin, 1799), pp. 9–11. (This book is not in the bibliographies. A copy of it is to be found in the Jews' College Library, London.) The difficulties had been foreseen by some of the opponents of Jewish integration. See Hartmann, *Untersuchung, ob die bürgerliche Freiheit den Juden zu gestatten sei*, pp. 176–179, 183–186. The experience of some decades taught the lesson also to a Jewish apologist. See Jost, *Offenes Sendschreiben an Herrn Geh. Ober-Regierungs-Rath K. Streckfuss zur Verständigung über einige Punkte in den Verhältnissen der Juden* (Berlin, 1833), p. 82.

27. Schnee, *Die Hoffinanz und der moderne Staat*, II, 146–148. See also p. 122.

28. [Michael Benedikt Lessing], *Die Juden und die öffentliche Meinung im preussischen Staate* (Altona, 1833), p. 79.

29. Printed with the letter quoted in note 14 above. See *ibid.*, pp. 39–42.

30. The collection of money by Geisenheimer mentioned in the text is perhaps the indication of such a step. From the second decade of the nineteenth century, societies for the furthering of artisanship among Jews were founded in almost every community of any importance. The history of these societies is still to be written. Much material on it is to be found in the records of *Sulamith* as listed in Siegfried Stern, "Die Zeitschrift 'Sulamith'," *ZGJD*, VII (1937), pp. 223–224.

31. See chap. x above; Wenzel Gustav Kopetz, *Allgemeine österreichische Gewerbs-Gesetzeskunde* (Vienna, 1829), pp. 322–323.

32. Halphen, *Recueil des lois*, pp. 46–47.

33. An early testimony is given by Schiffner, *Gallerie der Personen Böhmens*, p. 344.

34. Kopetz, *Allgemeine österreichische Gewerbs-Gesetzeskunde*, pp. 322–324.

35. Pribram, *Urkunden und Akten*, I, pp. CXVIII–CXXIX.

36. *Ibid.* The same practice was in vogue in Bavaria, where the Jew was not free to buy and resell property. Accordingly, a non-Jewish person used to be employed as a silent partner. See Buchholz, *Aktenstücke*, p. 135; Alexander Lips, *Über die künftige Stellung der Juden in den deutschen Bundesstaaten* (Erlangen, 1819), pp. 86–87.

37. Pribram, *Urkunden und Akten*, I, pp. CXI–CXII.

38. Täubler-Stern, *Die Emanzipation der Juden in Baden*, pp. 51–52, 54.

39. *Ibid.*, pp. 95–96. The number mentioned is 570 artisans.

40. Pribram, *Urkunden und Akten*, II, 5.

41. Posener, "The Immediate Economic and Social Effects," pp. 294–302.

42. Karl Gutzkow, "Börne's Leben," *Gesammelte Werke* (Frankfurt a.M., 1845), VI, 85–91.

43. Edmund Silberner, *Sozialisten zur Judenfrage* (Berlin, Colloquium Verlag, 1962), pp. 109–112.

44. On Austria see note 33 above. On Prussia see Selma Täubler-Stern, "The Jews in the Economic Policy of Frederick the Great," *JSS*, XI (1949), pp. 141–152. In Baden, Täubler-Stern, *Die Emanzipation der Juden in Baden*, pp. 95–96.

45. Buchholz, *Actenstücke*, pp. 115–116, 134, 137; Kopetz, *Allgemeine österreichische Gewerbs-Gestezeskunde*, pp. 317, 326–327; Bergl, *Geschichte der ungarischen Juden*, p. 87.

46. A moralizing attitude is assured even by jurists and economists like Günther Heinrich von Berg, *Staatswissenschaftliche Versuche* (Lübeck and Leipzig, 1795), II, 255–263. Similarly, Johann Ludwig Ewald, a theologian and advocate of Jewish rights, remained critical of traditional Jewish business practice. Johann Ludwig Ewald, *Ideen über die nöthige Organisation der Israeliten in christlichen Staaten* (Karlsruhe, 1816), pp. 177–181. It is seldom that the economic usefulness of the hawker — who brought the commodities to the consumer and bought up what otherwise would have been wasted — was recognized. But one exception was Ignatz von Rudhardt. See his *Über den Zustand des Königreichs Bayern nach amtlichen Quellen* (Stuttgart, 1825–1827), I, 63–68. Gabriel Riesser quoted him in support of his vindication of Jewish business practice. Gabriel Riesser, *Gesammelte Schriften* (Frankfurt am Main–Leipzig, 1867), II, 126.

47. This was one of the complaints of the Frankfurt burgher [Schreiber]: *Über die Ansprüche der Judenschaft in Frankfurt a.M. auf das volle Bürgerrecht dieser Stadt* (Frankfurt a.M., 1817), p. 56. Ludwig Börne in his anonymous *Actenmässige Darstellung des Bürgerrechts der Israeliten zu Frankfurt a.M.*, pp. LXX–LXXI, minimized the Jewish economic expansion but did not deny it. For Bohemia see Schiffner, *Gallerie der Personen Böhmens*, p. 350. In the forties, Ludwig Philippson declared the adaptation of the Jewish merchant to the Gentile type to be the most outstanding result of the process of readjustment. Ludwig Philippson, *Wie sich der Statistiker . . . Hoffmann verrechnet*, pp. 34–35.

48. The situation was described, unsympathetically but not incorrectly, by von Bricevitz in *Minerva*, II (1812), pp. 165–169, voicing strong reservations concerning the Prussian edict of that year in favor of the Jews. In similar terms is the observation of Conrad Friedrich von Schmidt-Phiseldeck, *Ueber das jetzige Verhältnis der jüdischen Nation zu den christlichen Bürgervereinen und dessen küftige Umgestaltung* (Copenhagen, 1817), pp. 46–49, 62–63. The first part of this book appeared in the original Danish version as early as 1811, and was translated into German in 1816 (printed in Wiesbaden). The book has been extensively reviewed and points relevant to the discussion here have been emphasized by Ch. H. Pfaff, "Ueber das Verhältniss christlicher Regierungen und Staaten gegen die Juden in dem gegenwärtigen Zeitpunkte," *Kieler Blätter für 1819*, I (1819), 127, 141–142, 145–146.

49. See chap. iii, note 10.

50. The most famous case of the fall of a court Jew is that of Joseph Süss Oppenheimer, known by the name Jud Süss, who served his master Karl Alexander of Würtemberg. When the duke died in 1737, the opposition party of the aristocracy came to power. They impeached Jud Süss and he was condemned and hanged (Selma Stern, *Jud Süss* (Berlin, 1927); Schnee, *Die Hoffinanz und der moderne Staat*, IV, 109–148). The Rothschilds in France survived the Restoration, the Revolutions of 1830 and 1848. Another example of the court Jew's insecurity is that of Samuel Oppenheimer in Vienna: Max Grunwald, *Samuel Oppenheimer und sein Kreis* (Vienna and Leipzig, Braumüller, 1913), pp. 117–137. Another case is told by Schnee, *Die Hoffinanz und der moderne Staat*, III, 99–106. Schnee summarizes the cases, *ibid.*, p. 204, but minimizes the precariousness of the court Jew's position.

51. Louis Poujol, *Quelques observations concernant les Juifs en général, et plus particulièrement ceux d'Alsace* (Paris, 1806), pp. 55, 61, 66–67, 150–151.

52. See the memorandum quoted above, note 6, pp. 13–14. The edict of 1753 (in the memorandum erroneously dated 1751) did in fact not grant more than the right of residence to a limited number of Jews. Lorraine Jews were quick to refute the allegation of the Strasbourg memorandum in a pamphlet *Réponse des Juifs de la Province de Lorraine à l'adresse présenté à l'Assemblée Nationale par la commune toute entière de la ville de Strasbourg*. A German translation has been published by David Friedländer in the *Berlinische Monatsschrift*, XVIII, 1 (1791), pp. 351–392. I have seen only the German translation. See M. Ginsburger, "Nancy et Strasbourg," *REJ*, LXXXIX (1930), pp. 79–85. The alleged bad experience of Lorraine with the Jews served as an argument against granting citizenship in Prussia for one of the high officials in Berlin in 1810. Freund, *Die Emanzipation der Juden in Preussen*, II, 300.

53. Berr, *Lettre*, p. 12.

54. The first scholarly analysis of the facts was given by the Prussian statistician Johann Gottfried Hoffmann in the 1830's and 1840's when enough experience was accumulated. See his *Die Bevölkerung des Preussischen Staates nach dem Ergebnisse der zu Ende des Jahres 1837 amtlich aufgenommenen Nachrichten in staatswirtschaftlichen, gewerblichen und sittlichen Beziehung* (Berlin, 1839), pp. 81–83; Idem, *Zur Judenfrage; Statistische Erörterungen* (Berlin, 1842). Against Hoffmann's analysis is directed the attack of Ludwig Philippson quoted above (see notes 25 and 47), but his arguments are on an apologetic level. Hoffmann's analysis comes very near to the conclusions of the best treatment of the problem in our day by Simon Kuznets, "Economic Structure and Life of the Jews," *The Jews, Their History, Culture and Religion*, ed. Louis Finkelstein (Philadelphia, Jewish Publication Society of America, 1960), II, 1597–1666.

55. Schmidt-Phiseldeck, *Über das jetzige Verhältnis*, pp. 24, 62; Pfaff, *Über das Verhältnis*, pp. 127, 129, 141. (Schmidt-Phiseldeck is apparently on the lookout for an adequate expression and once (*ibid.*, p. 18) he uses the newly coined word "Familienvolk.") Friedrich Rühs, *Über die Ansprüche der Juden an das deutsche Bürgerrecht* (Berlin, 1816), p. 6; Jakob Friedrich Fries, *Über die Gefährdung des Wohlstandes und Charakters der Deutschen durch die Juden* (Heidelberg, 1816), pp. 3, 5, 12, 15, 17, 18.

56. Ludolf Holst, *Judenthum in allen dessen Theilen aus einem staatswissenschaftlichen Standpunkte betrachtet* (Mainz, 1821), p. 78. Holst attributes the expression to Ludwig Börne, who however denied using it but found the expression not inappropriate. Ludwig Börne, "Der ewige Jude," *Gesammelte Schriften* (Nuremberg, 1880), V, 10–11.

57. See Jacob Katz, "The German-Jewish Utopia of Social Emancipation," *Studies of the Leo Baeck Institute*, ed. Max Kreuzberger (New York, F. Ungar Pub. Co., 1967), pp. 61–80.

XII. PROFILE OF EMANCIPATED JEWRY

1. On this and the following, see Jacob Katz, "The Term 'Jewish Emancipation'," pp. 1–25.

2. Jacob Toury, *Die politischen Orientierungen der Juden in Deutschland, von Jena bis Weimar* (Tübingen, Mohr [Siebeck], 1966), pp. 1–28.

3. Jost, *Neuere Geschichte der Israeliten*, II, 160–165.

4. *Ibid.*, I, 110–129, 271–310.

5. See chap. ix above.

6. Moshe Rinott, "Gabriel Riesser — Fighter for Jewish Emancipation," *LBIYB*, VII (1962), 11–38; Katz, "The Term 'Jewish Emancipation'," pp. 21–25.

7. Katz, "The Term 'Jewish Emancipation'," pp. 16–21.

8. It is worthwhile to quote this in full: "Ein kurzes aber starkes und eindringliches Wort, ganz aus dem Gefühle eines constitutionellen Staatsbürgers hervorgegangen, nicht aus einem so oft als kränkelnd und charakterlos getadelten falschen Humanitätsgefühl," Jost, *Neuere Geschichte* I, 196. Jost also pointed here to the English origin of the term and the Catholic context — a fact that escaped me when I wrote my above quoted article.

9. The opponents will be treated below.

10. See Katz, "The Term 'Jewish Emancipation'," pp. 23–25.

11. The struggle for Jewish emancipation in England has often been described. See Albert M. Hyamson, *A History of the Jews in England* (London, Macmillan, 1928), pp. 260–272; Cecil Roth, *A History of the Jews in England* (Oxford, Clarendon Press, 1964), pp. 241–266.

12. Jost, *Neuere Geschichte*, I, 78–93, 158–177.

13. Salo W. Baron, "Impact of the Revolution of 1848 on Jewish Emancipation," *JSS*, XI (1949), 195–248.

14. Ismar Elbogen, *A Century of Jewish Life* (Philadelphia, Jewish Publication Society of America, 1944), pp. 3–17; Otto Jöhlinger, *Bismarck und die Juden* (Berlin, Reimer, 1921), pp. 6–26.

15. Elbogen, *A Century of Jewish Life*, pp. 17–29.

16. The polemic that arose around Rühs's and Fries's writings has been described by Jost, *Neuere Geschichte*, I, 46–47. A modern analysis of the opponents' weltanschauung is offered by Selma Stern-Täubler, "Der literarische Kampf um die Emanzipation in den Jahren 1816–1820 und seine ideologischen und soziologischen Voraussetzungen," *HUCA*, XXIII (1950–51), 171–196.

17. Katz, "The Term 'Jewish Emancipation'," pp. 19–25.

18. Bruno Bauer, *Die Judenfrage* (Brunswick, 1843), An analysis of Bauer's attitude is given by Nathan Rotenstreich, *Judaism and Jewish Rights* (In Hebrew; Tel Aviv, ha Kibbutz ha Meuhad, 1959), pp. 9–25.

19. Théophile Hallez, *Des Juifs en France, de leur état moral et politique depuis les premiers temps de la monarchie jusque à nos jours* (Paris, 1845), pp. 230–238; Henry Lucien-Brun, *La condition des Juifs en France depuis 1789* (Paris-Lyon, Retaux, 1901), pp. 217–224; Paul Leuilliot, *L'Alsace au debut du XIXe siècle: essais d'histoire politique, économique et religieuse [1815–1830]*9 (Paris, S.E.V.P.E.N., 1959–60), III, 233–246.

20. Silberner, *Sozialisten zur Judenfrage*, pp. 56–62.

21. Toussenel's book appeared in Paris in 1845, and was reprinted in 1847.

22. Toussenel's ideas were analyzed by Silberner, *Sozialisten zur Judenfrage*, pp. 28–35.

23. Katz, *Jews and Freemasons*, chaps. 2–4.

24. *Ibid.*, pp. 63, 74–75.

25. *Ibid.*, pp. 82–91.

26. *Ibid.*, pp. 73–81, 84–91.

27. Heinrich Eberhard Gottlob Paulus, *Die jüdische Nationalabsonderung nach Ursprung, Folgen und Besserungsmitteln* (Heidelberg, 1831), pp. 2–3, and elsewhere in this book, which is Paulus's main publication concerning the Jewish question.

28. Karl Streckfuss, *Über das Verhältnis der Juden zu den christlichen Staaten* (Halle, 1833), pp. 21–22.

29. Salo Baron, *Die Judenfrage auf dem Wiener Kongress* (Vienna and Berlin, 1920), pp. 125–130.

30. Conte Corti, *Der Aufstieg der Hauses Rothschild* (Vienna, 1953), pp. 117–120; The splendid house and society of the Rothschilds in Naples and Frankfurt is also described by Moritz Oppenheim, *Erinnerungen* (Frankfurt am Main, Frankfurter Verlagsanstalt, 1924), pp. 44, 75–77.

31. Heinrich Heine, *Sämtliche Werke* (Hamburg, 1862), XIII, 296–297; Joseph Dresch, *Heine à Paris (1831–1856), D'après sa correspondance et les témoignages de ses contemporains* (Paris, Didier, 1956), p. 73.

32. Rudolf Vierhaus, *Am Hof der Hohenzollern, Aus dem Tagebuch der Baronin Spitzemberg 1865–1914* (Munich, Deutscher Taschenbuch Verlag, 1965), pp. 34 35.

33. There is a vast literature on intermarriage. The latest summary and extensive bibliography on the subject is Moshe Davis, "Mixed Marriage in Western Jewry: Historical Background to the Jewish Response," *JJS*, X (1968), 177–220.

34. The sociological definition of the Jewish community as pariah-people by Max Weber has the same starting point as the more impressionistic namegiving by the anti-Jewish critics. Weber's definition has been much discussed and censured, recently by Efraim Shmueli, "The Pariah-People and its 'Charismatic Leadership'. A Re-evaluation of Max Weber's 'Ancient Judaism'," *PAAJR*, XXXVI (1968), 167–247. Whatever one thinks of the evaluation of Jewish existence that is involved in Weber's definition, the factual basis of the castlike structure of the Jewish community remains valid.

35. Some of the participants of the Assembly of Notables in Paris convened by Napoleon in 1806 proposed to answer the emperor's question concerning Judaism's attitude toward intermarriage in the affirmative: *Collection des actes de l'assemblée des Israélites de France et du royaume d'Italie* (Paris, 1807), pp. 143–144. Similar opinions were voiced by members of the first reform rabbinical assembly in 1844 in Braunschweig; see *Protocolle der ersten Rabbinerversammlung abgehalten in Braunschweig vom 12ten bis zum 19ten Juni, 1844* (Brunswick, 1844). The anonymous author of the pamphlet *Ein freundliches Wort an die Christen zur gänzlichen Beylegung ihres Streits mit den Juden* (Königsberg, 1804), pp. 45–46, fancied that intermarriage could be enforced by the state.

36. This attitude is reflected in the discussion of the rabbinical assembly of Braunschweig quoted in the previous note. See also the article "Zur Mischehe," *AZJ* (1847), pp. 485–487.

37. This was repeatedly stated by those who fought mixed marriages by Jews. (Kinorhe) [Isidor Ludwig Chronik], "Ueber die Ehe zwischen Juden und Christen," *Kirchliche Reform* (October 1846), pp. 6–7.

38. Michael Hess, *Freimüthige Prüfung der Schrift des Herrn Professor Rühs über die*

Ansprüche der Juden an das deutsche Bürgerrecht (Frankfurt am Main, 1816), pp. 55–57. Rühs reacted to this argument in his *Die Rechte des Christenthums und des deutschen Volkes, vertheidigt gegen die Ansprüche der Juden und ihrer Verfechter* (Berlin, 1816), pp. 12–14.

39. Rinott, "Gabriel Riesser," pp. 17–19.

40. Solomon Schechter, "Abraham Geiger," *Studies in Judaism*, Third Series (Philadelphia, Jewish Publication Society of America, 1924), pp. 69–77.

41. I cannot list here the bibliography pertaining to this subject. An excellent survey and analysis of the conception of Judaism in its new setting is given by Max Wiener, *Jüdische Religion im Zeitalter der Emanzipation* (Berlin, Philo Verlag, 1933).

42. Martin Philippson, *Neueste Geschichte des jüdischen Volkes* (Leipzig, 1900), II, 175–180; Leopold Löw, *Zur neueren Geschichte der Juden in Ungarn*, pp. 274–296.

43. On the historical significance of the Wissenschaft des Judentums, see Wiener, *Jüdische Religion*, pp. 175–208; Meyer, *The Origins of the Modern Jew*, pp. 144–182.

44. Jacob Katz, "The Influence of Religion and Society on each other at the Time of the Emancipation," *European Judaism*, I (1966), 22–29.

45. See chap. viii above.

46. The historical role of the philosophy of Judaism and Jewish historiography is well analyzed by Wiener, *Jüdische Religion*, pp. 114–174, 209–228. Among the historians, Heinrich Graetz's influence is especially notable. On this see the latest evaluation by Shmuel Ettinger, "Introduction" to H. Graetz, *Essays, memoirs, letters* (In Hebrew; Jerusalem, Bialik Institute, 1969), pp. 7–36.

47. Theodor Mommsen, *Auch ein Wort über unser Judenthum* (Berlin, 1881), pp. 15–16.

48. See chap. x, note 36.

49. But there were limitations on the rabbis' mobility. The école rabbinique in Metz, established by the state in 1829, accepted only French students. Halphen, *Recueil des lois*, p. 82. In Württemberg the rabbi had to be a citizen of the state; only in exceptional cases had a foreigner access to the examinations which were a precondition for accepting a rabbi's position. Mayer, *Sammlung der Württembergischen Gesetze in Betreff der Israeliten*, p. 85.

50. Graetz, *Geschichte der Juden*, XI, 384–385.

51. Barouh Mevorah, "Effects of the Damascus Affair upon the Development of the Jewish Press, 1840–1846" (In Hebrew), *Zion*, XXIII–XXIV (1958–59), 46–65.

52. Philippson, *Neueste Geschichte*, II, 300–309.

53. Narcisse Leven, *Cinquante ans d'histoire L'alliance israélite universelle (1860–1910)* (Paris, Alcan, 1911); André Chouraqui, *L'alliance israélite universelle et la renaissance juive contemporaire, 1860–1960* (Paris, Presses universitaires de France, 1965), pp. 1–141.

INDEX

Absorption, 3, 6, 36, 124; and post-medieval thought, 37; of converts, 123; of Jewish community in Prussia, 171; and emancipation, 214

Academy of Science, Berlin, 51

Acceptance, social, 58, 74, 104, 161, 193; Gentile objections, 80–103; through conversion, 104–143; Hezel's assumptions, 109; and anti-Jewish attitudes, 201

Acculturation, 32, 34, 43, 64–66; of Ashkenazi women, 84; through conversion, 109

Act of Emancipation, Prussia, 121

Adaptation, cultural, 6, 161, 166; and Jewish citizenship, 63, 77; and religion, 118; and Liberal movement, 196; and Jewish sociability, 203

Adler, Nathan, 154

Admittance, see Residence, right of

Agriculture, 60, 61, 100, 169, 176, 179, 189; and free choice of residence, 184; and Baden *Oberrat*, 185

Alexandria, 216

Algiers, 3

Alliance Israélite Universelle, 3, 216

Alsace, French, 22, 70–73, 139–140, 167, 169; Jewish occupations in, 177–180, 182, 188; anti-Jewish attitudes in, 200

Alsace-Lorraine, 9, 11

Altona, 137

Amalgamation, 2, 196; and Jewish emancipation, 201; and Jewish sociability, 203

Amsterdam, 25, 30, 70, 146; traditionalists of, 155–156

Anderson, Reverend James, 45

Anglican church, 12, 195

Anticapitalism, 200

Antiquity, 83; and Jewish traditionalism, 5

Anti-Semitism, 80–103, 193, 199–200, 217

Apology of the Westphalian Rabbis, 151

Apostasy, 25, 134

Aristocracy, landed, 182

Army, see Military service

Arnheim family, 204

Arnstein, Adam, 110–111, 112

Arnstein, Fanny von, 56, 110, 112

Arnstein family, of Vienna, 31; and conversion, 110–112

Artisans, 179–183, 185–186, 189–190

Asch, Abraham, 139

Ascher, Saul, 133–134, 209; his *Leviathan*, 133; and autonomy of personality, 134–135; outline of reform, 135–136, 212; demand for positive reformation, 138–139, 141

Ashkenazim, 9, 10, 42, 138; in Buda, 13; in France, 42, 168; Gentile stereotype of, 80–81; and Freemasons, 84; seeds of acculturation, 146

Assimilation (assimilationists), 2, 34, 168, 196; and maintenance of Jewish organizations, 212–213

Associations, 21; craftsmen's, 44–45, 99; of enlightened Jews, 113. *See also* Guilds

Atheism, 147; as basis for anti-Jewish attitudes, 89

Attitudes, 57, 64; Jews, 35–37, 96, 140; Gentiles, 37–41; anti-Jewish, 80–103, 193, 199–200; remolding of, 124–126; of traditionalists, 156; and Jewish emancipation, 200–201

Aurore Naissante, Frankfurt Jewish Freemasons, 153

Australia, 3

Austria, 2, 3, 22; size of Jewish community in, 9; *non tolerandis Judaeorum* privilege, 12; Edict of Tolerance, 30, 42; educational reform, 127, 128; and Jewish right of residence, 183; and Jewish occupations, 184, 186; and Jewish citizenship, 192; and Jewish emancipation, 198

Austrian Empire, 10, 198; size of Jewish community, 9

Azulai, Hayyim Joseph David, 126, 137

Baden, 166, 167, 186; *Oberrat*, 173, 184; Edict of *1809*, 185

Baer, Israel, 146

Bankers, 22, 187–188; influence of, 31

Baptism, 112, 117, 119, 121, 123, 210; among court Jews, 122

Batavia, 74

Batavian Republic, 168

Bauer, Bruno, 200

Bavaria, 166, 176, 186, 194

Behavior, social, 1, 62, 93; and Jewish community, 20, 31, 148, 173; and traditionalists, 148, 156. *See also* Morality

Belgium, 168

Bendavid, Lazarus, 132

Berlin, 57–69, 80, 105, 202; extent of conversion from Jewish community, 121–122; establishment of *Freischule*, 126–128; and secularization of education, 128

Berlin Burial Society, 151

Berlin, Nahman, 154

Berlin, Saul, 137–138

Berr, Berr-Isaac, 180, 183, 188

Bertolio, Abbé, 74

Bible, 4–5, 36; and educational reform, 129–130

Bing, Isaiah Berr, 73

Bingen on the Rhine, 181

Bismarck, Otto von, 197–198

Biur, 129

Bleichröder family, 204

Böckel, Ernst Gottfried Adolf, 122

Body tax (*Leibjoll*), 104, 155, 162, 166; abolished in France, 167; abolished in Prussia, 170

Bohemia, 9, 10, 13, 18, 174; Jewish associations, 20; and Edict of Tolerance, 162–164; and *Judenpatent* of Francis II, 164–165; post-emancipation restrictions, 174, 198; and Jewish occupations, 183, 186

Bonn, 75

Bonnet, Charles: his *La Palingénésie Philosophique*, 107; attempts to convert Mendelssohn, 107–108

Books, publication of, 125, 128, 148–149

Bordeaux, 126, 128

Börne, Ludwig (Juda Löb Baruch), 186

Bourbons, France, 169

Braunschweig, 181

Bremen, 180

Breslau, 70, 121; educational reform in, 127, 128, 152

Britain: Freemasonry in, 44–46. *See also* England

Buda, 13

Bureaucracy, 31–33

Burial, early, 113, 137, 144, 150, 151, 156

Burial society, in community organization, 21

Businessmen, 22

Capitalists, Jewish, 15, 18–19, 177, 186, 187, 190; contacts beyond local boundaries, 23

Catholic church, 5, 163; and Napoleon, 172

Catholics, 39, 217; and romanticists, 120; Irish, 195

Catter, Herr, 114

Censorship, 147, 149

Cerf Berr, Isaac, 70, 178, 179

Character, Jewish, 68–69; transformation of, 64–65, 124–125; Humboldt's view of collective, 76–77; and reform of Jewish status in Prussia, 101, 102

Charity, 21, 35, 213

Chief Rabbi, 20, 78

Christianity, 14, 15, 25, 214; in Gentile's ideology of rejection, 87–90; converts to, 104–123; Mendelssohn's view, 108. *See also* Conversion

Church, 38, 39; in von Dohm's thinking, 59; and state, 59–60, 171; warnings re Judaization of, 123

Cicero, 98

Circumcision, 77, 135, 139

Citizenship, 30, 32, 33, 87, 142, 153, 155; for French Jews, 30, 70–75, 100–101, 140, 167–168, 171, 176, 192; for German Jews, 57–64, 68, 70, 122; effect on economy, 60–61; reconciliation with religious proscriptions, 61–64, 78, 91–92, 100, 166–167; and Dutch Jews, 74–75, 168, 192; implementation of reform, 75–76; Prussia, 76, 170–171, 192; and anti-Jewish attitudes, 91–103; and "State within the State" slogan, 99; and conversion, 122–123; and legislation, 161–162, 165–166, 168, 214; and legal status of Jewish religion, 174; and Jewish emancipation, 195–198, 214

City of London, 196

Civic betterment, 2, 68, 71, 72–73, 109, 161–162, 192, 198; in Humboldt's view, 77; through reeducation, 109

Civil rights, 58–59, 174 175, 199; restriction of (France, *1808*), 169

Civil service, 89, 170, 180, 186, 189, 194–195; in England, 196; in Prussia, 198

Civil status, 7, 32, 38–42, 57, 104, 192–193; in England, 12, 15, 38, 39; in Germany, 40–41, 57–64, 68, 70, 71; France, 70–74; Holland, 74–75. *See also* Citizenship

Cleves, 20

Cohen, Daniel J., 32

Cohen, Raphael, 136, 148, 194

Collective responsibility, 104, 116, 170

Cologne, 180

Comitate, 14

Community, Jewish, 19–20, 155; transformation of, 1–2; leadership, 20–21; means of control, 21, 155; social status and social mobility, 21–22; extension beyond local boundaries, 22–23; and

individual self-identification, 23; and traditionalism, 24–25; and conversion, 26, 110–111, 121–123; control over individuals dealing with outer world, 26–27; comparative independence and self-government, 31; and the state, 31–33; and acculturation, 34–36; collective responsibility, 104, 116, 170; and Friedländer, 116–117; in post-Revolutionary France, 171–172; and social exclusiveness, 204, 206, 208, 213; and preservation of interstate solidarity, 214–217; as social subgroup after emancipation, 216–217

Congress of Vienna (*1814–15*), 31, 71, 193, 199, 204

Conservatives, *see* Traditionalism

Consistoire, France, 172–173; discriminatory features, 173

Constitutionalism, 198

Conversion, religious, 2, 25–26, 72, 78, 104–123, 142; in Germany, 34; and acceptance of Jew into society, 38, 111; and anti-Jewish attitudes, 95; age for, 105–106; motives for, 106, 119–121; Christian expectations of, 106–107; and dissolution of traditional society and values, 110–111, 121; and parental authority, 112; attitude toward baptism, 112; and Enlightenment, 113–116; attempts at compromise, 115–119; emotional component, 119–120; among literati, 120; extent of defection, 121–122; by Jewish community elite, 122

Copenhagen, 70

Counter-Reformation, 15

Court agents, 22

Court Jew, 28–31, 43; influence of, 28–29; and Jewish emancipation, 30–31; effects of changes of times on, 31, 187; and conversion, 122; in Stuttgart, 180

Courts, 19; Jewish, 19; and court Jew, 29; rabbinical, 140, 156

Craftsmen, Jewish, 60. *See also* Handicrafts

Cranz, August Friedrich, 53

Cremieux, Adolphe, 216
Cromwell, Oliver, 12, 15, 39, 92
Culture, Jewish, 1, 2, 214–215; and Jewish society, 4; and traditionalism, 5; contacts beyond local boundaries, 21–22; Gentile interest in, 43

Dalberg, Grand Duke, 169
Damascus, 216
De Bonald, Louis Gabriel Ambroise, 101
Deism, rationalistic, 98
De Pinto, Isaac, 34, 69, 83
Dessau, 127, 128
Deventer, 11
Diaspora, 1, 37, 205
Dietary laws, 205–206; as issue in civil reform, 61, 63; and religious reform movement, 138; and traditionalists, 147, 153, 159
Discrimination, 169, 193, 203; legal, 10–12; political, 12–13; and intermarriage, 140–141; and *consistoire* and *Oberrat*, 173–174
Divorce, 19, 167
Dohm, Christian Wilhelm, 50, 57–64, 68, 70, 71, 73, 93, 95, 131; his *Uber die burgerliche Verbesserung der Juden*, 58, 192; and natural religion, 63–64; his "Civic Betterment," 68, 71, 109, 161–162, 192; and anti-Jewish attitudes, 90
Dresden, 17
Dubno, Solomon, 129
Dutch National Assembly, *see* Holland

Eastern Europe, 2
Economics, 15, 39; and Revolution, 179
Economy, 1, 10, 14, 213–214; Dutch, 11; Austrian Empire, 12–13; role of Jew in, 15, 18–19; and acceptance into social structure, 19; and horizontal social mobility, 22; and Jew's civil status, 38–41, 57, 60–61
Edict of *1808*, France, 184
Edict of *1809*, Baden, 185
Edict of *1812*, Prussia, 30–31, 121–123, 170; and legal status of Jewish religion, 174

Edict of Bavaria, 176
Edict of Expulsion, France, 10–11
Edict of Expulsion, Prague (*1745*), 31
Edict of Nantes (*1598*), 99
Edict of Tolerance, Austria, 30, 42, 53, 66–67, 70, 71, 161–162, 170; and conservatives, 147, 155; stipulations of, 162–163; legal significance of, 163–164; uneven character of, 163–164; and Jewish traditional occupations, 176; and Jew's acquisition of landed property, 184
Education, 5, 20, 166; and community status, 21; and social mobility, 21, 22; and Jew-Gentile social relationships, 43–44; and transformation of Jewish character, 64–65, 68–69, 124–125; secularization of, 65–66, 127–128, 147; reform, 66–69, 124–134, 215; Wessely's views of, 66–68; and perpetuation of Jewish "type," 84; and conversion, 109, 119; curriculum content, 127; civic, 127; and the traditionalists, 130–133, 152, 158–159; criticism of, 161; and Edict of Tolerance, 162, 164
Egalitarianism, 70–75, 104; and *Judenpatent* of Francis II, 165
Eibeschütz, Jonathan, 24, 36, 143
Eisenmenger, Johann Andreas: his "Entdecktes Judenthum," 44, 93, 94, 96; his misrepresentation of Jewish views and attitudes, 96–97
Eisenstadt, 13
Emancipation, Jewish, 2–8, 30, 42, 100, 191–218; and national influence, 4; as political slogan, 4, 195–196; and traditionalism, 4–6; and destruction of stereotypes, 7–9; and intervention of state in Jewish community affairs, 32; and dissolution of autonomous community, 33; Humboldt's recommendations, 77–78; and reemergence of idea of Christian state, 90; as slogan of Liberal movement, 195–196; differences from country to country, 196–199; and reemergence of anti-Jewish attitudes, 199–200; and Jew-

ish social exclusiveness, 201–206; and definitions of Judaism, 206–212; expectations for, 213–214; and signs of disintegration of Jewish nation, 214–215

Emden, Jacob, 36, 143–145

Emigration, 3, 6, 170–171, 215–216

Endogamy, 204–205

England, 1, 3, 9, 22; size of Jewish community, 9, 196; civil status of Jew in, 12, 15, 38, 39; acculturation of Sephardim, 34; Jewish emancipation, 196–197

Enlightenment, the, 30, 90, 107, 189; penetration into Jewish circles, 54; and reform, 57–59; and conversion, 113–114; and education, 124–127, 131–132; and definition of Judaism, 210

Estates General, France, 73

Esterhazy, Count, 13

Ethics, 130

Exclusiveness, Jewish, 95, 96, 98, 201–202, 213–214; conflicting interpretations of, 202–205; and endogamy, 204–207; as defense mechanism, 205–206; and Jewish attitudes, 207

Expulsion, 33, 170

Family life, 20, 189; and conversion, 113; and intermarriage, 205; and social exclusiveness, 206, 207, 214

Fichte, Johann Gottlieb, 99–100

Fleckeles, Eleazar, 147, 149–150

Florence, fictitious synod of rabbis at, 136–137, 139

France, 1, 3, 9, 22, 146, 193; size of Jewish community, 9; size of general population, 10; restrictions on Jewish immigration, 10–11; economy, 15; citizenship to Jews, 30, 70–75, 100–101, 104, 140, 167–168, 171, 176, 192; National Assembly, 30, 42, 73–74, 168, 176; acculturation of Sephardim, 34; Freemasonry in, 44, 46; Estates General, 73; and implementation of social reform, 75; anti-Jewish attitudes in, 100, 200; reform

legislation, 167–168, 171; the *consistoire*, 172–173; Jewish occupations, 177, 186; Jewish emancipation, 198; and interstate solidarity of Jews, 216

Francis II, of Austria, 164; his *Judenpatent*, 164–165; and military service by Jews, 165

Frankel, David, 47

Frankel, Zechariah, 211

Frankfurt am Main, 25, 70, 75, 202; educational reform, 127, 130; citizenship for Jews, 168–169; Jewish occupations, 177, 180, 186; Jewish emancipation, 197

Frankfurt an der Oder, 70, 137

Frankists, 112–113

Frederick II, of Prussia, 51, 102, 170

Frederick the Great, 30, 105

Freemasons, 44–47, 80, 81, 83–84, 153; social basis, 44–45; and religion, 45, 89, 114; and the Jews, 45–47, 201–202; Scottish rite, 47; Mendelssohn excluded from, 50; and Order of the Asiatic Brethren, 55, 84–85; and "State within the State" slogan, 99

Freischules, Berlin, 126–127

French National Assembly, 30, 42, 73–74, 168, 176

French Revolution, 4, 28, 57, 70, 71, 100; and Jewish status, 167–170, 171; and economics, 179; and Jewish occupations, 188

Friedländer, David, 30–31, 75–76; and conversion controversy, 115–119; and dissolution of Jewish communal organization, 116–117, 121; and establishment of *Freischule*, 126

Friends of the Hebrew Language (*Dorshe Sfat Ever*), 125

Fries, Jacob Friedrich, 199

Fürth, 12

Galicia, 2, 10

Geiger, Abraham, 207, 211

Geisenheimer, Siegmund, 127, 181

Gellert, Christian Fürchtegott, 69

Gentiles, 37–38; attitudes of, 38–41; and social relations with Jews, 42–56; resistance of to integrating Jews, 80–103, 104; description of common Jew, 81–83

Germany, 1, 3, 9, 10, 19, 22; reaction to Jewish integration in, 7; size of Jewish community, 9, 10; controlled population growth, 10; *non tolerandis Judaeorum* privilege, 12, 13; and court Jew, 15; intervention in Jewish community affairs, 31–32; acculturation in, 34–35; Jewish-Gentile social relationships, 44–57; Freemasonry in, 44, 46–47; and social reform, 57–64, 75; Jewish stereotype, 80–81, 85; extent of conversion in, 122–123; and naturalization, 194; and Jewish emancipation, 195, 197–200, 202

Gesellschaft der Freunde, Berlin, 113

Ghetto, 6, 20, 109–110, 153; educational institutions, 126; and changes in traditional occupations, 176. *See also* Community, Jewish

Gouda, 11

Grand Lodge (Freemasons), London, 45

Grattenauer, Karl Wilhelm Friedrich, 85–86, 88, 101; his *Wider die Juden*, 101–102; observations on female conversion, 111; dissenting views of conversion, 123

Grätz, Heinrich, 122

Gregoire, Henri, 71–73

Guilds, 21, 60, 99, 183; and Edict of Tolerance, 162

Gumperz, Aron, 49–50

Gurlitt, Johann Gottfried, 119

Hagiz, Moses, 37

Hahn, Jacob George Hieronymus, 74

Halakah, 25, 135–136, 138-141, 156, 157, 159; and endogamy, 204; and Orthodox view of a Jew, 210; and historical view of Judaism, 211, 212. *See also* Law

Halberstadt, 12, 14, 152, 181

Halle, 25, 105

Hamburg, 22, 24, 215; anti-Jewish reactions in, 80; Jewish occupations, 177

Hameasef, Hebrew periodical, 69, 125–126, 136

Handicrafts, 17, 60, 61, 176, 179, 184, 189; and Edict of Tolerance, 162

Hapsburgs, 13

Hardenberg, Karl August von, 121

Hartmann, Friedrich Traugott, 90, 93–95; admiration of Eisenmenger, 97; and Voltaire, 99; and converts, 106

Hasidism, 24

Haskalah, 191

Hebrew (language), 125, 214. *See also* Language

Heder, 84

Hegelians, 199–200

Heidenheim, Wolf, 151

Heine, Heinrich, 210

Heretical movement, 23–24

Herz, Henriette, 56, 118; and conversion, 120

Herz, Dr. Marcus, 50, 114, 150

Hess, Michael, 207

Hessen, Karl von, 55

Hezel, Wilhelm Friedrich, 108–109

Hirschfield, Herr von, 114

Historical criticism, 211–212

Holland, 3, 4, 9, 22, 168; National assembly, 4, 30, 74; size of Jewish population, 9; size of general population, 10; Jewish immigration to, 11–12; acculturation of Sephardim, 34, 37, 146; Freemasonry in, 44, 46; social reform in, 74; acquisition of citizenship by Jews of, 168, 192; Jewish occupations, 177; Jewish emancipation, 198

Homiletics, 36, 145

Horowitz, Zvi Hirsch, 153, 154

Hourwitz, Zalkind, 72–73

House of Lords, Britain, 196–197

House of Orange, 30, 155

Huguenots, French, 6–7, 99

Humanism, 72, 82

Humboldt, Alexander von, 56, 76

Humboldt, Wilhelm von, 56, 76–78, 102; and converts, 106

Hungary, 3, 9; size of Jewish community, 9, 10; size of general population,

10; *non tolerandis Judaeorum* privilege, 12–14; and Edict of Tolerance, 162; Jewish occupations, 186; Jewish emancipation, 198; Orthodox-reform schism, 210; Jewish immigration, 216

Ideology, 1, 23, 25; and admission or rejection of Jews, 14
Identity, social, 213
Immigration, Jewish, 215–216; to England, 9–10; to Hungary, 10, 216; to Austria, 10; to Germany, 10; to France, 10–11
Industrialization, 193
Industry, 186
Inheritance, 19; and conversion, 112
Institutions: Jewish, 19–20, 21, 57; public, 12
Institutum judaicum, 25, 105
Integration, 3, 6–7; political, 32, 38–42, 57–79, 170; social, 42–56; Gentile objections, 80–104; religious, 118 (*see also* Conversion); and educational reform, 129–131; and Jewish occupations, 176–188; and Jewish emancipation, 199, 201, 206–207, 214
Intellectuals, 193; conversion of, 120, 122; and remolding Jewish attitudes and mentality, 124–126. *See also* Enlightenment
Intermarriage, 2, 110, 140, 156, 203; and tendency toward endogamy, 204–205; criticism of resistance to, 205, 207
Investment, financial, 18, 189–190
Iraq, 3
Ireland, 195
Iselin, Isaak, 51
Islam, 24
Isolation: social, 181–182, 189, 214. *See also* Exclusiveness
Israel, 37, 62; and Jewish patriotism, 92
Israel, Levi, 40–41
Israelites, Biblical, 5; Puritan identification with, 15
Italy, 22, 44
Itzig brothers, 114

Jacobson, Israel, 75, 76, 138, 139, 152, 181, 182
Jeitteles, Baruch, 136, 151
Jerome Napoleon, of Westphalia, 168, 173
Jesuits, 99
Jew Bill, England, 40, 195
Jewish-Gentile relations, *see* Social relations, Jewish-Gentile
Jewish nation, 14; commitment to concept of, 23, 37; Orthodox view of membership, 210; trend toward disintegration of, 214–215
Joseph II, of Austria, 30, 42, 70, 155, 186; and conversion, 106, 110; and promulgation of Edict of Tolerance, 161–164, 166; and Jewish military service, 165
Jost, Isaac Marcus, 195
Judaism: attempts to define, 206–212; insurance of continuity of, 212–214; preservation of interstate community, 214-215. *See also* Religion

Kabbalists, 23, 55
Kant, Immanuel, 134
Klopstock, Friedrich Gottlieb, 162
Knigge, Baron Adolf von, 81–83
Kojetein, Moravia, 147
Kölbele, Balthasar, 52
Königsberg, 69, 70, 121; converts from, 122
Körner, Theodore, 56
Kossuth, Lajos, 198
Kuh, Ephraim, 54

Ladino, 214. *See also* Language
Landau, Yehezkel, 145, 147, 149–150, 154; and Edict of Tolerance of Joseph II, 155, 162
Landgemeinde, 19–20, 31, 32
Land ownership, 163, 179, 181, 182, 184
Landtag, 197; of Prussia, 198
Language, 65, 80–81, 84, 86, 125; and cultural isolation of Jewish society, 157; diversification after emancipation, 214–215

Lavater, Johann Caspar, 51–53, 107, 143

Law, 1, 19, 27, 30; and Jewish traditionalism, 5; in France, 10–11; in Holland, 11–12; in England, 12; Talmudic, 19, 64; rabbinical, 135–136; and traditional Jewish occupations, 179–184

Law of Kabbala, 55

Legislation, 161–175; in Austria, 161–166; and diversion of Jews from traditional occupations, 166, 169; and French Revolution, 167–168, 171; Prussia, 169–171; discriminatory features, 173–174; and status of Jewish religion, 174; and status of Jewish occupations, 176. *See also* Law

Leibjoll, see Body tax

Leipzig, 12

Leopold II, of Austria, 164

Lessing, Ephraim Gotthold, 48, 50, 69

Lettre Patente (*1784*), 188

Levant, 22

Levies, *see* Taxation

Levy, Banker, 114

Liberal movement, 193–194, 196, 199, 202

Lissa, 154

Locke, John, 38, 40

Lorraine, 188

Louis XIII, of France, 11

Louis XV, of France, 11

Lübeck, 180

Luxury, 34, 35

Luzzatto, Moses Hayim (RaMHaL), 25

Magdeburg, 12, 14, 181

Maimon, Salomon, 50, 80; and conversion, 114–115

Mainz, 20

Mantua, 136

Maranos, 9–10

Marcus, Jacob R., 139

Maria Theresa, Empress, 13, 105–106

Marriage, 19; restrictions on, 10, 194; and social mobility, 21, 22; and Edict of Tolerance, 163–164; and *Judenpatent* of Francis II, 164; civil, 167;

171; and occupational choice, 183; and Jewish exclusiveness, 204–205. *See also* Endogamy

Marx, Karl, 186

Maury, Abbé, 100

Mayence, 75

Mecklenburg-Schwerin, 144, 167

Mehemet Ali, 216

Menasseh Ben Israel, 15, 92

Mendel, David, *see* Neander, August

Mendelssohn, Dorothea, 113, 120

Mendelssohn, Moses, 4, 17, 36, 47–54, 57–66 *passim*, 68, 69, 70, 73, 80, 95, 102, 112, 114–117, 134, 158, 194, 209; background of, 47–48; his *Phädon*, 48–49; contacts with non-Jewish intellectuals, 49–50, 67; followers of, 50, 75–76; exclusion from Masons, 50; aloofness from some social and political societies, 51; and conversion, 51–52, 107–108, 114–119, 120; and religious tolerance, 52; and Lavater affair, 52–53, 143; and pamphlet *Das Forschen nach Licht und Recht*, 53; his *Jerusalem*, 53–54; as spokesman for Jewish expectations, 59; and Jewish citizenship, 59–66 *passim;* and separation of church and state, 59–60; and Jew's occupational limitations, 61; his translation of Pentateuch, 62, 65, 66, 129, 149, 150, 157, 158; and education, 65, 129, 131, 132–133, 157; Schulz's polemic against, 88; and religious observance, 134; and the rabbinical authorities, 143, 149–151; and early burial controversy, 144–145; and Edict of Tolerance, 162

Mercure de France, 101

Messiah, 5, 23–25, 135, 142; and Schleiermacher's suggested reform Judaism, 118

Messianism, 37, 62; in anti-Jewish attitudes, 92, 94–95

Metz, 11, 70–72, 178

Michaelis, Johann David, 73, 89–90; and rejection of Jews' citizenship, 91–92, 94; and increased Jewish population, 92–93; and Eisenmenger, 97

Middle Ages, 6, 18, 23
Middle class, Jewish, 177, 193
Migration, 180, 215–216
Military service, 165, 166, 170, 189; and religious proscriptions, 61, 63, 91, 100
Mishnah, 66
Mobility, 21, 22; and occupational choice, 178–184, 193
Mommsen, Theodor, 213
Money, 15, 18, 169, 176, 186
Montefiore, Sir Moses, 216
Morality, Jewish, 27, 68–69, 71–72, 93, 94; and educational reform, 130
Moravia, 9, 10, 18; Jewish associations, 20; and Edict of Tolerance, 162, 163, 164; post-emancipation status in, 174, 198
Moseiten, 132
Moslems, 3, 5
Münster, 11
Musar literature (moralists), 25, 35, 43
Mysticism, 24–25

Napoleon, 31, 100, 104, 168, 169, 188, 192; and Paris Sanhedrin, 139–141, 156–157; restrictions on Jewish residents, 169; concordat with Church (*1801*), 172; and Jewish occupations, 184; and Jewish emancipation, 198, 199, 201–202
Nationalism, 193, 199, 201
National property, 179
Naturalization, 2, 39–40, 57, 92, 168, 174–175; and change in status of Jew, 191–192. *See also* Citizenship
Naturalization Bill, England, 40
Natural rights, 76
Neander, August (David Mendel), 119
Nicolai, Friedrich, 50
Nikolsburg, 20
North German Federation, 197
Nuremberg, 12

Oath of Allegiance, 195
Oberrat, Baden, 173, 185
Observance, religious, 20, 189; and educational reform, 130, 132–133; and religious reform, 134; and traditional-

ists, 146, 148; and Liberal movement, 194
Occupations, 1, 39, 57, 100, 155, 197; restrictions on, 11, 18, 169, 178; and right of residence, 17–18, 178–180, 183–185, 186; and citizenship, 60–61, 63, 68, 77; and religious proscriptions, 94, 134; and Edict of Tolerance of Joseph II, 162; and *Judenpatent* of Francis II, 164; and legislation, 166; and Prussia, 170; and Baden *Oberrat*, 173, 185; post-emancipation flight from traditional professions, 176–190; competition in, 178; extension of, 179; and social contacts, 204
Odenburg, 13
Oppenheimer, Samuel, 13
Order of the Asiatic Brethren, 55, 84–85, 112
Organizations, 21, 212–213
Orthodoxy, 210

Paalzov, Christian Ludwig, 101
Paderborn, 20
Padua, 25
Palestinian Jewry, 37
Pappenheim, Salomon, 151
Paris: Sanhedrin, 139–141, 156–157, 172, 178; Jewish community, 178–179; Jewish artisans, 179–180
Parliament, British, 196–197
Passive resistance, 77; in innovator-traditionalist controversy, 151, 152
Patriotism, 140, 214; as issue in civil reform, 62
Paulus, Heinrich E. G., 199, 203
Peace of Luneville, 75
Peace of Westphalia, 13
Peasants, Jewish, 177, 180–186 *passim*
Peddlers, 22, 61, 68, 166, 177–178, 186, 188
Pentateuch: Mendelssohn's translation of, 62, 65, 66, 129, 149, 150, 157, 158; teaching of, 128–129
Periodicals, 125, 215
Pestalozzi, Johann Heinrich, 128
Pesth, 13
Philantropienists, 128

Philantropin of Frankfurt am Main, 127, 153, 181, 207
Philosophy, 36
Poland, 2, 10, 18, 22; Hasidism in, 24; emigration of Jews from, 215–216
Political status, *see* Civil status
Politics, 1, 2, 3, 19; and integration of German Jew, 32
Population, Jewish, 9–10; ratio between general population and, 10; controls on, 19, 32; increase as result of civil reform, 60; in anti-Jewish attitudes, 92–93; and legislation, 167
Pork, prohibition on, 61
Portugal, 10
Prague, 13, 18, 70, 146; expulsion of Jews from, 16; Jewish community, 20, 21; Edict of Expulsion repealed, 31; educational reform, 127; and *Judenpatent* of Francis II, 165–166; Jewish occupations, 180, 186
Prejudice, 7, 40, 41; Gentile view of common Jew, 81–87 *passim;* and Sephardim, 83; justification of attitudes, 87–100 *passim;* and Jewish emancipation, 199–200. *See also* Attitudes; Discrimination
Press, Jewish, 213
Pressburg, 127, 157–158
Professions, 179, 186, 190; and social relations, 204. *See also* Occupations
Protestantism, 120, 217
Proudhon, Pierre J., 200
Prussia, 12, 14, 30–31, 72, 176, 186; Jewish citizenship, 76, 170–171, 192; anti-Jewish agitation, 101–102; attempts to improve Jew's status in, 116–118; conversion in, 121–122; reform through legislation in, 169–171; restrictions on Jews in, 194; Landtag, 198; and Jewish emancipation, 202; Orthodox-Reform schism, 210
Public administration, 39
Public office, *see* Civil service
Public opinion, 14, 194; and civil status of Jews, 40, 70–71; and acquisition of estates by Jews, 182. *See also* Stereotypes

Publishing, books, 125, 128, 148–149
Puritans, 15
Purveyors, 22

Rabbi, 20; social mobility of, 22; and religious reform movement, 136–137; and enlightened laymen, 148–160 *passim;* and *consistoire,* 173
Rabbinical assembly, 139
Radical Order of the Illuminati, 81
Rashi (Solomon Yishaki), 129
Rationalism, 33, 36, 39, 108, 134; and anti-Jewish attitudes, 97–99; and conversion, 109, 114–117, 119; and education, 124, 131–133; and Philantropienists, 128; and definition of Judaism, 210–211
Reform, 2, 124–141; and Berlin group, 57–70; educational, 66–69, 124–134, 150; and Alsatians, 70–73, 167–169; and French, 73–74, 167–170; Dutch, 74–75, 168; implementation of, 75–76; and the Enlightenment, 76; Humboldt's view, 77; Gentile objections to, 80–103; religious, 124, 130–131, 133–141, 161; of ghetto educational institutions, 126; and the traditionalists, 142–160; legal, 161–175; as Continental movement, 215
Reformation, 14, 15, 131
Reform movement, 133–141, 189, 198; and Ascher, 134–136; and acceptance of innovation by community, 136–137; cooperation between rabbis and innovators, 137–138; and sanction for change, 139; and Paris Sanhedrin, 140–141; schism with Orthodox, 160; criticism, 161; goals of, 208–209; and definition of Judaism, 210–211
Reign of Terror, France, 171
Rejection, ideologies of, 87–103. *See also* Attitudes, anti-Jewish
Religion, 1, 4, 5, 10, 14; and Jewish community, 21–23; and acculturation, 34–35; and Jewish citizenship, 61–64, 78; and the state, 78, 171–174; and the rationalists, 108–109, 114–119; and cultural adaptation, 118;

and the romanticists, 120–121; and educational secularization, 129–131; reform, 133–141, 215 (*see also* Reform movement); Ascher's view, 134; post-emancipation status, 172–174; and Jewish occupations, 189; and social relations, 204–207; politicians' definition of, 207–208

Religious observance, *see* Observance

Resettlement, and occupational changes, 178–180

Residence, right of (admittance), 9–18, 58, 155, 166, 197; and France, 10–11; and Holland, 11–12; in England, 12, 15, 38, 58; and economic and religious forces, 15–19; political and legal inferences, 16; and status and position of the Jew, 17–18; Jewish occupations and, 18, 178–180, 183–186; and the court Jew, 29; and Prague, 31; and Dohm, 58–59; in Prussia, 170, 194

Restoration, 39, 193

Retailers, 22

Revolution, 167–169. *See also* French Revolution

Revolution of *1830*, 193

Revolution of *1848–1849*, 198

Ridicule, 152–154

Riesser, Gabriel, 194–197, 199, 207

Right of residence, *see* Residence

Rites, religious, 23, 77, 135, 203. *See also* Observance

Romanticists (romanticism), 120; and Catholicism, 121; and Jewish emancipation, 193, 199, 201

Rothschild, Baron Lionel de, 196–197

Rothschild family, 31, 187, 204

Royal Court (Hofgerecht), 29

Royal Society of Arts and Sciences, Metz, 71

Rühs, Friedrich, 199, 207

Russia, 2–3

Sabbatai, Zevi, 23–24

Sabbath, 135, 136, 139, 153, 154; as issue in civil reform, 61, 63, 167

Sabbatians, 24, 37, 113, 147

Salomon, Sir David, 197

Salons, literary, 56, 118, 120, 201

Sanhedrin, Paris, *see* Paris Sanhedrin

Satire, 152

Saxonia, 17

Scheintod, apparent death, 144

Schlegel, Friedrich, 120

Schleiermacher, Friedrich, 56, 118–119, 121; recommends formation of reform sect in Judaism, 118; his *Speeches on Religion*, 120; on conversion among Jewish community elite, 122; fears Judaization of church, 123

Schnee, Heinrich, 30, 122

Schönfeld, Thomas von, 112

Schools, 21, 65, 126; and Edict of Tolerance of Austria, 66, 162; *Freischule*, 126–127; differences in aims, organization methods, and curriculum, 128; laxity in teaching Jewish tradition, 129–132; and cultural adaptation, 166. *See also* Education

Schroetter, Baron, 102

Schulz, Johann Heinrich, 88–89; his anti-Jewish attitudes, 95–96, 99; and "State within the State," 99, 100

Schutzgeld (protection money), 29

Schwager, preacher, 89–90

Science, 36

Sectarianism, 113

Secularization, 87; of the state, 33, 38, 90–91; of education, 65–66, 127, 128, 147; and anti-Jewish attitudes, 90–91

Seesen, 127, 128, 130

Self-government, 19, 31; and state intervention, 32

Self-identification, 5, 23

Sephardim, 9, 69, 83, 146; clandestine entry into France, 11; in Buda, 13; cultural and religious connection beyond local boundaries, 22–23; acculturation of, 34, 37, 43; civil status in France, 42; and educational reform, 126; French, 168

Settlements, separate, 33. *See also* Ghettos

Shohet, Azriel, 34, 36

Silesia, 162

schism with Reform movement, 160; in definition of Judaism after emancipation, 211

Traits, Jewish, 83–84. *See also* Stereotype

Trier, 186

Turgot, Anne Robert Jacques, 60

Turkey, 10

Tychsen, Olof Gerhard, 112, 144

United States, 3

Universalism, 125; and educational reform, 130

University, 44, 194

Usury, 176, 177, 188, 200

Utrecht, 11

Varnhagen, Rachel, 56

Veit, Simon, 113

Vernacular, *Judendeutsch*, 65. *See also* Language

Vienna, 9, 12–13, 70, 184; expulsion of Jews from, 16; conversion of Jews in, 105; educational reform, 127; celebration of Edict of Tolerance in, 162; and Francis II, 164; post-emancipation restrictions, 174

Voltaire, 69, 83, 100; his *Essai sur les Moeurs*, 40; and opposers of Jewish integration, 97–98

Voluntary societies, *see* Societies, social and communal

Wealth, 21

Weber, A., 32

Wessely, Napthali Herz, 48, 57, 143; and educational reform, 66–69, 124–126, 131, 149, 150; and Mendelssohn's translation of Pentateuch, 66, 129, 149, 150; traditionalists and, 145, 147, 149–151; "Words of Peace and Truth," 150; and Edict of Tolerance, 162

Western Europe, 1–3

Westphalia, 75, 138, 159; acquisition of citizenship by Jews of, 168; *consistoire* of, 173

Wissenschaft des Judentums, 211

Wolfenbüttel, 127, 128

Wolfssohn, Aaron, 132

Women, 84, 86; and conversion, 111

Wurm (German actor), 86

Württemberg, 32, 166, 197

Yehieh, Ascher ben, Rabbi of Barcelona, 137

Yeshivot, 21, 22, 84

Yiddish, 81, 214; in transformed educational structure, 129. *See also* Language

Zunz, Yomtov Lipman, 211